DOING SOCIAL WORK
RESEARCH

Roger Smith

Open University Press

Open University Press
McGraw-Hill Education
McGraw-Hill House
Shoppenhangers Road
Maidenhead
Berkshire
England
SL6 2QL

email: enquiries@openup.co.uk
world wide web: www.openup.co.uk

and Two Penn Plaza, New York, NY 10121-2289, USA

First published 2009

A catalogue record of this book is available from the British Library

ISBN-13: 978-0-33-523564-3 (pb) 978-0-33-523563-6 (hb)
ISBN-10: 0335235646 (pb) 0335235638 (hb)

Library of Congress Cataloging-in-Publication Data
CIP data applied for

Typeset by RefineCatch Limited, Bungay, Suffolk
Printed and bound by CPI Group (UK) Ltd, Croydon, CR0 4YY

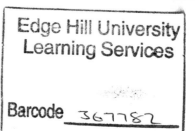
The McGraw·Hill Companies

CONTENTS

INTRODUCTION:

A CHALLENGING TASK?

The need for a baseline

It may be a little discouraging to start with the observation that social work research is by no means a clear or straightforward activity. This is reflected in continuing debates, disagreements and uncertainty at all levels of the enterprise, from students who often ask me, 'do I need a hypothesis?'[1] to apparently intractable disputes among even well-established academic practitioners about what counts as knowledge and how it should be measured. This kind of disagreement is not restricted to social work, and it is not necessarily unhealthy, reflecting as it does a series of dynamic and creative discussions within and between disciplines about how we can generate real and valid insights into human interactions and social phenomena. Tied up with these controversies is another set of questions about the most appropriate or legitimate ways of obtaining research evidence. These tensions are often associated with conflicts between 'qualitative' and 'quantitative' conventions in social science, it might be observed. However, they also have a distinctive 'social work' dimension which will be a central focus of concern for us, and which should be outlined briefly at the outset.

The specific challenges of doing social work research can partly be viewed as a corollary of the distinctive nature of this field of practice, which has also been a matter of significant recent debate. Explicit concerns have been raised, for example, about the relationship between theory, practice and research in social work (Trevillion 2008). Problems have been identified both in terms of the practical arrangements for sharing insights and creating an effective dialogue between research and practice, but it is also suggested that social work research has adopted a limited and essentially one-dimensional view of its own role and rationale, becoming detached from more fundamental concerns with theory development, or wider contextual challenges:

social work research in the UK generally focuses on ways of improving

service outcome to particular client groups. With some honourable
exceptions, it has not for some years sought to extend or develop the core
knowledge base or central underpinnings of the social work tradition.

(Trevillion 2008: 448)

According to this line of argument, there has been a persistent failure to
make appropriate and useful connections between the different facets of the
theory–research–practice triad, which is partly accounted for by the prevailing climate within which social work practice (and training) is constituted.
The need to establish a rationale for any kind of research practice which
goes beyond the immediate and practical may, of course, be a feature of
any applied discipline, and is not necessarily restricted to social work by
any means. Similar challenges may well confront those involved in nursing
(Giuliano 2003) or education research (Elliott 1990), for instance.

In seeking to define the appropriate terrain for research activity, though,
there do appear to be good grounds for airing this kind of concern. Social
work agencies, for instance, do not appear to have a substantial degree of
commitment to the research process, above and beyond quite localized evaluative projects, usually intended to justify a particular form of intervention or
new initiative; and this rather limited conception of the research arena also
seems to be shared by government and its outposts. The recent history of
'official' research in youth justice, for example, is replete with examples of
such work, from which only positive findings are cherry-picked; sometimes,
indeed, new practice developments are 'rolled out' before pilot evaluations
have been completed (see Holdaway et al. 2001, for example). Social work
and governmental agencies do not, therefore, appear to have a substantial
commitment to the research process, either in the sense of commissioning and
utilising studies with a wider scope, or in terms of the support and resources
they could provide to encourage practitioner research with the potential to
offer immediately relevant insights into the impact of or need for services.

At the same time, though, we should accept that academic researchers can
legitimately be criticized for failing to seek proactive engagement with the
world of practice, with all its inevitable imperfections and pressures.
Researchers may be reluctant to 'get their hands dirty', in the sense of establishing working relationships with commissioners that are 'too close', or
where these might slant research projects in a particular direction. Academics
are criticized, too, for being too abstract, and not producing findings
which are relevant or accessible to practitioners or policy makers, as well as
service users:

It's not about whether existing research is worthless, but whether there
is a focus on policy and policy implementation that doesn't necessarily
address some of the questions that are taxing practitioners and the
people who use services.

(Amanda Edwards, Head of Knowledge services, SCIE,
Community Care, 10 July 2008)

Academic researchers have also been challenged for their apparent lack of willingness to support the dissemination process by converting their findings into useable outputs which can be applied in the practice arena (Shaw 2008).

In addition to these concerns, perhaps arising with some degree of inevitably given competing perspectives and research agendas, there is a danger that relying on in-built assumptions may create or perpetuate barriers between producers and users of research. For example, research often delivers findings which are not conclusive or straightforward; sometimes, indeed, these can be critical of practice or policy innovations. It is bound to be frustrating for agencies, service users and practitioners if the messages they receive are not clear cut, are predominantly negative, or actually complicate rather than simplify the task. This tension is not necessarily resolved where research is led or carried out by people who use services themselves, despite the likelihood that it will be seen as having greater credibility.

Researchers are sometimes criticized, too, for stating the obvious, which may fuel the belief that good practice in social work is no more than applied common sense which does not need expensive research to justify it. The problems of research relationships and mutual lack of understanding are further compounded by a number of other factors. The question of ownership and control is one such issue, given that there are likely to be a number of key stakeholders with an interest in the chosen topic, including service users, practitioners, the researcher(s), agencies, and the wider community. This is likely to lead to the absence of a clear and consistent view of the most appropriate research strategy and methods to be adopted. Intending researchers will see from this that there is little chance of them being able to carry out pure and unfettered enquiries into their chosen subject matter, even where the project is one that they have decided on for themselves. Of course, as Shaw (2007) acknowledges, these are not simply practical or contextual issues; they also reflect significant underlying questions to do with the politics of research and power imbalances which must be negotiated and where necessary challenged.

Beyond the immediate challenges of finding common ground on which to base research investigations, there are further important considerations to do with the scope and purposes of these activities. What kind of questions and subjects of inquiry do legitimately fall within the remit of social work research, and what should it be seeking to discover? The scope of social work research, for example, could be defined according to those roles and functions which social workers inhabit; in other words, the subject area would be bounded by conventional (often official) definitions of what the task is and how it is performed, which may, to a large extent, be determined by law and statutory guidance. Of course, this is not to be taken for granted, either in terms of the defining criteria of what constitutes the social work task, or delimiting what aspects of this task and the context should be the focus of social work research. The context would seem inevitably to have an important part to play, given what we already know about how the task is defined and managed. Research will be massively constrained if it restricts itself to the formal questions of determining user characteristics and evaluating existing practices. If this was the case, the many positive contributions to practice that research can generate from 'outside', for instance inspired by the disability movement, would not have been realized. Indeed, as we shall see, the lack of certainty about exactly what social work is itself suggests that we should try to avoid being too prescriptive about the scope and remit of research into the subject.

So, what is 'social work', or what might it be?

It does, indeed, seem reasonable that we should begin at least by reflecting on this kind of definitional question before going on to consider whether or not there are distinctive features to the research task as applied to the social work domain. Can we thus achieve any degree of certainty, or at least consensus on this fundamental issue? This is definitely no easy task, as the varying and competing attempts at defining the subject indicate. Davies (1981: 3), for instance, has for a number of years been associated with a fairly narrow, service-oriented conception of the task, which he has defined in terms of *'maintenance*: society maintaining itself in a relatively stable state by making provision for and managing people in positions of severe weakness, stress or vulnerability'. He suggests, too, that 'social work can only be understood by observing what it does and then by reflecting on the contributions that those activities make to the way society ticks' (1981: 4). Although he does not give much space to a discussion of research in this particular text, he suggests that it is best seen in its role of the contribution it makes to 'creating and developing' new and constructive forms of intervention (1981: 195). This characterization seems to offer us a vision of social work as an essentially *practical* task, even when the intervention takes the form of counselling or emotional support, which should be evaluated and judged in terms of its capacity to achieve and sustain socially determined objectives of well-being, happiness and usefulness.

However, it is clear that this view is not shared by others, who believe that the idea of social work as primarily about performing a 'maintenance' function is too limited:

> In our view, the notion of social work as 'maintenance' is too static . . . [T]he community is not a machine that is more or less carrying out its functions, requiring 'maintenance' to keep it running smoothly. Communities, however defined, are ever-changing living entities or human systems.
>
> (Smale *et al.* 2000: 7)

Thus, the variability and dynamism of the human world demand an approach to practice which is based on flexible understanding, recognition of diversity, and the avoidance of prescriptive solutions. Issues of power and inequality inevitably mean that people have different views about needs and appropriate interventions, with the result that these must be seen as provisional and negotiable, rather than fixed and determinate.

While it might be thought by some that this is a matter for pragmatic judgement, with different modes of assessment and decision making being applicable depending on the circumstances, others have suggested that there is a fundamental and critical distinction to be made between ways of thinking about and doing social work; an eclectic approach cannot resolve the problem, according to this perspective. For example:

> *Constructive social work* argues that social work is as much, if not more, an art than a science and proceeds on the basis that practice is better characterised as a *practical-moral activity* rather than a *rational-technical* one, and that attempts to increase realism and objectivity are likely to be misguided.
>
> (Parton and O'Byrne 2000: 3)

This argument has potentially far-reaching implications for the ways in which all aspects of the social work process are conducted from assessment, through decision making to case planning and intervention. It is seen as a creative and wide-ranging process, as opposed to a systematic exercise in measuring need and then determining the appropriate service, at the right level to meet this need. Because of this, social work intervention also needs to be conceived as relatively flexible and unbounded, starting from where service users are, and addressing the problems they face in their own terms and according to their own priorities. Smale and colleagues (2000: 234) conclude that this is an essentially 'idiosyncratic' process, which deals with the difficulties encountered on their own merits, and in the light of the broader social context which, itself, shapes the problems encountered by individuals 'downstream'.

These examples suggest that the approach to social work practice should be broad, systemic and creative, rather than immediate, situated and pre-determined.

We should be careful, however, to avoid setting up over-simplified polarizations of theoretical debates and practice orientations within social work because there is certainly a variety of positions that can be adopted. For example, the tension between individualized and 'social' responses may tend to suggest a degree of homogeneity about each of these which is not necessarily the case. The assumptions underlying certain forms of therapeutic intervention, for example, would be dissimilar in many ways to those of behavioural methods; however, both might tend to adopt an individualistic view of problem solving. We can accept, perhaps, that social work is about pursuing a problem-solving approach to the problems of people in their social settings, but there is much less evidence of agreement between proponents of very different ways of understanding and addressing these. While it is not really the place of this book to go into very great detail about these live and enduring controversies, it must be recognized that they also inform the ways in which social work research is thought about, designed and carried out.

'Positions' and values

Shaw (2007) is concerned that attempts to mark social work research out as distinctive have largely derived from a parallel rejection of positivist assumptions, which not only dismisses this view of scientific understanding, but also by extension certain forms of practice based around the principle of achieving measurable and agreed outcomes ('maintenance', for example). There appears to be an in-built belief in some quarters that social work itself *necessarily* incorporates a denial of the kind of principles of measurement and objectivity which inform certain types of knowledge generation and practice guidance. In other words, social work must be a critical enterprise, rooted in a certain set of values to which it alone can lay authentic claim:

> Lying behind claims to social work's special character is, I suspect, an old heresy that for many years was prevalent – the belief that social work has a basic value position that has greater merit/greater human authenticity/is more whole-person oriented, etc. than any other profession.
>
> (Shaw 2007: 662)

However, Shaw (2007: 663) suggests that this position is not sustainable, and is indeed rather unproductive if it makes us 'disinclined to listen to the voices of colleagues in other disciplines and professions'. Nonetheless, he also argues that 'good research' in social work will aim to 'promote justice, social change and social inclusion' (2007: 665). In other words, one of the key criteria for determining research quality in the discipline is apparently rooted in the aspiration to achieve social justice. This point develops Holman's (1987) earlier exhortation to recognize and promote 'research from the underside', which would give a direct voice to people experiencing social deprivation, and enable them to 'express their needs and demands and to campaign for their purposes' (1987: 682). In this important paper, Holman set out a number of principles which should underpin such research, from the 'bottom up', suggesting that it should be people from the population in question who define the 'scope and purposes' of the investigation, as well as its methodology and practice (1987: 681). Similar sentiments continue to be expressed, articulating the view that research which does not fully involve its subjects cannot gain a full or fair picture of the questions it addresses. The goal should be to

> democratize ways of knowing, so that the knowledge of marginalized groups will attain similar status to that of scientific 'knowers'. *Then the*

focus can more legitimately be on choosing the right methods for the
research question.

(Humphries 2008: 194 emphasis added)

It may be that this kind of value base is not exclusive to social work, as Shaw (2007) indicates, but it nonetheless has powerful implications for the approach we take to determining the suitability and worth of particular research strategies.

Of course, the position is somewhat complicated by the evidence of tensions within the value base of social work itself, reflected in documents such as its professional codes of practice (GSCC 2003). Social work practitioners are expected to respect service users' autonomy, for example, while also exercising a protective function on behalf of both them and the wider community. In this context, to privilege the position of disadvantaged groups in general becomes problematic, since there may be competing interests and indeed harmful behaviours displayed within these groups. We cannot just assume a uniform community of interest or ignore the need to make judgements about the consequences of conflict or oppressive behaviour. Shaw, again, observes that some models of research have demonstrated qualities of appreciativeness, but have not at the same time taken account of 'asymmetries of power and divisions of interest' (2007: 666). In other words, research which respects and indeed privileges the perspective of disadvantaged people and those who use services may not always take account of the issues of 'power, space, place and time' (2007: 667) which impact on and shape their experiences and their differing needs and interests.

Social work research, therefore, is bound up with and problematized by the same tensions which are to be found in attempts to articulate a set of values which does 'justice' to people in a variety of circumstances, whose interests and perceptions do not always coincide and sometimes come directly into conflict (young people on the streets seen as a threat to the community, for instance). This, in turn, suggests that there are practical as well as ethical challenges to be faced in trying to use 'values' as the basis for operationalizing the concept of 'social work research'.

So, where should we start?

At this point, of course, it may be more helpful to try to identify key questions to be considered, rather than to elaborate a precise definition of terms at the outset. We may perhaps find it helpful just to set out at this initial stage some of the ways in which social work research *could* be understood, while leaving normative decisions about which is the best approach to take to the side for the moment. This, at least, will lay the basis for subsequent discussions about research strategy and practice without necessarily predetermining the outcome or foreshortening the decision-making process.

At its most simplistic, what makes social work research 'distinctive' (Shaw 2007) is that it purports to be principally *about* social work. However, as we have already seen, this is to presuppose that we have a clear view about what constitutes the terrain of social work itself. Firstly, then, as Holman (1987) and others have suggested, the task may be to determine the kind of contextual questions which might be asked, such as what are the origins and determinants of social problems? In this sense, then, the questions to be considered are less about what social work does but about the focal point of its interest – how are needs identified and measured, for example? In this respect, the student I supervised who decided to consider the impact of housing needs of African-Caribbean families could claim to be investigating a topic of relevance to the domain of social work, despite its ostensible subject matter. Similar questions could be asked of the criminal justice system, too, given the recent experience of changing patterns of service in this sphere.

In addition to considerations of the *scope* of social work, it is also possible to think in terms of research into its structures and *organization*. How social work is constituted as a form of organized (and professionalized) practice can be seen as a legitimate topic of enquiry. Clearly, however, this also poses additional questions in terms of the interdisciplinary nature of inquiry (it overlaps with psychology, sociology and organization studies, for example), and the methodological questions associated with this; while, at the same time, we are again faced with definitional problems in determining just what kind of activity is or is not, social work.

More conventionally perhaps, research might be carried out into the application and outcomes of social work *methods* such as behavioural or therapeutic interventions. It might be felt that this has, up to now, been the primary orientation of much investigative activity in the field. It also appears to form the backdrop to core methodological debates and controversies, reflecting wider disputes on the relative merits of qualitative and quantitative approaches, for example. Humphries (2008: 8) acknowledges the centrality of this debate in social work, while stressing that they are not necessarily exclusive and that 'both methodologies may be used within any single research study'. Nonetheless, she does go on to suggest that part of the reason for the assertion of the value of qualitative methods has been because of a sense that only the 'quantitative domain' has been seen conventionally as legitimate. In this way, some important approaches and 'forms of knowing' have been excluded from consideration, such as those which reflect personal experience and meanings. Indeed, this kind of approach might be particularly well suited to another possible sphere of enquiry for social work research which is that of the nature and quality of *relationships*.

In considering the range of possibilities, in terms both of subject matter and investigative strategy, it immediately becomes clear that the terrain of social work research is not easy to navigate, either conceptually or practically. This may indicate that approaching the question of how to 'do' this kind of research is fraught with danger. However, precisely because it is multi-faceted and contested, the silver lining is that, in any given context, there is almost certainly no one 'right' way of going about the task. In approaching their subject matter, social work researchers may need to apply a rather different set of criteria than those of whether what they are doing is correct or incorrect. Indeed, it may be better to think in terms of whether they are acting in ways which are 'appropriate' or 'justifiable', not only in strict methodological terms, but also in terms of the sort of values articulated by Shaw (2007) which we considered previously, and which are underpinned by principles of 'social justice' (Humphries 2008). What we can perhaps conclude from this discussion is that it is not, in the end, possible to avoid making choices in approaching and conducting social work research (or any other kind of research, for that matter). As Humphries (2008: 15) argues: 'research is both contentious and political'. It cannot rely on pure objective benchmarks against which its quality or value can be judged, and therefore researchers cannot realistically aspire to this sort of approach. It therefore remains for them to be clear and explicit about their own 'starting points' and what assumptions of beliefs underpin these. In the specific context of social work, of course, this tends to imply that research must necessarily be conducted in a way which is consistent with and supportive of its underlying values (although, as we have already seen, these are not unproblematic). Social work research must therefore deal with three distinct types of question:

- is its focus consistent with the broadly defined field of 'social work' itself?
- is it informed by values which reflect those to which social work aspires?; and
- in light of these, is it conducted in ways which are reasonable and justifiable, both methodologically and ethically?

Box 1 Researching social work values

I once carried out a study of the values held by child welfare practitioners and the impact of these on their practice (Smith 2005b). This involved interviewing practitioners and analysing documents in each of four distinct organizations, in order to ascertain whether or not they thought and behaved differently according to each organization's stated principles and purposes.

I used methods based on the use of Weber's (1957) abstract model of 'ideal types' in order to find out how closely each agency and its staff compared to its explicit goals, and to determine what factors might lead them to depart from these commitments.

In fact, in most cases, there was a close relationship between organizational values and individual practice.

While there is inevitably much emphasis on methods and strategy when we consider the practice of research, the relationship between practice and values remains as important to social work research as it does in direct intervention in the field. Carrying out this kind of inquiry must therefore address both methodological and moral challenges.

The structure of the book

The aim of this book is to enable intending researchers in social work to prepare the ground and carry out their work. In order to do this, the book will identify key strands informing contemporary practice in the field, before considering the practical implications for the organization and management of the research enterprise itself. It is therefore divided into three parts, moving from the 'big picture' issues of how we formulate research questions, and how different approaches can be justified (and criticized), through the process of constructing a research strategy to the practical task of planning and managing the process of enquiry and dissemination of what we find.

The first part, then, considers some of the main strands in contemporary social work research, considering the drivers for these, and their implicit and explicit assumptions about what counts as knowledge and how our inquiries should be carried out.

Chapter 1 will introduce the key contemporary challenges for applied social work research, identifying the policy context, and growing interest from a number of influential quarters in 'what works' in social work and social care.

The emergence of bodies such as Social Care Institute for Excellence (SCIE) has clearly sharpened the focus, emphasizing the aim of identifying and disseminating 'good practice' through evaluations, knowledge reviews and guidance. At the same time, interest in drawing in a wider range of constituencies, including service users, providers and community groups, has also served to problematize conventional understandings of the purposes and outcomes of social work interventions.

Relatively constrained definitions of what counts as credible and reliable research are rendered problematic by the increasingly diverse range of stakeholders involved. Critically, of course, it will become clear that we need to understand the differing perspectives brought to bear on the questions of what research is for, what approaches are legitimate, and how 'effectiveness' is to be defined and measured. These essentially political and contested questions of legitimacy and accountability will lead us to consider the implications for constituencies such as service user interests, and the implications of power imbalances and competing agendas. Perspectives on social work research will thus be shown to be open to debate.

Chapter 2 will explore in more detail the assumptions and ideologies which underpin research strategies linked to the search for 'evidence-based practice', which have tended to dominate in terms of policy and resource allocation. Links can be made here with underlying methodological assumptions, which tend to be empiricist and behavioural. Much recent research in youth justice sponsored by government and bodies such as the Youth Justice Board reflects this preoccupation. The ways in which these infuse the construction of research activities, from the formulation of the initial question through the design, implementation and dissemination phases will be explored, as will the wider uses of this kind of study.

In considering the impact of this particular research 'paradigm', this chapter will also reflect on its potential consequences, in terms of the ways in which certain types of inquiry and evidence are deemed to be less or even unscientific, and its place in setting the benchmark against which all other types of research activity are likely to be judged, especially by major funding bodies and sponsors.

In fact, it will be important to distinguish between the relative dominance of this kind of orthodoxy in research and its pragmatic uses, on the one hand, and its methodological strengths and weaknesses, on the other. From a practitioner perspective, such influences only become problematic if they threaten to define alternative approaches and findings as invalid. While some attempts have been made to recognize and incorporate alternative viewpoints such as those of service users within this perspective, it is still defined by its preoccupation with 'what works'.

An alternative perspective will be introduced in Chapter 3, which will, in particular, consider the potential contribution of more exploratory and critical approaches to investigation. These will often be informed by a sense of uncertainty, and will involve problematizing prior assumptions about what it is we should be measuring and against what criteria. Different types of theoretical assumption and investigative strategies will operate in this context, which may seek to avoid taking anything for granted. The kind of research question asked in this context is less likely to be about seeking to provide evaluative evidence to support good practice, and more likely to seek to explore and explain social processes and the meanings attributed to their experiences by key participants. This approach to knowledge generation will be shown to have significant advantages in challenging prior assumptions, validating the perspectives of research subjects, paying attention to their meanings and explanations, and developing new theoretical insights.

However, it will also be important to address potential criticisms of this orientation. It can be challenged to the extent that it relies on insufficient evidence and subjective interpretation rather than material 'fact', and that it produces findings which are not easily applicable to concrete problems. While a critical approach helps to lay bare in-built preconceptions, it may be seen as self-indulgent and uncommitted.

At the present time, as Chapter 4 demonstrates, there is a growing interest in social work in drawing on user perspectives directly to inform knowledge development as well as practice, and this may be seen to have inspired an emerging body of 'committed' research. This can be seen as being informed by established perspectives such as those of feminist and action research. These approaches have, in different ways, challenged conventional notions of objectivity, suggesting that it is neither possible nor desirable to stand outside the subject of enquiry. Indeed, they would consider it a distinct advantage for the researcher to be directly engaged with those who are the focal point of the investigation. Research effectiveness is thus to be judged in terms of its contribution to achieving specific, usually emancipatory outcomes. Like the first perspective, committed research usually takes the view that research should be outcome focused, and should be judged according to its ability to promote change. At the same time, however, it expects research practices themselves to be informed by principles of rights, participation and social justice. Thus, the growing level of support for 'user-led' research is partly attributable to a commitment to promoting the rights of disadvantaged groups, and seeing the research process itself as a means of securing this end.

The attractiveness of this approach should not lead us to be uncritical, however. It is clearly open to charges of being partisan and therefore selective in its use of evidence. It may also be the case that it is not as open as it should be to alternative explanations, and possible conflicts of interest *between* distinct service user interests. Nonetheless, its powerful impact should be recognised here.

The second part of the book draws on these broad orientations to research in order to begin to sketch out different ways in which research strategies can be developed in order to pursue specific investigative projects.

Chapter 5 draws on the earlier discussion of empiricist and evidence-based approaches to social work research, in order to sketch out some of the methods by which this kind of strategy is typically implemented, including: experimentation, secondary analysis of large-scale statistical data, longitudinal studies, surveys, evaluations and comparative investigations.

Concrete examples of the application of such methods in social work will be considered, such as the evaluation of parenting programmes, the application of behavioural methods with young offenders and surveys of practitioners and service users. As with subsequent chapters, illustrative examples will be provided of research of this kind which could be undertaken by lone or student researchers. These will provide the basis for an exploration of the form, rationale and application of a series of methods, allowing for a discussion of their relative strengths and weaknesses and applicability to different research questions and settings.

Chapter 6 will likewise elaborate on the earlier discussion of critical methodology, enabling a range of methods and strategies to be considered, including: grounded theory, experiential, ethnographic and narrative accounts. These are predominantly qualitative approaches, and it will be possible here to consider their value and applicability both in their own right and collectively.

By focusing on the methods associated with this perspective, intending researchers will also be able to make connections between their aims and objectives and the practical tasks associated with planning and undertaking research projects.

As in Chapter 5, the application of different approaches will be illustrated by reference to concrete examples, such as the author's own study of diversionary practice in youth justice, studies of the experience and outcomes of residential care, the impact of domestic violence, and the issues involved in caring for disabled children.

There is now emerging a range of research strategies which reflect a common desire to achieve change with and on behalf of specific (usually oppressed or disadvantaged) interests, and these are the focal point of Chapter 7. Thus, the methods to be considered here will include those drawing on feminist principles, action research, user-led research and other emancipatory methods. This chapter will also provide an opportunity to discuss the potential of applying research explicitly as a means of securing desired changes, and the challenges of justifying this as opposed to apparently neutral and 'objective' forms of enquiry. Examples to be considered will be participative research on young people's health needs, a developmental evaluation of a training project led by people with learning difficulties, and other service-user-led research initiatives.

It will become clear that the methods associated with this perspective require a rethinking on the part of the researcher about her/his relationships with the 'researched', including the ways in which research questions are conceptualized, who 'leads', the nature of power relationships involved, and who decides what happens to the work when completed.

Exercise 1 What sort of researcher are you?

Inevitably, we all start from a personal 'position', incorporating our individual preferences, values and views about what we feel comfortable with.

It may be helpful to spend a few moments thinking about where you are coming from as a researcher:

- Do you, for instance, think that it is essential to involve service users in all aspects of your research?
- Do you believe that certain types of evidence and some kinds of knowledge are more valuable than others?
- Are there aspects of the research process that you feel ill-equipped to engage in or to understand?
- Are you interested in exploring subjects to find out what is going on, or are you more interested in solving existing problems?

It helps to give this kind of question some thought before setting out on a research project, because a good 'fit' between the researcher and the investigation is clearly important.

The final part of the book will offer some ideas as to how varying method-ological approaches may be operationalized in the conduct of particular research investigations. It will have a practical focus on planning, manage-ment, using research and dissemination.

Chapter 8 will consider the tasks of planning and preparing for research projects. It will set out some of the essential considerations for the intending researcher, in particular, the importance of generating a manageable research question, deciding on the appropriate method, considering key practical challenges such as ethical approval and permissions, timetabling and contin-gency planning.

Most successful research projects depend on effective and comprehensive plans of this kind, and this chapter will therefore go into some detail, based on the author's own experience as researcher and supervisor, in order to ensure that readers appreciate the scale of the task, and the importance of getting it as right as possible at this stage.

This chapter will incorporate a discussion of the relationship between the methodological approaches introduced earlier and the kind of pragmatic and practical choices which intending researchers will have to make. It will also explore further the potential benefits of strategies which integrate alternative methodological assumptions into a coherent project, using 'mixed methods'.

Chapter 9 will consider the operational requirements of carrying out social work research, in light of our earlier discussion. The key steps of 'scoping' the field (literature reviews), carrying out fieldwork, recording and analysing findings, critical review and 'writing-up' will be considered, in order to elaborate the connections between choice of strategy and the route towards implementation. For example, the relationship between these stages in an 'action research' project is demonstrably different from one which follows a standard experimental design, or a mixed-methods approach. The sequencing of work and the ways in which findings are recorded and used are clearly dependent on the choices made here. Thus, the reader will be able to make concrete and realistic connections between aims and intentions and the practical tasks of carrying out and documenting a credible research project.

As the previous chapter suggests, in social work the research process does not end with the completion of a report, or with a single output, particularly where it is seen as part of a wider project, for instance working towards empowering service users or communities. Once again, the orientation of researchers (and those who commission or utilize research) will have signifi-cant implications for the ways in which it is disseminated, perceived and used. The uses to which it is put and the impact on those concerned are essential questions, and it will be important here to consider the relationship between social work research, dissemination and practice, in its widest sense. In the case of students carrying out relatively small-scale or personal projects, the potential outcomes of their research in terms of service-user benefit, influencing systems or achieving change in policy and practice should not be overlooked. Every research study will leave a 'footprint' of some kind, even if this only affects participants.

This discussion will enable us to conclude with a fuller appreciation of the positive value of research activities and a sense of the interactive relationship between academic enquiry and practice. The need for practitioner-researchers and researcher-practitioners may be considered here as an illustration of this point. Research will be shown to be a powerful and constructive tool to improve understanding and action in the social work field.

Key points

- Social work research is eclectic, based on a range of academic disciplines and subject to a variety of interests and influences.
- Ideas about social work research are changing rapidly, notably with the increasing influence of user-led, participative approaches and the impact of other changes, such as the 'professionalization' of social work and growing interest among policy makers and research bodies.
- There is therefore a need to appreciate and interpret evidence obtained in a variety of different ways, both in order to understand and evaluate existing research, and to be able to develop and apply new research initiatives.

Note

1. The short answer is 'no', but more of this later.

1 DRIVERS, DEMANDS AND CONSTRAINTS IN SOCIAL WORK RESEARCH

Approaching social work research: not just a matter of choice

As we have already seen, social work itself is a contested and complex project. It is therefore inevitable that research in the field will also be the subject of competing demands and alternative agendas. At present, it is possible to identify a number of key influences which are likely to play a crucial part in shaping ideas and debates about the subject. Some of these can only be seen as positive developments, but this does not mean that they are any less of a challenge to us.

It is clear, for example, that messages about the centrality of service users' views has permeated thinking in policy and practice and, as a result, we have been required to reconsider how we formulate and address research questions, too. In some cases, indeed, it may be appropriate for service users themselves to take the lead from the start, but this represents a fundamental challenge to previously held ideas about researcher expertise and methodological issues such as validity, reliability and objectivity.

We have also seen the recent trend towards 'professionalization' in social work practice mirrored by a growing recognition of its distinctive identity as a research discipline. This has been reflected in current developments supported by the Economic and Social Research Council (ESRC), especially, which has sponsored a number of initiatives in this respect (for example, the seminar series on 'Theorising Social Work Research' in 1999–2000).

These trends within the field of social work must also be viewed within the context of a time of considerable activity at government level and in the broader policy arena which has had a very significant impact on the terrain of practice, and involves major implications for the process of knowledge generation, the articulation of ideas about 'good practice' and evaluation of service interventions. For many in the field, of course, this interest has been viewed as a double-edged sword. Substantial levels of investment in practice developments have been paralleled by an unprecedented sense of 'micro-management' which many practitioners have found to be deeply unwelcome and, indeed, counterproductive (Jones 2001).

At the same time as a number of major changes have affected policy and practice, longer-standing debates about the value and legitimacy of different types of research have continued, acting as a moving backdrop. It is not surprising, then, that social work is characterized by continuing uncertainty about the relationship between research and practice, and, indeed, the underlying value of research. For those in the field, who are subject to continual pressure to respond to requests from evaluators, researchers and managers for information about what they are doing and how, with little obvious sign of any direct benefit to their own work, this may seem little more than an unwelcome distraction, while the *real* work proceeds on the ground. As we shall see, one of the major challenges for researchers, whatever their starting point, is to establish credibility with their colleagues in the field and people who use services, as well as methodological legitimacy.

Interests and expectations: driving the research agenda?

Of course, research does not take place in a vacuum. In social work, as in other spheres of welfare intervention, the active involvement of a range of interests, or stakeholders, inevitably means that there will be competing viewpoints. It is too simplistic to seek to quantify the level of influence exerted by different interests, but we need at least to gain an idea of what these might be.

As Pinkerton (1998: 33) has acknowledged, the 'development of social research in the UK' has been a political process which has been closely associated with the changing trajectory of government policy and the welfare state. It is clear that much of the funding available for research in the wider field of social work has its origins in government departments (Marsh and Fisher 2005), and as a result we might reasonably expect that these will have a considerable degree of influence over the research process at all levels, from agenda setting, through the selection of researchers, to the methodology, conduct and dissemination of findings. It has also been the case that in the past substantial research programmes, notably in children's services, have been influential in changing the focus of concern and influencing policy-makers and practitioners alike (e.g. Department of Health and Social Security 1985; Department of Health 1996, 2001a). Both of these series of research projects are seen collectively to have helped shift the emphasis in children's social services towards early prevention and family support and away from what was seen as an over-emphasis on child protection work.

Many other government research programmes can be seen to be informed by a particular policy agenda, and perhaps to be geared to producing outcomes which support this. Indeed, this is clearly the case with much recent research in youth justice funded by the Home Office and the Youth Justice Board (an arm's length quango, but still strongly government influenced). However, Pinkerton (1999) questions the extent to which government's influence can be seen as entirely monolithic or predictable, suggesting that there are other elements of 'civil society' and indeed tensions within government which may affect the ways in which official research is carried out and used. As an illustration of this point, he cites a study of leaving care in Northern Ireland, carried out in the 1990s and commissioned by government. The initial 'stakeholders' identified for this study were 'the academics', 'policy makers', 'practitioners' and 'service users', and its stated aims were to provide a 'baseline' of information and comment to support future service developments in this area of work. Noting that those concerned with service delivery had different agendas and timescales for the research, Pinkerton (1999: 4) also observes that the young people concerned were expected to 'benefit from the other stakeholders achieving their outcomes'. There was a clear 'hierarchy' of involvement in the study, as the researchers subsequently acknowledged, with their primary focus being on the expectations of the policy makers, 'not least because they were also the funders'. Although this piece of research did not initially accord a significant role to service users, awareness of this shortcoming became stronger as the work progressed, and attempts were made to promote a more participatory approach both in the conduct and outputs of the study. Despite the imperfect nature of this working compromise, the final recommendations and subsequent initiatives did produce positive outcomes in relation to the wider project of young people's participation. Pinkerton thus argues that:

> the research system needs to be recognised as part of the wider social care system and as a site of negotiations between a range of stakeholders – all with their own legitimate interests and ways of working.
>
> (1999: 6)

One aspect of this relationship has gained particular attention in recent years, and that is the emergence of service users and their 'movements' as significant participants in the research process. According to Beresford (1999), this development parallels the wider growth in the strength of service user organizations, fuelled by a recognition of their collective interests. As he also points out, it is not simply that 'mainstream' research had not properly involved service users historically, but that it was experienced 'as part of a structure of discrimination and oppression; an activity which is both intrusive and disempowering in its own right' (1999: 4). At the same time, the outcomes of research of this nature could also be used to perpetuate oppressive service-delivery processes. Two responses by service user groups are identified. First, they have established their own research bases and carried out independent studies of one kind or another, especially in the fields of disability and mental health. And, second, they have taken a much stronger role in seeking to influence and lead research originating from other sources. These developments have also been associated with a recognition that the question of influence and control over research is not just a 'one-off' issue which can be resolved at a certain point in the process; rather, it is a continuing issue which permeates the activity from beginning to end. From the point of view of service users, this brings the focus to bear

> on the degree of user involvement and control in all key aspects of research including:
>
> - the origination of research
> - who gains the benefits of research
> - the accountability of the research
> - who undertakes the research
> - research funding
> - research design and process
> - dissemination of research findings
> - action following from research.
>
> (Beresford 1999: 4)

This helpfully illustrates the point that for all participants, the research process is continuous, and relationships and agreements negotiated at one stage may have to be renegotiated and possibly fought over again. It also draws attention to the possibility that involvement may not (and need not) extend throughout the process, although there are further issues arising from this kind of partial involvement.

A service user organization known to the author has had at least three very different experiences of 'participatory' research relationships, for example. In one case, the organization originated the idea for the research, recruited a suitable research partner, obtained funding from a charitable trust and then maintained oversight of the design, process and dissemination. In another case, the organization was invited to participate in a national study for which the (academic) researchers concerned had already obtained funding; however, the organization was included very substantially in the design, conduct and dissemination of the study, including co-authorship of the accessible report that was produced of the outcomes. In both these instances, those involved clearly felt that they had been able to take part fully and to exercise a considerable degree of influence (or even control) over both process and outcomes. In a third case, however, the same organization was recruited as a partner in another study where the experience was much less positive, and this was because they felt they were not listened to but merely required to follow a pre-prepared script (literally), in carrying out a series of interviews with other service users. Thus, even though the research may have achieved its initial aim of ensuring service user 'participation', this was not the way it felt to those involved.

We must accept then that social work research is not, cannot and should not be treated as a pure or discrete exercise of discovery. This is because the field and subjects of inquiry will always include people who are likely to be affected by its outcomes, and may well be directly involved in its processes. Despite this caveat, much research in social work is, of course, carried out more or less independently by students at all levels, whose primary concern (apart from passing the course!) is to investigate an aspect of the field which is of particular importance to them. In other words, the 'origination' of the research may rest entirely with the investigator concerned. There is nothing inherently problematic in that, but it does not obviate the sort of challenges identified by Beresford (1999) in the ensuing processes. As in practice, researchers may find themselves negotiating difficult terrain in the interface between organizational interests and those of people who use services and carers, over who has control over different aspects of the project, and on what terms. For researchers in a relatively weak bargaining position, which is often the case for those carrying out individual projects, either as students or practitioners, the task of negotiating permissions and access may necessarily involve more or less uncomfortable compromises. It may seem reasonable at the outset, for example, to offer to share findings with the host agency in exchange for access to the specific research setting. However, this clearly does not obviate the need to adhere to ethical standards and social work values in carrying out the investigation. Service users may, for example, express highly critical views of agencies or practitioners which they do not wish to be attributed.

Of course, it is also important to be wary of making promises about the potential uses and impacts of research in order to secure participation when it is almost impossible to predict the outcome (Pinkerton 1999). Indeed, it would seem both morally and methodologically suspect to try to anticipate one's findings before carrying out a piece of research, in any case (some might feel that it is only government which does that!).

We must recognize, then, that the context within which social work research is conducted will necessarily involve differing and sometimes con-flicting interests. In all likelihood, these will reflect broader relationships of structural inequalities and differential power relationships. This, in turn, will generate both practical and ethical challenges for researchers themselves.

What is social work research intended to achieve?

Once we have acknowledged that the field is contested in terms of expect-ations and interests, it also becomes clear that there are likely to be compet-ing views about what social work research is intended to achieve. The importance of considering this question is underlined by McLaughlin (2007) whose account of his attempts to promote research awareness among practitioner colleagues fell foul of their apparent indifference to its possible uses. After failing to sustain their enthusiasm for a programme of seminars to disseminate findings among the staff of one local authority, despite initial enthusiasm, he comments: 'I wondered why my colleagues could not see that research would provide us with the answers to many of our questions and help us to become more effective practitioners and able to deliver a higher quality service' (2007: 150). He attributes this outcome to a range of possible reasons, including pressures of work, lack of skills in reading and interpreting findings, limited access, or the inconclusive and unhelpful nature of many outputs. Paradoxically, it seems, research both complicates the world when practitioners want workable solutions and, it simplifies problems by drawing neat conceptual boundaries round them while those in practice have to grapple with 'messy' reality.

This critical observation takes us to the focal point of the question here which revolves around the uses of research in an applied discipline with many potential interests to be considered. For some, it seems, the purpose can be stated quite simply in the form of certain 'basic assumptions'. Thus, for example: 'child care researchers are concerned to ensure that their work has an impact on policy and practice', even though 'this is not easy to achieve' (Pinkerton 1998: 42). There is a well-established tradition of inquiry which emphasizes the search for effective measures and evidence of positive practice outcomes (e.g. Sheldon 1983, 1984, 1986; Sheldon and MacDonald 1992). It has been argued that the prioritization of this concern with the nature and impact of intervention is one of the distinguishing features of social work research. A distinction is drawn

> between scientific research on causes (biological studies in the laboratory, for example), and research on what works in front-line practice (such as in the primary care clinic) . . . In social care, effective intervention in the front line requires research that derives directly from practice concerns and offers solutions designed and tested to be feasible in practice . . . As a practice research discipline, social work research (at its best) can do this.
>
> (Marsh and Fisher 2005: viii)

However, there have been some concerns expressed about the apparent preoccupation with this particular kind of objective in social work research (D'Cruz and Jones 2004). The limitations identified are partly of a methodological nature, and partly attributable to the 'political' nature of the research process. For the moment, it will be sufficient just to note that it is important to avoid taking too restrictive a view of what the objectives of investigative study should be, and to consider alternative viewpoints which might have different priorities. Lorenz (2000), for example, offers a radically different view of what research in social work might fruitfully seek to achieve, especially in light of recent developments in our understanding of emancipatory practice. For him, social work research is reconstituted more as a form of dialogue than as an exercise in establishing fixed understandings. It is 'really an exercise in inter-cultural competence' (2000: 7), which is essentially a project to articulate and appreciate mutual differences, and to utilize these as a basis to negotiate common understanding across potentially divisive barriers. In this context, arguably, it is the research *process* rather than its outputs which is the focal point of interest and where collaborative goals can be realized. Certain forms of action research and other participatory methods might be seen as reflecting this kind of principle. Most significantly, no attempt is made to pre-judge any aspect of the process but to ensure that the right conditions are created for mutual exploration of different (and shared) perceptions.

A third possibility would be to broaden the scope of inquiry, so that social work research could encompass contextual questions and the issue of problem definitions, which effectively precede approaches concerned with finding solutions to pre-determined 'problems', or focus primarily on interactive processes irrespective of the broader picture. A classic study of this type was carried out by Bebbington and Miles (1989) on the subject of the circumstances of children entering the care system. This wide-ranging study considered the backgrounds of 2528 children entering the care system in 13 local authority areas over a six month period in 1987. Using logistic regression analysis the authors found that the likelihood of children entering care was subject to massive variation depending on their personal and family characteristics.

Table 1.1 illustrates these probabilities for two hypothetical children from contrasting backgrounds. As Bebbington and Miles (1989) observed, this kind of generalized study could be expected to generate findings which would help to identify the proper scope and strategy for social work intervention. They tentatively concluded that the identifiable association between 'single-parent families' and admission to care could be explained partly by the absence of 'social networks', which might in turn suggest 'the salience of family support strategies to prevention' (1989: 364, 365).

Table 1.1 Odds of admission to care according to background

Child 'A'	*Child 'B'*
Aged 5 to 9	Aged 5 to 9
No supplementary benefit	Household head receives SB
Two-parent family	Single-adult household
Three or fewer children	Four or more children
White	Mixed-ethnic origin
Owner-occupied house	Private rented house
More rooms than people	One or more persons per room
Odds are 1 in 7000	*Odds are 1 in 10*

Source: Bebbington and Miles 1989.

Box 1.1 Using statistics in social work research

Usually, when I ask social work students about this, I find that many are uncomfortable with using or interpreting statistics. This means that there is a double-edged risk here: they may be inclined either to be unduly suspicious of numerical data, or, on the other hand, to accept these uncritically. In some circumstances, though, techniques such as regression analysis may offer real insights by showing how different factors in the investigation may be linked.

If we know what this relationship is in pre-existing cases, for instance, it gives us the capacity to predict what it is likely to be when future examples occur. Hence, in the Bebbington and Miles's (1989) example, it might give an indication of where preventive interventions might best be focused. 'Simple linear regression' (Weinbach and Grinnell 2007), for instance, straightforwardly captures the relationship between two variables in the form of the equation: $Y = a + bX$.

While statistical techniques can be highly complex in some cases, and may appear daunting, there is still considerable value to be extracted from the appropriate use of relatively simple methods as well as purely descriptive use of numbers. Useful questions include: how many are in the sample? How long did it take to achieve this outcome? What proportion of the sample has this characteristic?

In order to try and encompass the range of possible objectives for social work research attempts have been made to offer typologies to enable us to categorize these. Lishman (2000: 1), for example, has suggested that the 'development of knowledge for practice has to encompass' three distinct areas of activity: the task of developing contextual understanding of 'individuals and society'; the identification of 'effective social work interventions'; and, exploration of 'the meaning and experience' of social work processes for 'participants'. As she recognizes, it is likely that methodological choices on the part of researchers will reflect their 'perspectives' on social work and its aims but this does not, in her view, mean that we should fall into the trap of identifying with 'polarized' positions which dismiss the value of alternative approaches. Instead, what is needed 'is a realistic assessment of the relative strengths and weaknesses of contested methodological positions and judicious choice of method appropriate to the purpose of the enquiry' (2000: 1).

Shaw and Norton (2007: 8) offer a similar typology, but with an additional component. According to them:

General distinctions . . . can be made between:

- methods for providing evidence of effectiveness and improving social work intervention
- methods for enhancing theory and knowledge about problems, policies and practice
- methods for highlighting and advancing the quality of lived experience, practical wisdom, and personal and organisational learning
- methods for facilitating social inclusion, social change and justice.

In setting out these distinctions between possible aims of social work research, they also importantly caution against 'exclusivity' when linking methods with purpose. While there might be a tendency, for example, to associate qualitative or quantitative methods with one or other type of objective, they feel that this is too restrictive, and indeed, potentially compromises the quality and depth of understanding achievable.

Interestingly, though, this overview of social work research does not caution against taking 'normative positions' (Shaw and Norton 2007: 7), suggesting that it is 'rarely possible – or perhaps even desirable' to attempt to place oneself outside the subject matter as a researcher. It may be more appropriate, for example, for the researcher to make explicit her/his own perspective and beliefs, insofar as they are relevant anyway, rather than to attempt to bracket them out of the investigative process.

The position of Shaw and Norton (2008) is somewhat at odds, however, with that adopted in another wide-ranging review of the field, which argues that the 'best research is specifically designed to be as free as possible from bias in favour of any interest group or policy position' (Marsh and Fisher 2005: vi). Clearly, this apparent disagreement brings into focus the fundamental question in social work (and all other) research as to whether or not it is possible to aspire to a truly objective position and, even if it is possible, is this necessarily appropriate, especially in a context where practice is, by definition, concerned essentially with groups and individuals who are experiencing various forms of disadvantage and/or oppression?

This issue brings us back again to the question of what social work research is intended to, or should seek to, achieve. Given that this is an area of practice informed by quite explicit values about promoting equality and challenging oppression, there is clearly a case to be made for the argument that research into the subject should equally be informed by these goals of empowerment and rights. Feminism, for instance, has sought to articulate the positive value of taking a clearly committed position in social work research and practice (Hudson 1985). Thus, for example, the way in which the research process incorporates choices about how participants' views are made known may be important as a sign of commitment and an empowering act in itself. Ironically, perhaps, opting *not* to be heard may be a powerful statement. In one study involving women who were 'mental health service recipients', collective choices were made about whether and how to give 'voice' to their experiences:

Aware of the prospective pitfalls of voice, and that there are no guarantees that an audience will be amenable to hearing, . . . women's agency was demonstrated through their respective decisions and refusals to speak.

(Gray 2007: 427)

And what counts as 'social work knowledge'?

Having observed that social work research incorporates different assumptions about what it is important or necessary to find out, it is perhaps unsurprising that we should also encounter a range of views about what constitutes 'knowledge' in social work. Some, indeed, have given considerable effort over to the task of generating 'a general theory of social work knowledge' (Sheppard 1998: 778) which both connects it to, and distinguishes it from, other ways of knowing to be found in the social sciences. For both Sheppard (1995) and Parton (1999) the distinguishing features of social work as a discipline are to be found in its necessary and constant connection to 'something called 'practice' (Parton 1999: 1). For Sheppard, this is particularly important because it charts a path which enables the development of a specific body of knowledge and understanding which is not dominated by other disciplines such as sociology. He has developed the concept of 'practice validity' as a means of evaluating evidence and information, in order to test out whether 'the knowledge used is capable of being utilized in a way consistent with the nature and limits of social work' (1998: 772).

This project can be called into question, however:

What is it about social work that makes it distinctive from other professional practices, for example, law, medicine, therapy, counselling? And is there something about practice knowledge which differentiates it from attempts simply to apply knowledge from other disciplines, for example, the social sciences, to a particular area of social and professional activity?

(Parton 1999: 1)

Of course, these issues connect to much broader and very well-established debates about what can be known ('ontology'), and how we can uncover this knowledge ('epistemology').

It is unsurprising that the question of what constitutes social work knowledge and how it can be obtained in valid and reliable forms is clearly influenced by wider debates, even if it has its own distinctive characteristics, too. Different conventions are clearly identifiable within the discipline, according to Parton (1999), including the 'positivist' tradition associated with Sheldon (1978), on one hand, which sees knowledge as a 'product', and the idea of knowledge as 'process' (Sheppard 1998), revealed through 'reflection-in-action' (Schon 1983), on the other.

Sheldon (1983) has claimed that it is most appropriate to approach the

---

Exercise 1.1 What counts as social work 'knowledge'?

Social workers often have to deal with documents and records which claim to provide factual evidence about people, their characteristics and circumstances.

It is possible to take these at face value, as a direct representation of those concerned and key features of their lives; or, they may be viewed as approximations, in the sense that the means by which this information is gathered are likely to be imperfect; or, they could be seen as 'constructs' derived as much from the beliefs and attitudes of those creating the records as from any external source.

Which of these is likely to be your starting point? In what ways do you think it would influence your choices about how to carry out research into the preparation and maintenance of social work records?

---

quest for knowledge in social work as a practical task, geared towards solving recognized social problems, without necessarily being able to rely on clear or comprehensive 'explanatory theories' to explain 'why and how' particular methods 'might work' (1983: 477). It is important, in his view, for evaluation and research in social work to avoid being too ambitious. Instead, we should be addressing the question of 'whether our small bits of intervention . . . come out roughly as predicted' (1983: 479). However, these modest goals should not deter us from the task of developing rigorous methods for testing the effectiveness of practice where possible, he would argue. It is important to avoid over-complicating relatively straightforward issues, it seems:

> As to what 'effectiveness' actually means, I am puzzled by the difficulty many colleagues seem to have with this concept. It simply means describing carefully the *status quo* and its likely effects, saying what it is you think you can do to alter this and why it would be beneficial to try; describing how you think you can bring this off, saying in advance what kind of tests could be applied to back up the view that something along these lines has been achieved; getting on with it and then defending your results against criticism.
>
> (Sheldon 1983: 480)

According to this characterization, the knowledge generated by social work research can be clearly delineated through a linear process of setting up a test with (more or less) known variables under (more or less) known conditions to produce identifiable, consistent and replicable outcomes. In fairness to Sheldon, he also acknowledges that there are circumstances where a 'softer' methodology (1983: 480) might be required to acquire useful understanding of social work processes, although it still seems that his principal concern is to generate a particular kind of knowledge based around identifying impact and effectiveness of practice interventions.

Sheppard's (1998) view, on the other hand, is that especially in a practice discipline like social work, knowledge is not really fixed but is continually generated, revised and improved upon through the social work process. Indeed, he goes so far as to suggest that this is an inevitable part of everyday experience, and that 'social science understanding' is no different from what we learn from 'everyday life' (1998: 767). Although in some ways he draws on the kind of methodology espoused by Sheldon, seeing people as inevitably 'hypothesis testers', he suggests that this is a continuous or 'progressive' activity, which leads to continual revision and reformulation of ideas and knowledge which is good enough for practical purposes. We must, however forego the possibility of ever achieving 'certainty' by these means: 'We must also recognize that such knowledge is provisional – we must always be prepared to revise out hypothesis in the light of further evidence' (Sheppard 1998: 768).

Although he does not refer to their work at this point, this formulation bears a distinct similarity to the methodological strategies incorporated in 'grounded theory' (Glaser and Strauss 1967), which seeks to develop a systematic basis for the conduct of research which explores its subject matter, allowing new ideas to emerge while simultaneously subjecting them to testing in light of the cumulative evidence available.

Importantly, the form of knowledge articulated here can be distinguished by its situated, concrete and practical characteristics, even though it can also be seen as having certain limits in terms of both its temporal and spatial context, and its uncertain nature. It is 'real for the time being'. Its specifically 'social work' quality is accentuated by certain key aspects of the social work task itself, notably the readiness of practitioners

> to forsake the formality of their roles, and to work with ordinary people in their 'natural' settings, using the informality of their methods as a means of negotiating solutions to their problems rather than imposing them. Imposed, formal solutions are a last resort in social work, whereas they are the norm in other settings.
>
> (Parton 1999: 4)

This echoes an earlier point made by Jordan (1987) about what he saw as the essential qualities of the social work task, and how it should address the question of elaborating working knowledge and mutual understanding with people who use services. Thus, social work uniquely 'pays close attention to individuals' own understandings of their needs' (1987: 141), and recognizes that these perceptions form part of the evidence which informs assessment and intervention processes. In this sense again, social work knowledge does not come from outside, but is developed, explored and analysed from within the interactive process. Of course, this also returns us to the question of where that knowledge can be seen to reside. If it is the product of an interactive process, it would seem that it cannot sit exclusively with one or other participant. As Beresford (1999: 6) observes, 'this raises the question of what the relationship should be between social work theorising and service users and their knowledge'. Drawing on the observation that there is not 'necessarily' any antagonism between the understandings of service users and practitioners, he does pose the question of the means by which 'service users' knowledges' can be included in the process of building understanding and theoretical insights in social work. The issue here goes beyond that of determining the most appropriate model for generating ideas and understanding to that of the relative status of different forms of knowledge. What gives a particular form of insight its legitimacy? Is it the 'rigour' with which the investigative activity is carried out? Is it the extent to which the evidence generated confirms or challenges prior understandings? Or, is it the authority and credibility which rests with the source of a particular piece of social work wisdom?

Thus, the question of what counts as social work knowledge appears to depend on a number of criteria, some of which are related to the way in which we go about gathering our evidence and constructing theoretical insights, and others which depend on the relationships between those engaged in the process of creating understanding.

The important point at this stage in the journey is not to express a clear preference for one or another approach to the generation of social work knowledge, but to recognize that it depends on a series of interlocking choices, about both the means we use and the sites and relationships we rely on as sources of evidence and understanding. When it comes to making these choices researchers necessarily have to take a committed position *because* the

---

Box 1.2 'Kinds and quality of research'

Shaw and Norton (2007) make an important distinction to be borne in mind when assessing the value of social work research. This can be captured in the form of two separate questions to be addressed to any particular study:

- Was the method used appropriate to this particular research question and research environment?
- Was the research carried out to an acceptable standard, according to the requirements of the chosen method?

Research may be carried out well but still be of limited value if it does not address the subject of inquiry in a way which makes sense methodologically.

Can we capture a sense of the 'quality of life' for older people, for example, merely by inquiring into their material circumstances?

subject of inquiry is a form of social practice, but the first element of the task is to be clear about the nature of these choices and the factors which are likely to influence them, including those which are contextually influenced. These decisions are, of course, not made in a vacuum, or by individuals without prior experience or 'positions'.

Methodology, power and legitimacy

In light of the previous observations, it is important to recognize that the relationship between methodological choices and the politics of research has long been seen as a matter which requires consideration. For instance, Trinder (1996) has suggested, like the present author, that research in social work can broadly be categorized according to three influential perspectives, which are informed by essentially 'political' judgements. In other words, apparently technical choices about strategy and method must be seen as at least partly dependent on wider assumptions about social structures and relationships. According to Trinder, the distinct perspectives which could be identified are: 'empirical practice' based on principles of 'rigorous measurement'; 'pragmatism', geared towards practical problem solving; and 'participatory/critical research' with a focus on empowerment through research practice. For her, the links between these and prevailing ideological currents could be made explicitly, tying forms of practice and social work 'knowledge' to particular social developments. Thus, empiricist agendas could be located in a specific historical context, namely the 'collapse of a self-confident modernism' (1996: 234), and the emergence of the 'risk society' (Beck 1992). The assertion of the merits of scientific methods could be seen as an attempt to reclaim credibility and coherence, rather than a timeless articulation of good practice in research:

> What we have is a reframed modernist 'back-to-the-future' project tied to neo-liberalism, where a science of confidence, discovery and exploration is replaced by a science of defensiveness, discipline and control.
>
> (Trinder 1996: 234)

Thus, the search for certainty in the sphere of social work research is mirrored by an increasing sense of insecurity and threat in the wider social world, according to this account. For Trinder, the model's claim to 'truth' is closely linked with an attempt to assert political 'power' by sectional interests: 'Rigorous it may be, but neutral it is not' (1996: 235).

The second distinct research tradition suggested by Trinder (1996) is that of 'pragmatism', which almost explicitly seeks to avoid making political choices, and is preoccupied with seeking the best possible fit between identified problem and investigative strategy and method. Pragmatist approaches tend, according to this view, to 'suppress' contradictory aspects of their inquiries, such as the tension between 'social constructionism' and the idea that the social world can be systematically understood as a fixed entity. Avoiding awkward epistemological questions such as this is associated with a tendency for this type of research to be descriptive rather than analytical. Thus, we might find (as we often do), that 'intervention' is taken as a given, rather than analysed in terms of its specific construction and impact; this is often found to be the case in investigations of social work practice in criminal justice, for example.

While suspicious of the potential for experimental or 'empiricist' methods to do justice to the complexity of the social world and social work processes, the pragmatist approach does not discount the possibility of drawing on these methods, or those of participatory research, where these can be utilized conveniently. The net effect is to produce a rather anodyne, and certainly incomplete, model of research practice in Trinder's (1996: 237) view: 'Research deals with surface not depth understanding, explanation or causation. Complexity is rendered into realism. Politics and power are excluded as researchers/practitioners pursue a strategy of change within the system'.

The third position identified by Trinder is the 'participative/critical' model of research practice which emphasizes the subjective experience, voices and knowledges of research participants. For researchers in this tradition, the project is one of 'power and empowerment', whose aim is to express opposition and resistance through enabling oppressed groups and individuals to articulate their own truths and understandings. Unlike the pragmatist approach, this model of research does not eschew analysis but views it not as something imposed by the researcher, rather as something which emerges from shared insights derived from the process itself. This strategy clearly finds echoes in certain strands of social work practice:

> within an analysis of oppression, the social worker or researcher works alongside members of oppressed groups in a non-hierarchical way drawing links between an individual's situation and structural factors, as a means of creating change and challenging oppression at individual and group level.
>
> (Trinder 1996: 238)

There is a problem with this approach, however, and this is that giving the 'voices of the oppressed' privileged status and uncritically accepting their truths does not enable the investigator to uncover how these truths 'come to be established' nor does it provide much guidance when (as they sometimes will) they are found to be inconsistent or impossible to reconcile.

Trinder (1996) concludes from this overview that research is, indeed, 'political', and that there is a discernible link between specific 'social work perspectives' and associated research methodologies. Thus, dependent on one's starting point, different questions will be asked, different investigative strategies will be applied, and, most significantly, different forms of judgement will be brought to bear on 'truth claims' (1996: 241). In essence, a series of related points is being made here. First, research in social work necessarily involves making political choices. Second, the methodology to be applied will thus depend on the ideological starting point of the researcher. Third, these will vary according to certain distinctive characteristics. And, as a result, there is no possibility of mixing methods.

It is with this final point that Little (1998) has subsequently taken issue, arguing on the basis of his own experience that it is entirely possible for the same piece of research to draw on a range of methodological perspectives. He believes that 'assigning researchers or their individual studies to these categories, as if they could be spotted in the street by the colour of their coats' is not appropriate (1998: 49). While he accepts that it is 'right to identify different types of research' (1998: 55), he resists the argument that there is little room for 'overlap', or that 'political considerations' have a significant part to play in determining the approach to be selected. They are 'of minor importance' (1998: 55). Instead, choices about method are a matter of 'rummaging' in the 'tool-bag' for the best equipment for the task in hand. Partly because social work itself is essentially practical and geared towards problem solving, he suggests that

> the choice and construction of research approach is a technical matter reflecting the middle-range theory and intellectual reference point applied by the investigator to a research problem. Good researchers tend to pull methods out of the tool kit as they are needed.
>
> (1998: 52)

Of course, Trinder (1996) could dismiss this as merely the argument of a committed 'pragmatist', but underlying this is a critical question for the research practitioner. Is it possible, or desirable, for social work research to adopt an entirely neutral position in relation to her/his intended programme of investigation? If not, is it possible, or acceptable, to 'bracket off' one's own beliefs in order to carry out the study in a competent and value-free fashion? Or, is it possible to work from a committed position, and still draw on a range of methodological options and apply them capably?

For Little, the answer to these questions might depend on the circumstances, citing his own experience of researching some subjects on which he did not hold any prior views, while acknowledging that his work could be identified as drawing on certain 'intellectual reference points' (1998: 51); although, as he points out, these too might derive from different methodological and, indeed, ideological traditions.

Certainly, in my own experience, I would suggest that it is possible to utilize widely different methods within the same research initiative and yet achieve a coherence of purpose and outcome. In one instance, a study of the impact of the Social Fund on poverty at different times incorporated a detailed analysis of spending decisions and budgets, on the one hand (Cohen et al. 1996) and, on the other, drew on the detailed personal accounts of claimants affected by those decisions (Smith 2003). Both, incidentally, were carried out in the context of a strongly held personal belief that the arrangements for meeting emergency financial needs incorporated in the Social Fund were (and remain) fundamentally unjust.

We can accept Trinder's (1996) argument that social work research is essentially political, and that certain broad ideological tendencies might underpin both strategic orientation and choice of methods, without necessarily drawing the conclusion that these are fixed or immutable relationships. Indeed, perhaps the appropriate conclusion to be drawn from this discussion is that we should rather adopt a position which 'eschew[s] hierarchies' (Shaw and Norton 2007: 34). Insofar as this is a political position, it is one which questions the perceived dominance of certain modes of enquiry, focusing, for example on the 'difficulty of applying standard (medical) hierarchy criteria of quality to social work research, such as using randomised control trials'.

If this is the case, it seems that judgements of quality and credibility of research should be made in terms of its internal reference points, and the competence with which methods are applied, rather than by reference to predetermined external criteria rooted in either political choices or assumed methodological hierarchies:

> Methodology/method should be fit for purpose and be used to best answer the research questions. Innovatory methods are significant but should be judged in that context. Hence, methodological quality should be judged according to the type of research being carried out. Not every type of research will fulfil all quality criteria, but research should be primarily fit for purpose and then as robust and transparent as possible.
>
> (Shaw and Norton 2007: 35)

Framing social work research

We have explored in this chapter some of the ways in which research in social work is shaped and driven by a variety of influences and interests. There are clearly a number of powerful forces in play, and changing trends in the ways in which the task in general is organised and managed (Corby 2006). In identifying different ideological and methodological positions, the aim has been to enable intending researchers to acknowledge that these are inevitable features of the landscape; to locate themselves in relation to these; and then to make considered and explicit choices about their own rationale and methods. However, it also seems clear that some aspects of the terrain are negotiable, and we should not necessarily expect specific research practices and assumptions to flow automatically from the adoption of a particular 'position' or methodological orientation.

In reaching this position, I have tried to suggest that we should recognize the significance of the kind of influences to which we are subject, but that there is also scope for rethinking apparently fixed and constraining methodological orthodoxies. Corby (2006: 175), for example, is concerned that social work research is becoming 'so top-down organised that only certain types and methods of research which provide useful but uncritical material for policy development are deemed relevant'. For example, he suggests that this means that there is very little material on certain aspects of 'disempowerment', such as the 'issues of gender or sexual orientation' (2006: 174) which is sponsored by government.

However, at the same time, there are other, countervailing influences, such as the growing articulacy of service user movements, which not only offer a focal point for resistance but also incorporate alternative models of research practice. They also help us to recognize the kind of criteria to be applied both when evaluating existing research and when planning to initiate it. For example:

• In what ways is this research consistent with social work values, in its approach as well as its substantive findings?
• Is this research clearly practice-oriented?
• Whose interests are being (should be) served by this piece of research?

It is important too for the practising researcher to recognize that these and related questions are not simply to be asked on a 'one-off' basis at the outset of any particular inquiry, but they continue to apply and should be brought to bear on the process, just as much as the aims and objectives. Whatever the worthy intentions of the study which exploited the service user organization referred to earlier, the reality was that this organization, and probably others involved, were adversely affected by the experience. This kind of tension may be experienced acutely when, for whatever reason, external pressures or expectations become more insistent; possibly, this could be due to lack of time, or to research commissioners' expectations of the kind of outcomes they would like. However, for social work, this is the point where research and practice come into close alignment around their shared values: service users' interests cannot be compromised in the process. One workshop member in the overview study undertaken by Shaw and Norton (2007: 35) expressed this point in terms of 'the need for a social justice agenda to underlie social work research and a clear statement in any quality criteria that good-quality social work research will not exploit or disempower people'.

This suggests that one very specific test of social work research 'quality' should be the extent to which it adheres to underlying professional values, albeit that these, too, are subject to variable interpretation.

Key points

- Like practice, social work research is subject to a range of influences, including policy drivers, academic conventions, service user interests and power dynamics
- The purposes and context of research will inevitably (and should) influence methodological choices
- It is important to retain a degree of flexibility in order to avoid pre-empting these choices, given the range of interests and alternative approaches available.

2 'WHAT WORKS':
EVIDENCE FOR PRACTICE?

Types of social work research

Having initially outlined a number of possible approaches to social work research, we will now proceed to explore several of these in rather more detail. The aim here is to sketch out, in somewhat 'idealized' form (Weber 1957), alternative ways of conceptualizing and undertaking the research task, specifically in the social work context, although many of the underlying principles are applicable across a wider range of disciplines. In the first part of this exercise, I will set out some of the central assumptions which inform (and tend to differentiate) each model, before going on to consider their application in the research setting.

While it is possible to be over-prescriptive in assigning particular research strategies to distinctive 'paradigms', the aim here is not to establish a 'hierarchy' (Shaw and Norton 2007) of methodologies, nor is it to set up artificial oppositions and conflicts between methods when there may be considerable benefit to be gained from productive interactions. However, by setting out some points on which different models can be distinguished, it is hoped that the purposes and practicalities of the research task itself can be clarified, and that intending researchers will be able to glean some helpful ideas about obtaining the best possible 'fit' between their intentions and the methods to be applied.

Initially in this exercise we will consider the model of enquiry which has in recent years been encapsulated within the term 'what works' (McLaughlin 2007), and which is associated with the search for evidence to support the development of models of good practice (or to identify and eliminate bad, or ineffective, practice). Unlike other models, then, this perspective is associated with an essentially 'technical' approach, concerned with the impacts and changes effected by particular forms of intervention, or with the antecedents of certain problematic social phenomena which merit attention (such as the 'causes' of youth crime, for instance). In other words, the focus is very much on problem identification, and, problem solving. This approach to social work research is held to be associated with medically dominated traditions of clinical practice, and it is suggested that it has been progressively applied to correctional programmes in probation, and then social work (McLaughlin 2007). It is commended because it 'rightly reminds us of the importance of outcomes', and it is noted that there has been a recent proliferation in the number of studies which purport to investigate the important question of the influence of social work practices on the lives of children. The focus on practice and its effects obviously makes this orientation to research attractive to those in the world of policy and service delivery who are concerned with the value and effectiveness of alternative forms of intervention; as a result, there appears to be a fairly close relationship between government and other policy interests and the promotion and commissioning of research studies of this kind. Indeed, there has been a series of 'waves' of research carried out into children's services, for example, which appear to be located within this paradigm (Department of Health and Social Security 1985; Department of Health 1996, 2001a).

In order to identify its key features, we will now consider four dimensions of 'evidence-based' research (Pawson 2006) which distinguish it from other approaches: knowledge claims, methodological assumptions, research strategy and potential criticisms – a similar framework will also be applied in the following chapters.

Knowledge claims: the search for certainty

Given that this perspective is often concerned with the quality and effectiveness of social work (and other) interventions, it is unsurprising that it should prioritize the search for evidence of 'effects' of one kind or another. This necessarily leads us in the direction of certain assumptions about the nature of that evidence, as well as the appropriate methods for capturing it. Research can be expected to offer us answers which are concrete and 'real'. For Humphries (2008: 10), this viewpoint is associated with a belief in the model of knowledge generation offered by 'the physical sciences'. According to this perspective, what we can know consists of a set of fixed, substantive phenomena, and like the physical world

> social reality is external to the researcher, to be grasped and understood through appropriate methods that are rigorously examined and applied to remove all kinds of bias, including the prejudices of the researcher.
>
> (2008: 10)

Thus, irrespective of the skills and qualities of the researcher, it is believed to be possible to generate formal and complete knowledge of social phenomena from the outside. Properly applied methods of enquiry would be expected generate the same evidence and understandings regardless of the identity or characteristics of the investigator.

Underlying this position is the belief that there is no necessary distinction between the type of knowledge we can generate about the natural world and that which we can glean about social reality. As McLaughlin (2007) observes, these assumptions can be identified with the 'positivist' tradition in the social sciences. According to this, social phenomena could be seen as being determined in their substance and outcomes by 'invariant laws' of cause and effect, in just the same way as physical reality: 'The differences between them occurred because of their respective subject matters, which were little more than irritants to overcome by developing appropriate research techniques and methods' (2007: 25).

Giddens (1974) has identified a number of key principles underpinning positivist methodologies, in particular that reality consists of the sensations available to the senses, and so cannot be established by way of mental constructs; that there is no difference in applying this assumption between natural and social sciences; and that 'facts' should be clearly distinguished from beliefs and values. Irrespective of their significance, phenomena in the latter categories cannot be clearly delineated, and therefore cannot claim the same evidential status as empirical knowledge.

Improving our knowledge of the social world, according to the positivist view, depends on the 'incremental' process of discovering and explaining new data and connections between them (McLaughlin 2007). The extent of our knowledge is always likely to be determinate, but these limits are fixed by our physical capacities to create the necessary investigative tools and use them to gather more and better evidence.

It is this kind of logic which informs significant developments in social work such as the establishment and development of what purport to be comprehensive information systems, covering the needs of children, for example (DfES 2003). What appears to be a means of generating better information and promoting efficiency in the service context must also be recognized as importing certain key assumptions about what counts as valid knowledge to the heart of social work practice.

This kind of initiative is characterized by an intense level of attention to detail (DfES 2003), which relies on carefully constructed tools of definition, measurement and scaling in order to ensure accuracy and, importantly, replicability. Standardization of tools and processes is of considerable importance here because it is only by this means that we can be sure of what we are measuring. In this respect, human characteristics are held to be essentially similar to any other measurable phenomenon:

> The beliefs we hold and the values we subscribe to are as factually 'brute' as atoms, velocities or simple harmonic motion. If social scientists or social workers would only use carefully constructed apparatus

– questionnaires, Likert scales and the like – inner mental states could, in principle, be researched empirically.

(McLaughlin 2007: 26)

It thus becomes possible, in the social world, to test assumptions about the relationship between two or more phenomena, and to begin to identify potential associations and even causal links. For instance, much work has been done over recent decades to develop and refine our understanding of 'attachment' processes in order to improve assessment and practice (Howe *et al*. 1999).

The search for regularities and predictable links in human interactions perhaps predisposes those who adopt this approach to ally themselves with 'behaviourist' perspectives on 'social action' (Johnson *et al*. 1984). It is thus through their behaviour and that alone that we can gain an insight into the mental states or psychological drivers which inform human action. This is not to suggest that these unobservable states of mind do not exist, but that we must rely on what we can observe to inform our understandings of human behaviour and its antecedents. It is argued that all 'that can be publicly observed is the behaviour of the human organism under varying conditions or stimuli' and that therefore the methods to be applied are 'logically similar to those of the natural sciences' (Johnson *et al*. 1984: 33). As a result, we should be able, through observation and experiment, to develop a set of laws and principles which apply consistently to human behaviour and provide us with operational insights to be applied in practice settings. Indeed, models of intervention have commonly been developed which draw on this kind of behaviourist underpinning (e.g. Buchanan 2002). This underlying set of assumptions clearly has important implications for the kind of methods to be undertaken in social work research (and practice), especially if we also take the view that this means that other forms of inquiry have less (or even no) value in terms of generating meaningful and valid knowledge and understanding.

A further level of sophistication has been offered to empiricist knowledge claims by Popper (1980), who helps to deal with the issue of incomplete knowledge, which is a continuing problem for researchers in every field, not just the human sciences. A particular challenge for modern societies is the speed with which apparently obvious 'truths' become modified, superseded or simply disproved (Beck 1992), and this in turn appears to create difficulties for those who hold to a view of knowledge as fixed and certain. The problem seems to be that all assumptions or principles of behaviour we hold are, in effect, provisional. We cannot therefore claim to know anything with absolute certainty. However, this, in turn, helps us to make another important distinction between different forms of evidence, and, indeed, knowledge. Some forms of belief which may, indeed, inform our actions are necessarily speculative, such as 'intuition' and 'divine revelation' (Johnson *et al*. 1984) but it is only those which are capable of being observed and tested which can, in principle, be proved wrong, or 'falsified'. In other words, it is the capacity for 'falsification' which determines whether assumptions or hypotheses have any material value.

This argument is extremely important to the empiricist position for two reasons. First, it helpfully accounts for the possibility of being wrong. More importantly, though, it provides support for methodological approaches which rely on the development of ideas or hypotheses and then the establishment of processes for testing these and refining them. It enables those who start from this standpoint to attempt to pre-empt arguments that their findings and conclusions are typically inconclusive or incomplete. As McLaughlin (2007: 27) puts it, it is in fact 'by trial and error that science progresses' so that 'only those theories that have passed the best tests available are hung onto', if only until such time as they, too, are called into question by new and more rigorous tests.

Acknowledging that certainty is unattainable has further helpful implications for researchers who wish to assess the possible effects of interventions on outcomes, and to identify 'what works' (Newman et al. 2005). It is possible, for example, to argue that the quality of the tools available and the standards of evidence achieved cannot themselves be judged against absolute standards of accuracy or rigour. They must therefore be subject to continual improvement and revision, and they can also be seen as being of different levels of strength, without necessarily being inherently unsound. These are essentially *technical* matters rather than being dependent on our views about the underlying validity of our assumptions about what constitutes knowledge itself: 'We have argued that some forms of evidence may be stronger and more reliable than others' (Newman et al. 2005: 19). This, in turn, appears to enable those who adopt an evidence-based approach to social work research to accept and indeed value a wide range of methodological strategies, and to weigh them differently according to their origins and uses. Thus, it is argued, 'some sorts of information can provide a higher level of certainty than others that an intervention is likely to lead to a particular outcome' (2005: 19). However, certain kinds of investigation are more useful than others for answering some questions; and, it 'can also be seen that not all methods are practical, possible or ethical when investigating certain' topics (2005: 14). Thus, for example, surveys of service users' opinions about an intervention may offer 'valuable insights', while other methods such as quasi-experimental study can provide more 'powerful' evidence of 'the impact of an intervention' (2005: 16, 17). In this way, perhaps the door is opened to a kind of 'soft' empiricism, which does not rely simply on the observable effects of actions or behaviour in order to reach a rounded view of the effectiveness of particular practice interventions. While this may appear to be something of a compromise to the extent that it reintroduces subjective experience and opinion into the investigative frame (Johnson et al. 1984), it does not represent a rejection of the view that certain forms of externally valid and 'objective' tests can be established in the social sciences, and specifically in social work research.

Methodological assumptions: what is the problem?

Although as we have seen, researchers in the empiricist tradition sketched out here are likely to accept that the 'cultivation of uncertainty is a basic principle of scientific inquiry' (Newman *et al.* 2005: 9), and there are no ultimate answers, it is still important to seek out what 'is the best for the time being' (2005: 12). It is a perspective which is dominated by practical concerns about the causes of social and personal problems and the consequences of certain types of intervention to tackle these. There will thus be a concern to identify and characterize key aspects of a particular phenomenon, to find ways of quantifying both 'problems' and the effects of potential solutions and achieving an appropriate means of assessing 'effectiveness' (2005: 5). The end point will be a set of findings and explanations which will assist in clarifying and enhancing the performance of the social work task; indeed, this is the kind of resource which should inform the workings of any professional enterprise:

> First and foremost, social care is a practice discipline and, while it requires research from other areas to underpin it, it also requires research based in its own practice for its development . . . it needs social work research that is practice-based and that will deliver practice change.
>
> (Marsh and Fisher 2005: 10)

Here there does seem to be a preoccupation with practice and its effects, and it seems to be suggested, too, that this is an essential characteristic of social work research, which will have certain consequences for problem formulation, clearly.

Even if we restrict ourselves in this way to focus solely on the practice setting, this does not necessarily simplify the task of defining our research question, however (Lishman 2000). It is acknowledged for example that social work 'itself is a complex, uncertain and ambiguous activity' (Lishman 2000: 2) involving a number of dimensions of accountability, decision-making and intervention. It necessarily involves processes rather than operating at a fixed point and it is clearly interactive, and increasingly expected to be responsive to service users, if not led by them.

Nonetheless, researchers working from the 'what works' perspective incorporate an implicit assumption that it is possible (and desirable) to achieve some degree of clarity about the focus and objectives of practice-based research. For instance, it is likely that this kind of inquiry will be concerned with the success or otherwise of specific types of intervention, and so will seek to establish specific 'success criteria' (Lishman 2000). Clearly, too, there will be an implicit requirement to create some definitional limits around the object, processes and effects of practice. Thus, for example, effectiveness studies will wish to establish a range of 'baseline criteria' which will be used to establish the circumstances obtaining prior to any intervention taking place. So, there may well be a need to decide upon and set up recording procedures for a range of prior information about individuals or groups and their characteristics and circumstances. If, say, we wish to consider the impact of certain forms of mental health treatment on diverse ethnic groups, then it will obviously be important to establish robust mechanisms for recording ethnicity. However, even this single criterion for distinguishing individuals is by no means unproblematic, and this poses, at the very least, significant practical problems for researchers. What is necessarily being undertaken in this example is a form of 'abstraction' (Pawson 2006), which must be undertaken with considerable 'care' in order to avoid misrepresentation or corruption of the data. As Pawson (2006: 76) observes, in respect of 'systematic reviews' of research findings:

> In devising and evaluating interventions, simple distinctions between a 'programme', its 'implementation', its 'outputs' and its 'outcomes' are made routinely . . .
>   It is simply assumed that the review will track this type of 'programme' aimed at this type of 'subject' seeking that type of 'outcome'. However, the precise coinage of such abstractions is of immense significance in determining the appropriate evidence base.

This is still, however, seen as a technical task, requiring careful and skilled attention, rather than as invalidating the evidence-based approach itself.

Two distinct approaches to this challenge can be identified among researchers operating within this methodological framework. Some will attempt effectively to 'bracket off' the subject of study, attempting to create or specify a field of study which can be defined according to a set of regular features, and which is not substantially altered by external influences. In some institutional settings, for example, it may be considered that the nature of the regime itself is so pervasive that prior external factors can be more or less disregarded in terms of measuring the impact of different forms of treatment on residents. Alternatively, attempts may be made to develop investigative and explanatory mechanisms which incorporate contextual factors within the research model. For Pawson (2006: 25), for instance, this leads to the articulation of a rather more complex framework, which seeks to integrate different levels of evidence and explanation:

> Interventions offer resources which trigger choice mechanisms (M), which are taken up selectively according to the characteristics and circumstances of subjects (C), resulting in a varied pattern of impact (O). These three locations are the key sources of evidence.

There are a number of good examples of this kind or research, notably in the field of youth justice, where contextual factors such as policy and organizational structures are linked with practice interventions and then outcomes in order to provide a global view of particular reform programmes (e.g. Burnett and Appleton 2004). Clearly, this calls for quite elaborate approaches to formulating and investigating the research question(s) (e.g. Holdaway *et al.* 2001), and it still involves choices about what is or is not a relevant contextual factor, but it does seem to provide the basis for developing a wide-ranging, soundly based and essentially plausible explication of forms of practice intervention (Pawson 2006).

Although, as we have seen, current methodological thinking appears to offer us some grounds for working on the basis of 'probability' rather than absolute certainty (Lishman 2000), there are a number of challenges to be considered in adopting this kind of methodological framework. First, there is the question of what we mean by terms such as 'success' when we come to evaluate a particular intervention. Is it, for example, in the case of substance misuse, to be judged in terms of achieving total abstinence, a reduction in levels of use, less harmful behaviours, better health, or reintegration into the community (work, relationships and employment)? Even if we argue that it is all of these, we face the question of which take precedence and how they are weighted against each other. Second, we have to face up to the task of specifying interventions in sufficient detail and accurately enough to be able to distinguish them from other forms of practice: 'research, even in randomised control trials, may examine practice in so broad a way that details of difference in methods of practice and intervention, of importance to the individual practitioner, cannot be correlated with effectiveness' (Lishman 2000: 4).

Nevertheless, research concerned with establishing practice effectiveness (or lack of it) relies on the underlying assumption that it is possible to specify the field of study and the mechanisms in play with sufficient precision to be able to establish patterns and regularities, which in turn help us to understand and explain social work processes. If we think in terms of probabilities and tendencies, this is perhaps more realistic than the achievement of a certain and fixed connection between an action and its consequences. Again in the field of youth justice, tools developed such as the ASSET assessment schedule have been found to be successful in predicting reoffending at around the 70 per cent level (Baker *et al.* 2005). Research which obtained a more conclusive figure in this complex environment might indeed be called into question.

This kind of observation is particularly helpful for those interested in carrying out research into causal associations or correlations in social work practice. It is not that we have been released from our obligations to specify the object of study accurately or to develop good and reliable tools for measuring events and consequences, but rather that it is recognized that in a 'complex' world (Sheldon 1984), we are likely only to be able to achieve approximations both in terms of measurement and results:

> Human behaviour is . . . caused and determined, though it is usually indeterminable. Thankfully, as social workers and researchers, we are usually interested in . . . practical questions, i.e. do these people over here who are similar on a number of important variables to these

people here, commit less crime, suffer fewer relapses, attend school more frequently, attempt suicide less often following social work intervention?

(Sheldon 1984: 636)

In one sense, this is extremely helpful for the intending researcher, who is relieved of the (practically, if not theoretically) impossible task of developing an absolutely watertight framework for the conduct of research into 'what works' in practice. Defining ethnicity, for example, is a task which can be adapted to the precise subject of inquiry. In some circumstances, such as identifying discriminatory processes in problem definition or assessment, it may suffice simply to categorize the research population as 'white' or 'non-white'. In other settings, such as the influence of culture on informal care arrangements, it may be important to establish clear distinctions between and within minority ethnic groups.

Importantly, then, effectiveness researchers base their approach on the fairly reasonable assumption that social work practice can (and should) be judged in terms of its observable impact on a discrete problem area. These can be identified and measured with a sufficient degree of precision to command broad common agreement, and lead to shared understandings of actions and consequences; they need not be disqualified because absolute measures cannot be agreed upon given the huge complexity of the subject matter.

Designing effective research strategies

Given the kind of methodological assumptions set out earlier, effectiveness researchers have to face up to a number of key challenges in deciding upon the appropriate strategies and methods to be applied.

Any investigation which seeks to determine 'what works' can expect to undertake a number of tasks, some of which it might share with other approaches and some of which are distinctive.

To start with, unlike some approaches, particularly participative forms of enquiry, effectiveness research will require an initial formulation of the concrete research question to be addressed. Sometimes it is suggested that this should take the form of a 'hypothesis' to be tested; however, this is not necessarily the case. Where a hypothesis is introduced, it need not be too detailed. For example, where experimental designs are used which make comparisons between two or more groups, we need only conjecture that there will (or will not be) a difference between these groups without having to specify in great detail what this variation will be, or what its direction is. The important point, as Sheldon (1983) has observed is that the object of enquiry is 'testable', that is, that it has a material basis. It is likely that if the focus is on a particular aspect of practice that certain outcomes are expected or desired, and this might form the basis for certain assumptions about their potential value but these should not be too restrictive. Sheldon uses the example of a form of intervention designed to reduce family 'rows', which could be tested in principle against alternative criteria of 'frequency' and 'seriousness', leading to conflicting assessments of the outcomes identified. As he puts it: 'the advantage of hypotheses containing predictions about *amounts* of change is that they serve to anchor discussions about *kinds* of change too' (1983: 482).

What is also significant here is one sense in which this form of social work research is distinctive; it is concerned with measuring change, and in particular the resolution of situations involving social interactions which give cause for concern. This itself generates a number of strategic requirements in terms of planning a research study. As Sheldon again points out, it will be necessary to define the starting point, or 'baseline', clearly. This, of course, is essential if we are to be able to determine what changes in behaviour or relationships occur, and, more importantly, whether or not they can be attributed to a specific form of intervention. Thus, 'Having "dismantled" a problem into its concrete elements or found reliable indicators of these, the next stage in the sequence is to assess incidence *prior* to intervention' (1983: 484).

This may seem fairly straightforward on the face of it, but as Sheldon (1983) points out, there are two important assumptions underpinning this aspect of the process: first, that there are 'distinctly identifiable key items' of behaviour, feelings or characteristics which can be made available 'for counting' and, second, that the 'means and opportunity' are available to enable the researcher to 'carry out this task'. If we wish to ascertain the effects of an anger-management programme, for example, we have to identify indicators which can be quantified, and which in some way represent levels and frequency of 'anger'. So, we might think in terms of raised voices, demonstrative gestures, or signs of physical aggression, as suitable observable indicators in this context. As we shall see, these initial choices also have clear implications for the types of method and analytical tools to be utilized in this kind of study; consistent means of recording and quantifying data would seem to be required.

Having established the baseline, and the kind of indicators of change (or lack of it) to be applied, the next step will be to construct a framework within which the specific impact of the intervention in question can be identified, as far as possible. It may be possible, for example, to establish comparative studies, utilizing matched control groups, in order to evaluate the differential effects on similar groups of different types of intervention (Sheldon 1984), or of intervention as opposed to non-intervention.

There have been a number of highly influential studies of this kind carried out over the years, such as the Cambridge-Somerville Youth Study (e.g. McCord *et al.* 1969) and the High/Scope Perry Preschool Study (Schweinhart *et al.* 1993). In these cases, children and young people were allocated to different groups and then either provided with specific 'treatment' programmes or simply the normal range of services. In both cases, these groups were closely matched and then followed up over a period of years with the aim of identifying possible programme effects (on delinquency in both cases, and also on educational attainment, relationships and economic status in the High/Scope study).

Certain other requirements follow from this approach, such as the need to recruit sufficiently large numbers into the sample to be able to make meaningful comparisons between groups, primarily by way of statistical tests. It is also necessary to build in a sufficient and appropriate timescale to be able to identify changes that take place and, importantly, the extent to which they are sustained. The High/Scope study, for example, followed up its sample of young children well into adulthood, and was able to argue on this basis that certain types of intervention in children's early years can have very long-term beneficial consequences across a range of aspects of their lives. These findings provided the justification for the Sure Start programme in the UK initiated in the late 1990s, incidentally.

Such studies must also meet quite stringent demands in terms of the 'matching' process between control and programme groups, and they must also ensure as far as possible that there are no extraneous factors which could distort this selection process; this is the problem of 'context', identified by Pawson (2006). It may be thought that 'random allocation' to comparison groups is appropriate if the sample size is large enough (Sheldon 1984), but even this may be insufficient to negate any possible variable impact of societal or cultural influences which bear on the entire population in question.

Of course, researchers also face practical problems where the necessary sample size for valid results is simply too great, likely to be the case where the study is being conducted alone. As an alternative, Sheldon (1983) has suggested that 'single-case' studies may also be feasible, as long as the baseline data are sufficiently clearly enumerated, and the intervention itself is specified precisely. Such studies can be devised with varying levels of sophistication to determine 'before and after' effects, or those which consider the impacts of different types of intervention applied sequentially, or staged interventions which are offered and then withdrawn periodically. Indeed, given a sufficient degree of rigour, Sheldon (1983: 499) argues (optimistically) that 'these designs hold out the possibility that in certain areas of social work we could see the emergence of the practitioner-researcher, or the evaluation-oriented team'.

This does indicate that sound and useful 'evidence-based' research in social work can be carried out by individuals as well as larger and better resourced teams of researchers, although it does not represent a deviation from the standards of rigour which are expected of such studies. Thus, it is important not just to specify in some detail the key 'baseline' data, but also to be detailed and explicit in elaborating just what a particular intervention comprises. Indeed, one of the limitations acknowledged by researchers responsible for the Cambridge-Somerville study was a substantial degree of uncertainty about exactly what 'treatment' of the programme group actually involved (McCord et al. 1969). Clearly, the nature of the intervention specified cannot be simply taken for granted, especially if it takes the form of in-depth and interactive practice between practitioners and service users. This is not an impractical task but it must be accounted for in the research design. Indeed, variation in treatment approaches may offer another dimension to the study:

> We cannot agree ... that uniformity is necessary for either effective treatment or for an evaluation of effectiveness ... Although treatment varied from counsellor to counsellor and from boy to boy, this variation can itself be studied by the investigator.
>
> (McCord et al. 1969: 7)

It has been observed, too, that when we focus on the content of intervention additional variables such as the service user's or practitioner's ethnicity or gender may become pertinent (Newman et al. 2005). The challenge of determining which are the most relevant to a given study must also be recognized by the researcher. Research designs looking for evidence of 'what works' are thus obliged to negotiate difficult terrain between the general and the particular, specifying baseline data, elements of practice and outcome measures in such a way as they capture common features or similarities between different aspects of the study, while also developing tools which are sufficiently robust and precise to differentiate essential features of practice and its effects. It is here that the empiricist researcher may well think in terms of 'replicability', and perhaps 'triangulation', so that the methods used and the findings recorded are subject to validation, in the sense that they can be repeated or varied and produce the same or similar results (Humphries 2008). Research designs will therefore incorporate a pilot stage, at which point tools, measures and techniques will be tested for reliability and validity; in essence, the aim will be to demonstrate that these can be applied consistently and effectively irrespective of the researcher.

Research design from this methodological perspective is thus concerned to develop a sufficiently robust mechanism for quantifying the nature, impact and effects of practice, and identifying the nature and direction of any change occurring. This generates a number of key challenges in terms of the tasks of specifying relevant and appropriate data and developing tools of measurement and analysis which are precise and reliable on the one hand, but generally applicable on the other. Importantly, social work research of this kind will seek to generate findings and conclusions which can inform practice developments and provide the basis for service improvement.

Evidence-based social work research: criticisms and challenges

Despite its centrality to much social work research and development, there are a number of critical observations which can be addressed to the 'what works' model of inquiry; and it is important that these are taken into account, both by research practitioners and those who are seeking to make sense of and apply research findings.

First, it seems that there are grounds for concern about the 'knowledge claims' of evidence-based research (McLaughlin 2007). It is suggested that 'randomized controlled trials' (RCTs) act as a kind of gold standard for this methodological perspective, acting as the benchmark against which the strength and quality of all social work research may be judged, but that this relies on certain unsustainable assumptions about what counts as knowledge and how it can be generated. Instead, there are both practical and conceptual limitations to this kind of model. It is both ethically and practically problematic, for example, to attempt to allocate service users to comparison groups, and the problem of specifying and quantifying different aspects of an intervention cannot be overestimated:

> If we were measuring the effectiveness of support groups to reduce the re-occurrence of domestic violence how would we know whether this was due to the model of domestic violence management, the charisma of the support group leader, the companionship of the other women or even changes to the violent partner that were most important in creating a change?
>
> (McLaughlin 2007: 80)

Devising comparable measures of the impact of these different aspects of the intervention, and then accounting for their interactive effects seems to be a highly problematic task.

As we have seen, this can be viewed as primarily a practical problem, that is, social work and its practices are essentially and in principle reducible to quantifiable and measurable data, but the very complexity of human characteristics and interactions means that the best we can hope to achieve are 'probabilities' and approximations, rather than exact representations of the subject of inquiry. In a sense, this position can be equated to a kind of 'soft' empiricism or a 'pragmatic' perspective (Trinder 1996); the focus is still on empirical investigation of effectiveness and practice outcomes. This position, as its characterization suggests, is not based in any explicitly ideological or theoretical set of principles, but itself is driven by a concern to find 'what works', for all practical purposes. We are no longer concerned here with what counts as knowledge but with what is usable and offers possible solutions; for 'pragmatists research design is therefore based on technical rather than epistemological or ontological grounds' (Trinder 1996: 236). This, in turn, enables them to co-opt a range of methods to their purposes, spanning the apparent divide between qualitative and quantitative methods, for instance. So, a 'classic pragmatist design would include surveys, file searches, and some psychological tests' (Trinder 1996: 236). Much of the government-sponsored research into child care and child protection in recent years seems to adopt this kind of eclectic model of design and data collection (e.g. Department of Health 2001a). Trinder (1996) also argues, however, that underlying this essentially practical (and possibly opportunist) approach to evidence-gathering and analysis, there does lie a discernible 'worldview', which links 'a vision of an ordered and understandable world with a passing glance to plurality and social constructionism' (p. 236). In other words, it manages to accommodate these apparently disparate and contradictory positions within its practice, 'suppressing' any inconsistencies which would otherwise emerge.

This approach clearly has certain advantages, not least that it enables us to move beyond debates about the legitimacy of competing methodological assumptions to focus on the often more attractive question of what social work is and does, and how it is experienced. Research of this kind tends to acknowledge that certain central concepts such as 'child protection' are socially constructed and contested, but still tends to take them for granted, concentrating instead on 'descriptive and evaluative' accounts of how formally defined problems of this kind are assessed and dealt with. Trinder's (1996) suggestion is that these inbuilt assumptions tend to feed through into both problem definition and methodological application, so that qualitative analysis tends to be either subordinated to, or reduced to, quantitative methods relying on 'frequency counts'. In the end, then, according to this view, this eclectic approach is no more than a variation on the theme of empiricism, based on convenience, and a recognition that the social world is complex and hard to quantify:

> Difficult epistemological questions and difficult substantive research questions are avoided. Research deals with surface not depth understanding, explanation or causation. Complexity is rendered into realism. Politics and power are excluded as researchers/practitioners pursue a policy of change within the system.
>
> (1996: 238)

The implication here is that researchers taking a pragmatic view are in danger for two reasons: first, they have no clear rationale for including or excluding particular methodological approaches, or indeed, findings and, second, that they are in danger of accepting dominant (official or formal) problem definitions and assumptions as they are, without subjecting them to critical scrutiny. The way in which 'outcomes' are defined or prioritized might be one illustration of this, given that concepts such as 'well-being' or 'quality of life' are open to such wide interpretation. Indeed, it could be argued that merely to focus on outcomes is to accept a particular understanding of the way in which human lives and experiences are structured, pre-empting alternative approaches concerned with processes and perceptions.

Despite such concerns, attempts have been made to address the problem of contested definitions. As long ago as 1992, for instance, it was being argued that constructs such as 'quality of life' could be operationalized for research purposes in order to evaluate services and outcomes (Cheetham et al. 1982). Thus, for example, external measures (such as standards of accommodation and income) could be utilized alongside more 'subjective' evidence to generate a composite picture of the service user's quality of life; in this way, experiential and perceptual data could be integrated into formal measurement schedules. In this example of a study of the suitability of supported accommodation, the researchers concluded 'that discussion of quality of life must balance the utility of a scoring device which can allow ready comparison against the evocative account of an individual's own words' (Cheetham et al. 1982: 88). The precise approach and measures to be used are not prescribed in such cases but depend on the context and nature of the study. The important point is that our evidence is incomplete if it does not utilize *both* subjective (internal) and objective (external) indicators of impact and benefits of service interventions. Pragmatism in this instance is not seen as a defensive response to complex methodological questions or knowledge claims, but as a positive attempt to reconcile competing strategies and perspectives, without necessarily prioritizing one over another. It has been argued, for example, that 'evidence-based' research in social work has responded to concerns about what type of knowledge is 'most valued' (Newman et al. 2005) by promoting the role and participation of service users 'in all parts of research production'. Thus, it is argued, recent developments have moved away from an emphasis on external measures of service user benefit, or 'opinion studies' which tend to follow a pre-ordained script towards an emphasis on ongoing involvement in the research process; for instance, this could include taking the lead role in specifying appropriate 'outcome measures'.

Despite the clear signs of pragmatic adaptation, a further problem arising from this for the empiricist model of social work research is the issue of the effect of compromise on the underlying principles upon which this methodological perspective is based. In other words, does its value as hard evidence become diluted as it adapts to the practical and theoretical challenges posed by the real world of social work practice? For those who see RCTs as the 'gold standard' in social research, it is problematic when 'research becomes driven by the availability of data rather than by the need to answer specific questions' (McLaughlin 2007; Gilbody et al. 2002: 14). The gist of the argument here is that ideas of a methodological 'hierarchy' are unhelpful, even for those who aspire to an essentially empiricist, evidence-based form of inquiry. This view is expressed particularly strongly by one advocate of evidence-based approaches:

> My main and radical charge against the hierarchy of evidence is that it fails to provide the gold standard for the job it purports to do: RCTs are

not the best basis upon which to make causal inferences in the world of social programmes.

(Pawson 2006: 51)

Pawson (2006: 182) goes on to argue that it is because 'human intentionality is the very medium through which' practice operates that this cannot be bracketed off when we try to make connections between interventions and outcomes, however closely they are specified. We thus need to adopt a 'multiplicity' of research methods, which themselves are judged against 'multiple standards' of authenticity. Pawson concludes that 'methodological supremacists' must be resisted. In the field of social work, then, it makes sense to accept that lack of precision is a given, and that even quantifiable events are only, at best, an approximate indicator of what actually happens (for instance, during the period of a young person's mandatory attendance at an Intensive Supervision and Surveillance Programme). However, this does not mean that material evidence is eternally elusive, but that we must accept a modified version of what counts as a 'fact'. Qualitative methods may be used, for example, to elicit concrete and specific evidence which, nonetheless, cannot be quantified in any strictly numerical sense, such as a service user's feelings of confidence or self-esteem.

Shaw (2003) makes a powerful claim along these lines for the recognition of the 'distinctive and indispensable' place of qualitative approaches in outcomes research, which can be identified in four distinct aspects of the process:

1 Design solutions.
2 Sensitivity to the micro-processes of practice and programmes.
3 Applications of symbolic interactionism and ethnomethodology.
4 Qualitative analysis.

Thus, we have not dispensed with the idea that practice and, in particular, outcomes can be evaluated in terms of their concrete impacts and benefits, but it does appear that such approaches must be guided by a range of evidential criteria and methodological approaches in order to gain a rounded and sensitized view of just what is going on when social workers intervene in the practice setting.

Evidence-based research: from methodology to method

This brief methodological overview has considered some of the challenges and possibilities of research which is concerned with uncovering what does (and does not) work in social work practice. Even if we restrict ourselves to this one strategic approach the task is clearly complex and challenging. However, it has been suggested that there is scope for developing a coherent and practical framework within which appropriate forms of evidence gathering and analysis can be situated. There is not necessarily an exact relationship between the empiricist methodological framework and the precise methods to be applied, as commentators such as Shaw (2003) recognize; however, the concern with interventions, change and outcomes does tend to point in the direction of evaluative techniques which are concerned with identifying, recording and specifying the level and direction of change to problematic aspects of people's lives. It is these strategies which will form the primary focus of the chapter in the next section which will consider 'evidence-based' methods in more detail.

Key points

- Empiricist research is driven by a search for certainty and definitive conclusions; it is often associated with the task of determining 'what works' in social work.
- The identification of appropriate methods and research tools is treated essentially as a 'technical' exercise under this paradigm.
- Empiricist methodologies have been criticized for over-simplifying and misrepresenting complex forms of human relationships and social dynamics.

3 CRITICAL PERSPECTIVES:

THE VIEW FROM OUTSIDE

Certainty and doubt

While researchers concerned to find out 'what works' in social work practice are unsurprisingly interested in obtaining definite answers, other perspectives are perhaps less preoccupied with 'certainty'. The adoption of a critical perspective can partly be attributed to a reaction against the hierarchies of knowledge and power attributed to the prevailing evidence-based orthodoxy (McLaughlin 2007). However, it is more than simply a position driven by a spirit of resistance and, as we shall see, there is a clear and sustainable independent set of principles underpinning the approach of the 'critical' researcher. It is important, too, to avoid seeing the problem simply in terms of opposing positions, and irreconcilable differences between one perspective and another, since there may well be considerable value in pursuing 'dialogues' (Shaw 2003) between differing methodological conventions.

Nonetheless, critical research perspectives do have a distinctive starting point, which as we shall see, infuses all aspects of their investigative processes. Put simply, this is about not taking for granted any prior assumptions, or indeed, forms of social organization or practice, thus exposing every aspect of social relations to question. At the same time, of course, what is called into doubt is not just what we know, but how we know it. Standardized forms of inquiry and evaluation become part of the researcher's field of study. In this way, the tendency of empiricists to treat certain features of their investigations as 'given', such as the constructions of child protection referred to in the previous chapter, these may become problematized and open to critical inquiry.

For researchers from a social work background, a critical perspective is attractive because it resonates with the professional values which promote anti-oppressive practice and non-judgemental attitudes. In other words, there appears to be a common resistance to the idea of problematizing service users, and a readiness to ask wider questions about the ways in which problems are defined and the contextual factors which may also be relevant: 'Research is not posited as a neutral fact-finding activity . . . Lives and life-stories are significantly structured by . . . unequal power relations, with significant implications for uncovering "truths" ' (Trinder 1996: 239) However, as we shall see, research undertaken from this standpoint is not unequivocally committed to the kind of participative models of inquiry which we shall explore in the next chapter. In casting a critical gaze over established and dominant structures of knowledge and power, it remains to a certain extent disengaged from the service user perspective. Clearly, a fully 'critical' perspective must avoid privileging any particular standpoint, which is a somewhat uncomfortable position, perhaps, as Trinder (1996) has acknowledged. However, for certain types of enquiry, it may still be valuable for the researcher to come to the problem without prior conceptions; for instance, this may be important in exploratory studies which seek to establish the key issues to be tackled in more detailed investigation. In practical terms, too, this reflects the reality that much research in social work originates with the individual researcher, and that we should be careful not to invalidate this source of original inquiry and insight simply because it is not directly inspired or led by service users.

Knowledge claims: is anything real?

While, as we have seen, empiricist research strategies can be questioned on the practical grounds that problem definition and measurement cannot achieve a sufficient level of precision, critical researchers suggest that the subject matter of social work needs to be conceptualized in a different way. It is not just a technical problem, but relates to the sources and content of knowledge itself. Because social work is fundamentally about feelings, relationships, meanings, and social interaction, we need to develop appropriate means of finding out about these and gaining an interpretive understanding. Because these are internal to human experience, transient and negotiated, our ways of gaining insight into them and making sense of them will necessarily be exploratory and interpretive.

Knowledge is therefore found to be embedded in 'subjective' experiences and feelings:

> Subjectivist sociologies stress that human action flows from subjective intentions and that social structure is, therefore, a subjectively based accomplishment. The social order is not a pre-given material structure, nor a determining normative set of rules. It is, rather, a continually emerging texture of meanings produced by individual human actors.
>
> (Johnson et al., 1984: 77)

Taken to its extreme, of course, this argument suggests that there is no way of making sense of anyone else's perceptions and emotions because they are held individually and are not directly accessible to observation from outside. Equally, there would appear to be no criteria of truth or validity against which to judge the evidence gained or the analysis derived from any particular research activity. Nor can any finding be seen as definitive, since new and different interpretations of what is observed are always possible. Interestingly, perhaps, the provisional nature of knowledge in this context mirrors Popper's (1980) argument that even hard evidence from the natural sciences is only valid for the time being, unless and until it is falsified.

In terms of modes of enquiry, this might be reflected in approaches to research which are concerned merely with articulating different viewpoints or experiences, rather than explaining or accounting for them, and thereby misrepresenting them. Thus, there has emerged a body of 'narrative research' (Tedlock 2000; Gould 2004), whose aim is to enable participants to articulate their own feelings and stories, which may be a good way of helping 'to show their capacity to identify the strengths and personal resources that individuals who have experienced adverse life events are able to mobilise' (Gould 2004: 135). This, in turn, it is argued is an approach which bears some resemblance to some therapeutic techniques in social work such as 'narrative family therapy'. Now recognized as a classic text, *The Client Speaks* (Mayer and Timms 1970) may be seen as an early prototype of this sort of study. Subsequent developments in postmodernist thinking have suggested that the loss of 'certainties' in social life generally are associated with a growing acceptance that knowledge can only be partial, complex and unstable (Humphries 2008). The aim of research in the context of this kind of assumption is simply to elucidate contradictions, ambivalences and irrelevances. In other words, rather than aspiring to certainty and closure, or even shared meanings and provisional agreement, the aim of research in the social world should be to expose and elaborate difference and dissonance.

While this kind of 'worldview' might sit at one end of the subjectivist or 'interpretivist' spectrum, McLaughlin (2007) rightly observes that this perspective is still 'nuanced' with a number of different methodological traditions falling under this broad umbrella. Most of these (ethnomethodology, symbolic interactionism, constructivism, for example) are concerned with investigating the processes by which shared meanings are achieved, without which the task of establishing a common basis for interaction would become highly problematic. As in the case of 'evidence-based' research, though, some compromise is necessary in order to accommodate theoretical anomalies.

The conceptual basis for the task of achieving and exploring 'shared meanings' lies in Weber's (1978) development of the notion of 'adequacy at the level of meaning'. In the absence of definitive means of achieving certainty about states of mind, and shared understandings, what we should instead be looking for are conventionally acceptable interpretations which constitute a ' "typical" complex of meaning' (1978: 11). In other words, we should be seeking consensual agreement as the basis for our analyses and knowledge claims about subjective human states. These shared meanings may be partial, incomplete and impermanent, but they offer us a sound and realistic basis for decisions and actions, at least 'for the time being' because they are based on mutually sustained beliefs. Critical research, notably ethnomethodology, is concerned with elaborating the processes by which this kind of consensual meaning is developed, and how it creates the basis for action. It enables us to identify the ways in which social work decisions are the product of negotiated processes (Hall *et al.* 2003). Typically (see Cicourel 1968), ethnomethodological research will record and analyse conversational exchanges in great detail, in order to track the construction and negotiation of meanings between participants. This could be a therapeutic encounter, for instance:

> In the analysis of the couple therapy conversation we observed the construction of Clienthood by tracking down some of the practices the conversationalists used to qualify what the therapeutic conversation should be orientated towards. The practices of the clients consisted of introducing new topics, blaming each other and thus offering each other the client position and finally a devotion to mutual dispute and blaming.
>
> (Kurri and Wahlstrom 2003: 77)

It should be noted here that despite their role in observing, recording and analysing these exchanges, the aim of the researchers, as ethnomethodologists, would be to elaborate the shared meanings of the participants and how these were achieved, rather than to interpret or impose their own (external) meanings on the exchange.

Others who use similar means of inquiry believe that it is possible to generate wider and deeper understandings from subjective accounts. Whereas for postmodernists, for example, there 'is no universal truth – all knowledge is relative and local' (Dyson and Brown 2006: 77), alternative perspectives suggest that individual perceptions and meanings can be taken to represent underlying material realities. In a sense, perhaps, this logical connection is necessary if we are to generate explanations of material social structures and influences which do not originate in the physical world, or in the decisions and actions of atomized individuals. We might, for example, take the view that this kind of perspective offers a useful starting point for an investigation of 'institutional discrimination' and how implicit conventions and decision-making mechanisms appear to produce oppressive outcomes in mental health settings.

This difference of approach within 'subjectivist' research reflects 'a key analytical dualism, namely whether the social world is an external world "out there" or an internal world "in here" (Dyson and Brown 2006: 54). Thus, these positions share the assumption that social reality is 'constructed', and therefore cannot be explained through externally imposed systems of quantification and measurement; however, they differ as to whether these socially constructed meanings stand for anything else, or should simply be enumerated and evaluated in their own right. For those who believe that there are underlying factors at play, there are important questions of how these can be identified and characterized through the representations of partial accounts. It also raises the associated question of the legitimacy of the researcher imposing meanings, rather than letting individuals' accounts speak for themselves. This is no less the case for researchers adopting this model of understanding than it is for empiricists applying pre-existing categories and instruments to attempt to confirm or disprove prior hypotheses. This is what Trinder (1996: 239) has referred to as 'the central tension' in critical research.

The problem here is partly to do with the imposition of meaning by the researcher, but it is also to do with the means at hand to achieve 'generalizations'. In the absence of concrete and fixed criteria of validity and reliability which appear to be offered readily by evidence-based research strategies, how can we go about providing meaningful conclusions or identifying common factors across a range of findings? How can we differentiate between knowledge and opinion? How can we avoid the researcher exercising her/his power to decide what matters in the subject under investigation? Dyson and Brown (2006: 165), for instance, suggest that research should be judged in terms of its 'credibility, trustworthiness and authenticity'. They distinguish between the 'strong form' of constructivism, which holds that truths are only transient and available '*in situ*', and alternative approaches which seek to generate accounts which 'ring true' and therefore offer plausible explanations which can be transferred to other settings: 'Transferability to other contexts is then assessable by those who read the reported cases, given sufficiently detailed description and interpretation in the research accounts presented' (2006: 174). In addition, they suggest, researchers should incorporate an account of their own 'positioning', setting out their own underlying assumptions and values. Again in contrast to the conventions of evidence-based research, this is a rejection of the view that 'value-free' research is possible under any circumstances. What helps the reader or user of the research is the opportunity to locate the situated knowledge claims it makes in relation to the perspective and acknowledged preconceptions of the researcher.

Box 3.1 Declaring your position

Some researchers believe that it is important to 'bracket off' their own beliefs and assumptions in order to avoid distorting either the process or their findings (Gearing 2004).

One research student felt that his own views about the discrimination experienced by travellers should not be allowed to pre-empt his study of this topic. He argued that it was important to clarify his own position at the outset in order to enable readers to take this into account; but this was also part of a process of disengaging one's own prior assumptions from the methods and thought processes to be applied in the course of the study.

While 'direct or literal replicability' of methods and findings is accepted as 'impossible', it is nonetheless realistic to expect broadly similar outcomes and understandings from researchers within 'a particular community' who choose to repeat a particular type of investigation. There are thus some inbuilt safeguards against pure speculation or fabrication, but the benchmarks here are not those of certainty and finality but plausibility and 'similarity'. The relationship between the knower and the known can be expressed in understandable terms, but this is not fixed and predictable in the way that it would be if it were to take the form prescribed by those applying empiricist principles. This is not to suggest that this type of knowledge is inferior or more partial, however; rather, it reflects a view that it is in a sense more realistic, being based on the negotiated and subjectively constituted meanings of the critical or interpretivist perspective. As a result, the implications for research methods do not mean a reduction in standards of rigour or conceptual robustness but the development of a quite different set of operating principles and criteria of soundness and quality.

Methodological assumptions: thinking round corners?

Once we accept the underlying assumption that the researcher is somehow *implicated* in the construction and interpretation of every aspect of the study, then a number of methodological consequences follow. In one sense, it might seem reasonable to outline these in terms of their opposition to certain operating principles underpinning evidence-based approaches: subjective meanings as against objective facts; qualitative, in-depth analysis rather than quantitative and generalizable findings; small-scale and purposive sampling strategies in place of randomized, non-selective research cohorts. However, we must be careful not to oversimplify these distinctions, or to assume that the methods to be used are necessarily exclusive to one or other perspective. There is an important distinction to be made, instead, between different phases of the investigative process, that is, between methodology, method of investigation, and analytical strategy. While the methodological starting point will have implications for the way in which we approach these different elements of the research process, it does not necessarily require us to include or exclude particular techniques which may be available to us. As we have seen, for example, Sheldon (1983) has made the case for the use of very small (single-case) samples in pursuit of empiricist evidence of cause and effect in social work practice. What is important, rather, is the way in which our initial orientations shape the ways in which we formulate the subject of study and then try to make sense of what we find.

Thus, for those adopting a critical or interpretivist perspective, the research question will necessarily be formulated in terms of socially constructed events, structures and meanings. This is because, from this viewpoint internal constructs, meanings, motives, perceptions, understandings have real consequences, and to that extent this viewpoint represents a sharp challenge to the notion that it's only a world out there, a reality external to us that has consequences.

(Dyson and Brown 2006: 83)

Thus it is clear that there are multiple facets of the subject of inquiry to be understood, and that these in turn reflect a rather messy, uncertain and incomplete grasp on reality. At one and the same time, we seem to have gained a considerable degree of flexibility about the kind of methods likely to be helpful in this kind of context, while we have also lost the ability to apply absolute standards or criteria against which to judge their worth, or whether or not they have been applied appropriately. These, second-order judgements about the skill and appropriateness with which research strategies are applied also become provisional and contested in the same way as the object of study is, too. Nonetheless, we must ultimately rely on some criteria for judging the quality and value of the investigations carried out, or else both our findings and methods will become compromised by the problems of relativism, which offers no basis for evaluating the merits of any particular set of findings or analysis.

In the same way that social work values establish an effective 'bottom line' in terms of the ways in which practitioners should operate and the outcomes they should aspire to, so research from an interpretivist or 'constructionist' perspective must also incorporate some basis on which to judge its inherent value or effectiveness. Indeed, for some, it is the fit between social work values and critical methods of enquiry which provides this sort of legitimation. Both methods and practitioner standpoint seem to overlap with aspects of the social work task, it would seem. As Corby (2006: 144) observes: 'the theoretical underpinnings of constructionism and the methods of research deriving from this perspective are those that seem to fit best with social work values'. Thus, for example, the kind of appreciative approach taken by researchers seeking to encourage respondents to explain their motives is closely compatible with the exhortation to social work professionals to be 'non-judgemental' in their approach to the behaviours of service users. Not only do these value orientations overlap, but there is also considerable shared ground when it comes to processes of investigation and analysis.

Social work assessments are very often based on processes of personal engagement and enquiry, seeking out service users' 'points of view in order to provide help for them with their problems' (Corby 2006: 145). Social work also very often involves attempts to make sense of complex problems based on piecing together partial and sometimes conflicting accounts of people's lives and circumstances. Scott's (2002: 924) characterization of the habitat of social workers as 'the swampy lowlands of practice' leads her to suggest that an eclectic approach to knowledge generation is a necessary element of the job:

For example, a social worker in an oncology unit of a hospital who is interested in establishing a support group for women with gynaecological cancers may ask herself many, very different questions, virtually simultaneously. As she glances at the names of patients in a particular ward or outpatient clinic she may ask herself the following questions. How many of these women have a similar diagnosis? How many with this diagnosis are at a similar stage in the trajectory of their condition? These are relatively simple questions to answer. At the same time she may ask herself the core hermeneutic question, 'What does such a diagnosis mean for each of these women and for the significant others in their lives at this point in time?'

(2002: 924)

These questions, posed to frame a particular practice initiative, could equally easily be developed to form the basis for a piece of exploratory research seeking to elaborate meanings and their relationship to other aspects of these women's lives and treatment.

Research strategies of this kind may be relatively open to different kinds of information as is suggested here, but their underlying strengths are believed to lie in their ability to reflect problematic issues in detail and with a degree of authenticity. However, as Scott (2002: 929) again points out, there is a difference between claiming a 'strong commitment' to social work principles such as 'social justice' and being able to demonstrate that one's research activities have been carried out in a manner and to a standard which matches up to this aspiration, especially in the face of 'unexpected or unwelcome findings'. Service users may, for example, express discriminatory attitudes in the course of research interviews, which must be accounted for and incorporated into the analytical framework rather than ignored. At this point, too, the researcher will have to consider whether or not to step out of role and express her/his concerns about the views being expressed, at the risk, possibly of losing valuable 'data'.

Exercise 3.1

As a social work researcher, what specific responsibilities do you have in terms of the rights and welfare of participants?

What criteria can you apply (such as, risk of 'significant harm', perhaps) to determine when to 'step out of role'?

When is it justifiable not to intervene in ways which you would if acting as a practitioner? And why might this be the case?

Despite such challenges, there do appear to be a number of methodological features which can be consistently associated with this strand of social work research activity. Such investigations are likely to be concerned to explore subjects 'in depth', using methods of inquiry which involve spending time around the focus of the study, and relying on detailed accounts and explanations of what is found. In order to deal with accusations of 'cherry picking' (Scott 2002: 929), that is, finding evidence to fit predetermined expectations, research of this kind seeks to establish credibility and authenticity in a number of ways. This may be by way of 'triangulation' (Denzin 1970) or 'crystallization' (Janesick 2000), which may use other findings, other sources, or even other researchers to provide fuller or confirmatory evidence; or, it may be achieved by testing out findings and analyses with research participants themselves ('Have I understood you correctly?') but the aim is to provide some kind of benchmark against which the 'quality of the research' (Scott 2002: 929) can be judged by its users.

It is further suggested that credibility can be enhanced by articulating in detail the place of the researcher in the process, 'by writing the researcher' into accounts of the study, rather than by trying to 'sanitize' it. This feature is unavoidable, so should be part of the account, and can be incorporated into the frame of understanding applied by the reader or user of the research. This is taken a stage further still by feminist researchers among others, who argue that their explicit, committed, position gives greater strength and substance to their findings (Cox and Hardwick 2002). In this respect, this position comes close to that espoused by our third perspective which aligns the researcher unequivocally with those who are the focal point of inquiry, that is to say, service users or carers. Thus, for example, feminist researchers are reported to be committed 'to non-hierarchical research techniques' (Hammersley 1995: 56). Associated with this is an emphasis on the value of 'experience' as opposed to 'scientific method', which in these terms is a specifically 'masculine' construction which implicitly devalues and disempowers women.

Given that issues of gender, patriarchy and oppressive masculine behaviour feature significantly at the core of much social work practice, the assertion of the power and relevance of experiential accounts may carry additional weight in this particular field of inquiry. Clearly, however, this does not mean that such 'committed' approaches will eschew the importance of approaching the subject of research in a disciplined and systematic manner; indeed, this may be felt to be even more the case where arguments must be developed in the face of the conventional wisdom or the comfort of the *status quo*.

In the end, critical research perspectives take the view that non-hierarchical and eclectic approaches to data collection and 'finding out' do not weaken but actually enhance the quality of the material gathered; at the same time, however, they recognize that sound research needs to apply explicit and recognizable strategies intended to achieve credibility and authenticity of analysis. These strategies are not abstract or random but can be found rooted in social work principles of engagement, listening and validating the wishes and feelings of service users; and in social work practices of purposive inquiry, and the construction of plausible accounts of problematic situations.

Exploring meanings: research designs

Given the underlying tension between an open-minded approach to what counts as knowledge and the countervailing need to demonstrate soundness and rigour of approach, there are some significant challenges for the 'critical' research perspective when it comes to generating research strategies and designs. Challenges which may well arise include ensuring compatibility of findings obtained from different sources or by different means; formulating questions which are broad enough to allow different and new perspectives to emerge, and yet specific enough to generate some organizing themes for the study; setting limits to the field or topics of inquiry; and dealing with problems of bias or selectivity. Given that this mode of enquiry tends to be associated with the generation of new insights, meanings, ideas and theory, it is faced with a practical challenge in terms of *focusing* the investigation, a problem which is not typically encountered by those studies which seek to test existing ideas or practices against expected outcomes. Whereas studies which are concerned to evaluate prior assumptions about 'good practice', say, can focus on specific predetermined events or actions, this is not necessarily the case for those who wish to explore underlying meanings or the quality of social relationships. Of necessity, their investigative strategies must be more wide ranging and, indeed, open ended. We do not know in advance what we will uncover, by way of feelings or perceptions among our research subjects; indeed this is the basis for underlying claims to 'validity'. Answers will not be manipulated or truncated to fit preordained categories: 'This claim is based on using an approach which allows subjects to express and develop their own interpretations of the situation (sometimes called an *emic* as opposed to an *etic* analysis' (Critcher *et al.*, 1999: 72).

However, this very commitment to openness and exploration in research of this kind generates a number of significant challenges. The need for some sort of organizing framework and a specific 'starting point' remains, otherwise the enquiry will be unable to go beyond unconnected descriptive accounts of experience and emotions.

For some, at least, the 'unifying themes' of social work research are to be found in its value base, and its 'broader missions' (D'Cruz and Jones 2004), although this does not necessarily enable us to determine what kinds of substantive questions are posed. It may help, though, to think in terms of three alternative approaches: 'exploratory, descriptive or explanatory' forms of inquiry. These can be seen respectively as means for generating new 'knowledge' about relatively unknown subject areas; gaining fresh insights into existing areas of practice; and developing insights and explanations of particular issues.

Social work is, indeed, characterized by a wide range of emerging social issues which are not well understood or analysed, and this may well indicate the value of these forms of inquiry. In contrast to the notion of testing out possible solutions through evidence-based forms of evaluation, there appears to be a need first to elaborate a detailed understanding of certain types of social problem, and how they are perceived and experienced by those affected. Indeed, we might argue that it is impossible to formulate potential solutions until we have acquired this kind of insight. Thus, for example, the important study by Mullender and colleagues (2002) into children's perspectives on domestic violence played an important part in opening up a poorly understood area of major relevance to social work practice:

> The primary themes of [this] particular research study . . . were children's general understandings and perceptions of domestic violence – including whether they saw it as affecting children, who they saw as responsible for it, and what they thought should be done – and, more specifically, the need to learn from children who had lived with domestic violence about how they had coped with it and what they considered to be the most helpful forms of response.
>
> (2002: 24)

More narrowly, this could also be characterized as a kind of 'needs assessment' (D'Cruz and Jones 2004), intended to determine the level of incidence of a particular 'social issue' and the 'extent' and nature of the needs arising from it.

As we shall see subsequently, this kind of research design may also be associated with certain methods in particular, such as in-depth and relatively unstructured interviewing. The aim throughout is to avoid imposing constraints on the type of findings which may emerge. However, it is also apparent that the very openness of such approaches may generate a wide range of possibilities in terms of methods and processes of inquiry. This, in turn, leads to further challenges in terms of ensuring both coherence and 'credibility' (Smith and Deemer 2000). Research into under-explored and potentially controversial subject matter faces real challenges in this respect, given that 'plausibility and credibility are social judgements' (Smith and Deemer 2000: 881). Given that this particular research paradigm rests, in part, on its rejection of empiricist means of evidence generation and testing, alternative ways must be found to ensure that we can judge whether (or not) studies are soundly based and generate authentic conclusions.

One approach which is widely acknowledged as valuable in this context is 'triangulation' (Denzin 1970) which is intended to achieve two purposes: greater confidence in research findings and greater depth and subtlety of analysis. At the very least, we are provided with the means of observing the object of study from a number of different perspectives through this approach, which gives a much more rounded view of the subject matter. This is not the same as seeking forms of objective proof of what we find, but of giving access to deeper understanding and a more complete grasp on the reality of what we are observing. It is best understood not as 'a tool or strategy of validation, but an alternative' which provides 'rigor, breadth, complexity, richness and depth to any inquiry' (Denzin and Lincoln 2000: 5).

Triangulation as a strategy can be applied in a number of different ways at the design stage. For instance, the use of different sites of study might be one straightforward way of achieving a wider range of perspectives, and not simply as a means of comparing findings between one and another. Differences in the meaning and uses of 'day care' dependent on the setting could usefully be illustrated in this way, which might help us to get beyond the somewhat monolithic assumptions sometimes made about these services (Cole and Williams 2007).

However, the principle of applying a range of perspectives to the research question can be pursued in a number of other ways, too. We could thus apply a variety of methods within the overall framework of the study; we could use a number of different researchers, not just for the purposes of validating data, but perhaps to gain additional insights, too; we could carry out fieldwork at different points in time; and, of course, we could vary the research sample so as to gain a further understanding of diverse experiences and viewpoints.

Importantly, here, the aim is to extend and add detail to our observations rather than simply to provide verification. Such detail may, indeed, help to generate a stronger sense of credibility in the findings and analysis, but this is not the same as seeking or claiming definitive proof. Indeed, our investigations may achieve plausibility through demonstrating a multiplicity of subjective truths rather than a uniform objective conclusion. Something which might from one perspective appear to be a weakness of this kind of research strategy is thus capable of reinterpretation as, in fact, a source of robustness. Additionally, combining qualitative and quantitative methods may seem at first glance an impractical exercise, but may instead offer real benefits in the context of the overall research aim (McLaughlin 2007). However, the research task is to some degree rendered more complex when the investigator opts to integrate different approaches or data sources. Thus

> using multiple methods and triangulation does not remove the responsibility from the researcher to ensure that these methods work together in such a way that they add additionality and address the research question. Using triangulation does not remove the responsibility for ensuring that generated data is analysed rigorously and methodically identifying both areas of correspondence and dispute.
>
> (McLaughlin 2007: 43)

MacDonald (1999b: 98) suggests that researchers using multiple methods must be 'explicit' about the underlying 'assumptions and values' which inform their approach, and that this should inform every stage of the study, so that these can be taken into account by users of the research. She also asks for a 'robust' approach to the methods used, in order to ensure the validity of the findings, although this does beg the question of how 'robustness' is to be judged in the context of combining methods with very different frames of enquiry and criteria of what counts as knowledge. It may be more reasonable to ask of those using multiple methods that they make a plausible and explicit case for their specific choices and at the same time make clear the means by which they will integrate findings from these alternative sources.

What also becomes clear from this discussion is the importance of distinguishing between 'methods' and the assumptions underlying them, on one hand, and 'methodologies' and the continuing debates around these, on the other. It may well be possible, on this basis, to incorporate a number of methods into a research study which give greater depth and substance to the subject under investigation, while at the same time certain of these appear to be incompatible with the underlying methodological principles informing the study. The application of specific methods of data collection will need to be assessed 'for trustworthiness' in their own terms (D'Cruz and Jones 2004: 133), while they can still be integrated in order to address an overarching research question. This is not just a matter of pragmatism; rather it illustrates the important point that data gathered for one purpose and by particular means are capable of being evaluated and interpreted from a range of different positions. The approach taken need only demonstrate logic and coherence rather than compliance with one or another 'pure' methodological standpoint.

Uncertain ground: some criticisms

In one sense, a research perspective which seeks to chart a path between other, more committed, positions is always liable to criticism for precisely this reason. On the one hand, it can be accused of lacking certainty about what does count as knowledge; while, on the other, it can be faulted for remaining detached and failing to take sides unequivocally.

Ironically, it appears to be the case that some of the strengths identified by proponents of critical research methodologies are viewed as shortcomings from other viewpoints. Bryman (1988), for instance, has suggested that 'qualitative research' in particular is characterized by a number of qualities which emphasize diversity and the lack of concreteness. Such characteristics as 'contextualism' a concern with 'process', 'flexibility and lack of structure' and theory building rather than theory testing are seen by their advocates as positive attributes. However, the provisional and imprecise nature of the 'knowledge' articulated under these conditions may also be interpreted as a lack of rigour or precision in the kind of methods and instruments used:

> Many social workers appear to think that because human behaviour is complex, we need lots of different explanations to capture the reality of its different parts (distinctions between theories, perspectives and empirical data are often glossed over). We must aspire to something better if we are not to be stuck with . . . a *knowledge-pile* rather than a

knowledge-base. We need a sophisticated and comprehensive approach to understanding complexity, but not at the expense of rationality.

(MacDonald 1999b: 96)

MacDonald's position is not dismissive of interpretive approaches to research, but she argues strongly that these are not appropriate in every conceivable setting. 'Randomized Controlled Trials' have 'the edge over' other evaluative methods, in her view (1999b: 100). Indeed, valid measures of 'effectiveness' can only be produced where social work interventions are 'tightly defined and controlled' according to specific criteria (1999b: 103). Interpretive, critical or qualitative research can therefore be questioned on two distinct but linked grounds. First, it is incapable of (and, to be fair, does not aspire to) generating sufficiently accurate measures or precise findings to enable us to draw justifiable conclusions, especially about the impact and effectiveness (or otherwise) of social work activities. And, second, this is not just a matter of inappropriate or inferior techniques, but also a problem of the way in which practice knowledge is conceptualised. For some, such as MacDonald, this might mean that such forms of investigation have their place, in terms of clarifying issues such as 'what it is like' for parents experiencing difficulties, perhaps in the sense of assisting with the task of problem definition; but when it comes to problem solving, that is, 'knowing the best way of effecting . . . changes in mother–child interaction', it is 'scientific methodology' that 'has an especial contribution to make' (1999b: 97). For others, though, the lack of certainty inherent in more subjectively based research methods may represent more fundamental shortcomings.

Relying as they do on attempts to explicate meanings and emotions, researchers using such methods are exposed to the challenge that they are merely imposing their own arbitrary 'interpretations' on the data they obtain (Bryman 1988). Although we have already considered the merits of triangulation as a safeguard against the attribution of unverified meanings to the responses of research participants, there remains the difficulty of choosing authoritatively between alternative explanations; thus 'we may question why one interpretation has been plumped for rather than another' (Bryman 1988: 74). We must also reflect here on the viewpoint of the researcher, and what bearing that might have, whether, for instance s/he is from a different background to those who are the objects of the research – a recurrent problem of anthropological studies as Bryman has reminded us, but of equal significance in the diverse contexts of social work practice. It could be argued, for instance, that use of more 'objective' forms of measurement might help to overcome potential biases arising from gender or ethnic differences.

Concerns, too, may arise about the relationship between situated subjective meanings, even if these can be elaborated faithfully, and the aspirations among many critical researchers to generate concepts and theories from their findings, in the way proposed by Glaser and Strauss (1967) for example.

Their particular approach, now increasingly central to many studies, aims towards establishing detailed and rigorous processes for developing theoretical 'categories' in the first instance and then utilizing these to develop more wide-ranging and comprehensive theoretical frameworks. This does offer the potential for developing systematic methods of data gathering and enquiry which can, in turn, support attempts to draw generalizable conclusions from them.

Grounded theory has thus provided researchers considerable assistance in enabling them to draw out themes and analytical categories from their investigations. In my own research, I have found grounded theory techniques very helpful in developing a range of explanatory concepts to account for the practice of 'diversion' in one particular youth justice setting (Smith 1987). It was possible to provide explanations for the achievements of this initiative in terms of agencies' and practitioners' capacity to negotiate compromises in principle and in practice about notions of 'inter-agency working', the 'tariff' of disposals, the meaning of 'diversion', and what constituted 'success' in this context. In broader theoretical terms, it was possible to link these themes with notions of 'hegemony' (Gramsci 1971) and 'relative autonomy' (Poulantzas 1975).

However, it remains unclear whether this kind of research strategy effectively achieves two objectives claimed for it: the avoidance of prior assumptions on the part of the researcher and, at the other end of the scale, the generation of linking theories which go beyond atomized concepts. The problem of 'generalization' from one's findings is partly a practical one.

Techniques aimed at discovering and detailing complex interactions and social meanings are likely to be time consuming and generate substantial amounts of data from relatively small samples, especially where there is only one researcher involved, as is often the case. In this sense, then, the capacity to draw out generalizable conclusions may be limited. At the same time, Bryman (1988) questions whether qualitative researchers interested

---

Box 3.2 Can we justify our conclusions?

My own study of juvenile diversion (Smith 1987) concentrated on one instance of a pilot initiative in juvenile justice. I tried to draw theoretical generalizations from it, based on Cohen's (1985) model of alternative policy rationales. In retrospect, though, I am aware that the attempt to base strong conclusions on findings from just one site could be challenged for making excessive claims.

On the other hand, the depth and detail involved in concentrating on one specific example or practice initiative might compensate for lack of breadth, analytically and theoretically as well as evidentially, mightn't it?

in subjective meanings are disinclined to shift away from their focus on direct personal accounts for fear of compromising the 'integrity' of such testimonies.

This in turn draws attention to another area of potential criticism which is the tension between the researcher's position and role and the research subject, typically the social work service user. Certainly, to the extent that the researcher seeks to make links between responses and to make sense of these collectively, it becomes necessary to draw out common features of individual experiences which may not, of course, reflect those individuals' own priorities or perceptions:

> It is an excellent idea that social work researchers involve key inform-ants, especially people who are normally silenced in relation to the development and effects of social policies, such as service users and sometimes even service providers. However, the real world is not that simple. You are more likely to find that there are different meanings and versions of the truth within groups (for example, service users) and between groups (for example, between service users and policy makers . . .).
>
> (D'Cruz and Jones 2004: 137)

Accounting for difference thus appears to be incompatible to some extent with the principle of remaining faithful to individual accounts. Attempts to do so can only add further to the feeling of distance between the researcher and those who are the focus of study. Not only does this raise the possibility of inaccurate or incomplete representations, but it also poses the question of whose 'knowledge' takes precedence (Beresford 1999). The research process may be argued to replicate other inequalities and forms of oppression to the extent that it involves outsiders imposing their questions (and answers) on those who use services. Equally, in a very practical sense, service users may well feel that they have very little input or control over what happens in the organization and production of research. This replicates long-standing con-cerns about their exclusion and disempowerment from the task of articulat-ing knowledge *about* themselves: 'Traditionally in social work as in other social policy areas, the social work profession tended to be the arbiter and interpreter of such knowledge, at theoretical as well as practice levels' (Beresford 1999: 6). However well intentioned and however skilled, we cannot make simplistic assumptions that the researcher will (or can) straight-forwardly represent the service user's position through the process of enquiry. Importantly, too, we need to acknowledge that power relations are also hugely significant in determining what counts as knowledge as well as how it is produced:

> The knowledge of disabled people has been dismissed on the basis of their perceived incapacity; that of survivors because of the assumed unreliability and irrationality of their perceptions and understandings

and those of people with learning difficulties on the basis of their perceived intellectual deficiencies.

(Beresford 1999: 5)

This is not to suggest that there is no place for the researcher who is not a service user (it would put me out of a job for one thing!), or that the service user is always right. Instead it poses some interesting and important new challenges on the subject of validity and credibility of findings. While the empiricist position might insist on the development of objective or external mechanisms for verifying data, the service user perspective might instead insist on verification procedures which involve participants directly, applying tests both of accuracy and 'authenticity'; in other words, checking observations squarely against the knowledge and experience of service users themselves. Interestingly, perhaps, this sort of strategy provides an alternative answer to empiricist criticisms about lack of rigour and validity, since it roots the process of testing findings against truth criteria in the process of dialogue and exploration with people who are the object of social work interventions and who are, arguably, ideally placed to judge the value and strength of the evidence generated.

Critical research: possibilities for social work

In conclusion, we can observe that there are both possibilities and challenges for those who choose to adopt a critical or interpretivist approach to social work research. First, this kind of approach appears to sit well with many of the conventions and contexts of social work practice. It is rooted in processes of investigation and assessment which are familiar to the profession and it necessarily problematizes knowledge and power relations in ways which find clear echoes in social work value statements. However, it faces difficulties in justifying itself in the face of methodological challenges from the empiricist perspective and, at the same time, it faces the charge that it remains detached and uncommitted.

Researchers adopting this kind of approach thus need to develop and apply methods which can be shown to be rigorous, and to meet acceptable standards in terms of their claims to generate authentic findings while, at the same time, they must also ensure that they reflect the service user perspective accurately and fairly, in line with the professional values of social work, in fact. This, as we have shown, does not mean eschewing principles of methodological soundness but adapting them to the specific context and types of knowledge which lay claim to legitimacy.

Key points

- Critical researchers do not take surface 'facts' as given but are interested in the feelings, motivations, meanings and social processes which lie behind them.
- Research from this perspective is more concerned with exploring its subject matter 'in depth' than obtaining broad and generalizable findings.
- Critical and interpretive methods face some challenges in demonstrating the credibility of their findings and analyses, since these are acknowledged to rely on their own interpretations and judgements.

4 LEADING THE WAY?

SOCIAL WORK RESEARCH AND

SERVICE USERS

Changing times and the place of service users in research

The contemporary era is one in which there has been a discernible shift towards recognizing the importance of giving service users a place in determining the nature and substance of the practice interventions of which they are the objects. A number of key drivers have been identified as contributing towards these developing trends, including the contrasting influences of free-market consumerism, and collective movements of resistance, pioneered by disability activists in particular (Oliver 1990). The consequences of these shifts have been manifested in a series of initiatives at the policy level, and also in terms of the principles informing direct practice. We can see, for example, 'direct payments' legislation as an explicit attempt to locate control over resource decisions directly with service users, and the recent emphasis on 'personalization' in service arrangements flows from a similar source, also influenced to a considerable extent by consumerist ideals. Other developments, however, can be viewed as being more clearly rooted in principles of rights and participation, such as the *Valuing People* initiative undertaken by the Department of Health (2001b). Despite these high-level and high-profile measures, many 'service users argue that [their] impact at local level is very limited' (Beresford 2007: 26).

Arising from this perception of a wide gap between rhetoric and reality, service users have also begun to question the ways in which their circumstances are judged and their 'problems' classified:

> Service users and their organisations have also developed their own thinking about issues affecting them, for example, their identity and how they are perceived, new ways of understanding their situation

and new (particularly non-medicalised) approaches to support and assistance.

(Beresford 2007: 28)

Assertion of their right to have some say about service interventions has thus been associated with a similar claim to exercise some say over the ways in which knowledge about them is generated. Service users have sought, with some success, to establish 'their own research approaches' and in some instances they have become active researchers themselves (Beresford 2007: 29).

The growing emphasis on the rights of service users to take the lead in knowledge production as well as service provision presents some significant challenges for the conduct of research in social work, especially for those who are not (or do not see themselves as) service users, including the present author. We are confronted with fundamental questions about the legitimacy and authority with which we conduct our investigations, on the one hand while, on the other, we must also deal with criticisms about the shortcomings of methodologies which are not rooted in the experience and expertise of those most directly affected at the level of practice. For the moment, however, we will focus on the specific claims made on behalf of research activities which are explicitly based on a 'committed' approach, prioritizing the knowledge and evidence claims which derive from the service user perspective, and which form the basis for user-led and participative research.

'Experts by experience'? Making knowledge claims

The concordance between social work values and the belief in the primacy of service users' understanding of their own circumstances should not be too surprising. The importance of taking a user-centred approach, of empathy, and of 'unconditional' acceptance have been at the heart of formulations of the discipline's core principles for a considerable period of time now (Biesetck 1961; Banks 2006). In light of this, it is arguably a short step to the adoption of an epistemological position which accords greatest weight and value to the subjective truths and insights of the service user. The strength of these forms of knowledge lies in their immediacy, and their direct relationship with lived events:

> One key quality distinguishes such knowledges from all others involved in social care and social policy provision. They alone are based on *direct experience* of such policy and provision from the *receiving end*. Service users' knowledges grow out of their personal and collective experience . . . Thus the introduction of service users' knowledge into the discussion, analysis and development of social work and social care brings into the arena a crucially different relationship between experience and knowledge and between direct experience and social

work and social care discourses ... the importance of this cannot be overstated.

(Beresford 1999: 3)

As a result, conventional assumptions about the source of understanding and insight are called into question. However well-intentioned are social work practitioners and academics, their ability to determine 'what counts' as legitimate and sound knowledge about service users' lives is no longer taken for granted. There are particular reasons for according recognition to such forms of knowledge 'from below', which are grounded in both political and methodological struggles. For some, indeed, this is a necessary (in both senses of the word) condition of social work practice, which is a 'political activity' that is inevitably 'un-amenable to consensus' (Butler and Pugh 2004: 55). In light of this, attempts to research its terrain and its practices must also be 'contested' and reflect the articulation of competing perspectives and interests. It is not possible to avoid making choices about taking sides. The recognition of social work as an intrinsically political and thus power-infused form of activity means that the search for knowledge and ideas cannot be viewed as a neutral operation; it also means that the context becomes highly relevant, particularly where this is characterized by an important historical omission, the service user perspective.

It is against this backdrop that a range of 'emancipatory approaches to social work research' (Butler and Pugh 2004: 63) can be seen to have emerged, with two clear foci: the rejection of 'narrowly instrumental' agendas, and a transformation of the relationship between research and the lives and voices of service users. In this sense, research itself can be seen as a liberating force in social work; it is no longer to be viewed as being just about testing ideas and the production of knowledge but as a vehicle for privileging users' insights and enabling them to secure change. Underlying this argument is the associated contention that certain types of knowledge are marginalized or suppressed because they are held by groups who are themselves socially excluded or adversely affected by unequal power relations. For Pease (2002: 141), for example, this may be a reflection of the 'privileging of some cultural practices over others', which then means that certain ways of knowing are also less likely to be accorded recognition or legitimacy in the face of 'the dominant truth'. This line of reasoning is attributed primarily to Foucault (1980), who argued that power and knowledge are essentially indivisible, and that one in effect constitutes the other (see also Gramsci 1971, and the concept of 'hegemony'). This means that the knowledge and perceptions of service users can, in effect, be disqualified through the impact of marginalizing power relations. At its starkest, this has meant that concerns expressed by those in institutional settings about the way they are treated may be dismissed as symptomatic of their 'condition', a pattern which has been found to be repeated across a range of residential services (Butler and Drakeford 2005).

Nonetheless, because 'power is relational' (Pease 2002: 141), it incorporates the potential for renegotiation and 'resistance'. In other words, other forms of knowledge can be counterposed to those which dominate and, indeed, it is suggested that the very form of power relations generates the possibility of resistance. Thus, it also becomes possible to assert alternative perceptions and subjective truths against the forces of domination and, it is further suggested, to support this kind of movement is entirely consistent with social work values (Pease 2002: 142).

For social work practitioners and researchers alike, this indicates the need to adopt new strategies of engagement with service users, which recognize the value of their 'interpretations'. In this way 'service users are not merely consulted but supply the interpretive framework that is necessary for determining intervention' (Pease 2002: 142). It is not just the evidence from service users which should be given prominence but also the ways in which they think of 'problems', for themselves and others. It is clear that this also provides the basis for challenging discriminatory assumptions and beliefs and the ways that these may problematize service users.

So, we have acknowledged the strong and compelling arguments for giving greater prominence and validity to the understandings and perceptions of service users themselves, both in practice and in the conduct of social work research. This is rooted in core social work values, and the belief that it is central to the discipline to find means of validating and empowering those who are the subjects of intervention. Significantly, the claims made here are not just about rights and legitimacy, but they are also about validity and the authority inherent in service user knowledge claims. In this respect, these are methodological assertions as well as acts of political resistance.

According to Beresford (1999), the proper recognition of these forms of knowledge is methodologically justifiable in two ways: they enhance the 'practical' task of evidence gathering and analysis, and they provide insights and theoretical perspectives which have at least as much claim to validity as any others.

Thus, for instance, closer engagement with service users in the research process helps to 'fill a key gap' (Beresford 1999: 6) in what we know and how we think about it. Involving young people in a study of their health needs, for example, helped us to gain more in-depth data than might otherwise have been the case, and also to draw on their insights into the evidence generated to highlight specific aspects of their lives which might not otherwise have gained prominence (concerns about stress and living with violence; Smith et al. 2002).

Beyond this, though, the involvement of service users in 'theorizing' presents fundamental challenges to other analytical perspectives. Drawing on feminist arguments and 'standpoint theory', Beresford (1999: 7) suggests that

> service users who are on the receiving end of social work theory and practice which directly relates to them are likely to be better placed

---

Box 4.1 Making choices in participatory research

Interestingly, our collaborative study of young people's health needs encountered a range of choices among young people themselves about the nature and level of their involvement (Smith *et al.* 2002).

In one area, for example, they played a full part in drawing up interview schedules, recruiting interviewers from among themselves, and then carrying out and interpreting the findings from these interviews. The research team had to resolve the methodological dilemma of whether or not to 'allow' partners to interview each other and how this could be managed, as part of this exercise.

In another site, the young people involved decided that they would willingly take part in the interviews, but chose not to contribute towards the process in any other way.

Ironically, then, adopting a participatory strategy might also mean having to come to terms with participants' decisions to interpret their own research roles in quite different ways.

---

to generate critical questions and knowledge claims about them than outside academics or practitioners.

At the root of this claim lies the assumption that first-person accounts have greater veracity and authenticity than those which are based on external observation or interpretation. I recall, for example, from my days in practice being informed by a service user with alcohol problems that I could not fully appreciate his perspective because I had not been in the same situation myself. Thus, my 'knowledge' of his needs, wishes and circumstances could not lay claim to the same degree of authority.

This position has been articulated more explicitly in the form of 'standpoint theory' (Swigonski 1993; Orme 2003), which 'builds on the assertion that the less powerful members of society experience a different reality' (Orme 2003: 136), and therefore only they can represent this experience faithfully. This is associated with feminist perspectives in social work which highlight historic tendencies to overlook and misrecognize key features of women's (and children's) experience such as violence and abuse in domestic settings. The important task here is to ensure that these critical issues of oppression are acknowledged, so the emphasis is on 'revealing' previously hidden accounts and evidence. This knowledge is explicitly set against 'empiricist' assumptions that there is an objective truth, especially in a context where the nature of the abusive practice incorporates an attempt to avoid discovery and suppress just this sort of factual material. In one sense, perhaps, it could be suggested that this is just a matter of method, and that the choice of which approach to take is purely technical. However, underlying the 'standpoint' argument is that the dominance of certain types of method is not just accidental, and that this is associated with an unwillingness (perhaps even an inability) to conceptualize or to conceive as possible the extent to which oppression is implicated in patterns of social life and impacts on particular groups within the community, such as women exposed to domestic violence.

There does seem to be some variation in the arguments of those who assert the value of service user knowledge, however. Whereas, for some, the direct experiences, ideas and insights of those groups might elevate their knowledge claims above those operating from other methodological positions, it seems for others that what is sought is parity rather than privileged status. Thus, for example, Beresford (1999: 6) suggests that 'none of this means that social work and service users' approaches to theory and its development are necessarily incompatible or antagonistic' (1999, p. 6), and Powell (2002) argues that what is important is 'dialogue' which respects and takes account of the diversity of perspectives encountered. This does seem to be quite an important distinction between the claim 'that service users' knowledge has an epistemically privileged status' (Butler and Pugh 2004: 64), and the somewhat less radical claim that these alternative knowledge bases should certainly be recognized and validated, but as the basis for dialogue rather than absolute truth claims. So:

> Where the researcher is working with a diverse range of participants to promote dialogue as a basis for generating knowledge claims, her task becomes one of facilitating the reflective and reflexive skills of those involved. All participants in the process, including the researcher, become engaged in reflection and learning.
>
> (Powell 2002: 29)

Knowledge production is a collaborative rather than an exclusive process according to this view, without implicit hierarchies in favour of any one interest.

The methodological basis for participative research

Given the particular knowledge claims of this research perspective, a set of quite distinctive (but not exclusive) methodological assumptions follow. First, and most importantly, there is an implicit (and sometimes explicit) expectation, that participative or user-led research is primarily concerned with action and change, rather than either theory testing or theory building. In other words, the criteria against which research of this type should be judged incorporate questions about if and how processes and practices have been improved as a result. In this respect, the common ground with social work practice and its focus on empowerment and positive change is clear; this is one of the reasons for the obvious attractiveness of action-oriented participative research to many associated with the discipline. This is not exclusive, of course, and it should be recognized here that such approaches are also evident in academic disciplines such as sociology as well as more practice-oriented ones such as education. Indeed, the inspiration for much work of this kind can be traced back to Freire (1970) whose primary frame of reference was educational.

Taking this as our methodological starting point, at least two important consequences follow: the requirement to pursue a participative approach from the start and the importance of adopting methods which achieve a degree of synergy between knowledge and practice, that is to say, they should be action oriented. If the research aim is to achieve change for (and with) service users, for instance, then they clearly should have a fundamental role in determining just what changes should be prioritized, and, in turn, how progress, or lack of it, should be assessed. This is more problematic in practice than it may seem in principle. Even 'critical' research which seeks to articulate the concerns and aspirations of oppressed groups may very often stem from the initial motivation of a research practitioner rather than from service users themselves. This is not to suggest that such research cannot be empowering of service users or inclusive, as the example of 'service user participation' by 'survivors of domestic abuse' cited by Humphries (2008: 114) aptly demonstrates. In this research, informed by 'a feminist perspective', a two-stage, multi-method approach was taken, with the first part of the study being initiated by the professional researchers, utilizing a range of conventional methods. Stage 2, however, 'focused on user participation by abused women' (2008: 115), exploring in detail the extent to which service users themselves were able to take an active part in strategies to address domestic violence. This research thus importantly gave a 'voice' to a group who face 'continued marginalization' (2008: 116), but it apparently stopped short of according this group an active role in the design, implementation and dissemination of the investigative process.

By contrast, fully fledged participative research would seek to ensure that service users and their organizations have a central role in determining the shape and content of the project, from the initial research question through to the process of dissemination and seeking change. In recent years, a number of groups have emerged which represent service user interests *and* set themselves a research agenda, including organizations such as Shaping Our Lives and Central England People First. Other organizations which may not be user-led have also used their role and resources to encourage the formation of *ad hoc* groups which are enabled to commission and carry out their own research, including The Children's Society and the (university-based) Centre for Social Action.

In practical terms, then, it is not inconceivable for the research process to be driven by people who use services, but giving substance to this aspiration is potentially problematic for a number of reasons, notably access to resources, and the establishment of working relationships between user interest and external researchers who may be used to 'leading' the investigative process rather than acting in a more consultative and responsive manner. In my own experience of being invited to support the implementation and evaluation of a particular user-led project (see Smith 2004), this involved a substantial rethinking of prior assumptions about the researcher–researched relationship, and the extent to which I could or should attempt to influence aspects of the project. At what point, say, does the offering of advice about the content of an evaluation tool become so intrusive as to change the nature of the inquiry? Of course, the answer to this question depends to a substantial extent on the nature of the working relationship between parties and the prior understandings and ground rules established. However, whatever the status of the working agreement, the temptation to 'tidy up' research instruments, or to add something which will provide more substance or depth, remains.

This particular study (Weeks *et al.* 2006) also sheds some light on the second methodological principle outlined earlier: that participative research should be geared towards change outcomes identified by and in the interests of service users. The aim in this case was to develop, deliver and evaluate a 'training for trainers' programme which would both empower participants to act as trainers in their own right, and also to create a robust programme template which could be delivered elsewhere. In order to achieve this, the evaluative element of the project had to be seen as an integrated element, which would feed in new insights and improvements as the initiative progressed, rather than simply measure outcomes on completion. In this sense, it is important to think not so much in terms of the 'snapshot' or 'summative' (Everitt and Hardiker 1996) model of evaluation but to consider it more as a developmental or 'formative' tool: 'The emphasis is on evaluating practice in context. The approach recognises that practice comprises a set of actors who may have very different values and expectations' (Everitt and Hardiker 1996: 89).

It is important at this point to observe that this kind of methodological assumption does not imply a lack of 'rigour' or clarity about the research process. Indeed, the task of establishing mechanisms and processes to enable continuous engagement and reflection on the emerging findings requires a considerable degree of systematization and sophistication, especially when we consider that this may involve dealing in forms of communication which are very diverse and do not necessarily include the written word.

Indeed, if we reflect again on the underlying assumption that all perspectives on the research process are potentially of equal validity, then the practical task of ensuring that this is made real must be recognized as quite challenging and time consuming. There will, inevitably, be a lot of testing ideas and checking-out with each other in order to arrive at conclusions which, in turn, will generate next steps and further development of ideas and practice. Thus, in one such example, an initial request from villagers in Burkina Faso in effect initiated a research project which was guided by the 'social work talent' of being able to 'transform personal connections into public issues' (Sulman and Dumont 2006: 16). Out of the process of engage-ment which ensued, a 'model of development' was established which in turn was based on 'an iterative social work process that "starts where the village is at" and blends established participatory research and development method-ology with culturally competent interventions' (Sulman and Dumont 2006: 116). This, it is made clear, was a systematic process, utilizing a suitable research tool (Méthode Accélérée de Recherche Participative), which enables participants to 'become the experts who explain their ideas and knowledge to the [external research] team, and they provide personal narratives to illustrate their experience' (Sulman and Dumont 2006: 12). The analysis emerges from this process, and is then utilised directly to 'arrive at a plan of action' (Sulman and Dumont 2006: 14) which is then capable of being implemented and evaluated in turn.

Exercise 4.1

You might find it an interesting task to try to map specifically social work skills and values onto the principles of participatory research being set out here. For instance, it seems fairly clear that ideas of autonomy and self-determination (Biesteck 1961) figure prominently in the expectations of research which involves service users.

Importantly, of course, it is the participants, in this case the village com-munity who are at the centre of each stage of the process, from identifying the initial research problem, through design, data gathering, analysis, dis-semination and implementation of their conclusions. This underlines another important methodological principle in participative research, which is that user involvement should be ensured at every stage of the process. Thus, for example, care should be taken to avoid certain types of expertise becoming pre-eminent in specific phases, such as data analysis. This is not to suggest that specialized research skills have no value, but that they should be exer-cised within a framework of continuing dialogue and 'checking-out', rather than being imposed on the data and effectively excluding some participants from crucial aspects of the investigation. For participative research to be recognized as meeting its own aspirations, then 'service users are not seen merely as social actors but as co-researchers collaborating and participating in the research process' (McLaughlin 2007: 96)

This test has to be applied not just to the overall research project, but to each stage in the process as well, if it is to pass the test of being a fully 'participative' exercise. This represents a significant challenge, as McLaughlin (2007) acknowledges, not least because of the prior assumptions and work-ing practices of 'professional researchers' who may find it difficult to accept the notion of 'shared power', or the implicit threat to their own standing or expertise involved in sharing or ceding control. He concludes, however, that although the 'research process' may be 'less open' to some participants because of their circumstances or characteristics, this does not mean that they cannot 'make an effective contribution'. However, it may be necessary to develop 'alternative research tools and techniques' to ensure full participation (2007: 102). The fundamental point, here, in line with social work values in general, is that it is vital to provide means and structures to ensure involvement rather than to opt out when it becomes problematic, for whatever reason, if participative or user-controlled research is to become fully realisable.

Participative research designs for social work

Following the previous discussion, we can see that in its pure form participative research requires a comprehensive and continuing commitment to including its subjects in all aspects of the process. This clearly has parallels in social work with the principles of empowerment and service user rights but, just as is the case in practice, this is a challenging aspiration to live up to. There are significant implications for both the form and content of research studies inevitably. D'Cruz and Jones (2004: 86) suggest that choice of research design sometimes involves finding 'one's way through the maze of possibilities', but that this is made simpler by initial consideration of whether the intended study is about 'exploring, describing or explaining'. However, in the present context, a fourth possibility arises, which is that research is about change; in other words, the process of discovery leads not just to new knowledge in the abstract but to 'knowledge in practice'. As D'Cruz and Jones themselves go on to acknowledge:

> Where the strategy is one of moving beyond the building of . . . knowledge to the immediate use of that knowledge-building for achieving beneficial change with and among the research participants, then other sets of decisions also come into play.
>
> (2004: 87)

Research of this kind is usually characterized as 'action research'. This form of investigative strategy attempts to bridge a number of troubling dichotomies in social work: 'theory–practice, ideas–action, researcher–researched and so on' (2004: 88). Alternative conceptualizations include: 'praxis, ideas-in-action, collaborative enquiry and co-researchers' (2004: 88). However, as these authors also go on to observe, action research may be self-evidently about 'change' but it is not necessarily constituted as a collaborative exercise (Humphries 2008). It is possible for the researcher to initiate a process of inquiry which encourages and evaluates changing social dynamics without necessarily involving participants in the construction of the study or analysis of its findings. It is thus necessary to extend the term to 'participatory action research' which imposes as a prerequisite democratic processes of engagement at the heart of the intended study (D'Cruz and Jones 2004).

Four stages are suggested for the conduct of action research of this kind, following the initial identification of a 'thematic concern'. This is distinct from the kind of research question to be found under other methodological paradigms, such as the testable hypothesis in evidence-based studies, or the theoretical problem underpinning critical inquiries. One such thematic concern might be the issue of 'how specialist service delivery teams can improve the quality of their services', specifically for D/deaf and hard-of-hearing adults (McLaughlin *et al.* 2007). This is a very practical question of course, and it immediately helps to clarify the role and functions of potential participants in the initiative. In the particular case identified, it was clear that a collaborative team would have to be established between researchers 'the social services team and the D/deaf and hard of hearing service user groups' (McLaughlin *et al* 2007: 292).

Once this is established, the design of the study itself should be 'set within a cyclical process of planning, acting, observing, reflecting' (D'Cruz and Jones 2004: 88). By its nature, as a participative exercise, the design of the project itself should be seen as provisional and subject to revision based on mutual reflection on the findings which emerge. It is important therefore not to think of research of this kind as linear, since the process of reflection and dialogue may lead to quite fundamental revision of both its aims and methods of enquiry. Since these elements of the process are so central, this also indicates the necessity of establishing effective and inclusive means of communication and sharing, so that evidence and ideas can be appraised from all sides, and that contributions from all parties will be heard and acted upon. The practical importance of avoiding jargon and creating a sound basis for mutual understanding is clear. Hierarchies of knowledge or expertise cannot be allowed to distort the ongoing research process, and this is difficult given prior assumptions and pre-existing relationships. In the case example cited, this necessitated a 'transition to viewing the social workers and the D/deaf and hard of hearing service users as social actors' which was both ethically significant and methodologically important, in order to avoid the possible criticism of the professional researchers that they had 'failed adequately to engage with the social culture' of the marginalised group involved in the study (McLaughlin *et al.* 2007: 292).

There are risks here, too, for in making real efforts to ensure that the process is inclusive, the possibility of being 'captured' by the methodology emerges (D'Cruz and Jones 2004). By this is meant that the task of continually 'checking out' perceptions and mutual understandings may inhibit the aspect of the project which is about initiating and evaluating change: 'There is a complicated interplay, then, in the process of designing for action between constructing trustworthy research and facilitating change' (D'Cruz and Jones 2004: 89). It may help, in fact, to formalize arrangements to some extent, as Humphries (2008) indicates, with the implementation of a number of 'research cycles' which both ensure that collaborative engagement takes place and situates it within a wider framework of action-reflection. One example of this approach is to be found in an account of an action research project involving foster carers (Metcalfe and Humphreys 2002). A series of 'critical conversations' took place as this study progressed which enabled social work practitioners and foster carers to exercise a progressively increasing influence over the structure of the study and the investigative processes: 'as the work progressed, the action research cycles became the engine that drove the research, a process that took it out of the hands of one practitioner, and involved team members and foster carers' (Metcalfe and Humphreys 2002: 441). It was the carers' proposal for a change in practice to include 'information evenings' which became an important element of the practice innovation at the hart of the study, and it was these information evenings which subsequently demonstrated their value as a 'recruitment tool' (Metcalfe and Humphreys 2002: 444).

Similar processes of renegotiating established assumptions and power relations can be observed in other examples of practitioner research, too. For one researcher who, as an Approved Social Worker in mental health had been able to 'overrule (and effectively suppress)' the views and 'understandings' of service users, a completely new approach was needed:

> My position in these early discussions [about the research project] had to be one of humility and tentativeness – listening to what service users saw as important issues and, when sharing my perceptions, checking out whether or not these rang true . . . I felt that it was necessary to reverse the previous power relations between different perspectives: instead of the professional deciding whether the perspective of service users was sufficiently 'sane' in order for them to take decisions regarding their care, it would be for service users to determine whether my professional 'knowledge' fitted with their experiences to be useful in framing research questions.
>
> (Tew 2008: 276)

Thus, the user researchers in this case felt enabled to express criticisms of professional behaviour and to formulate research questions which seemed to fit in with their own central concerns about the topic (compulsion in mental health care). This was a crucial starting point because it offered service users a way into the research process, which might otherwise have seemed rather opaque and perhaps even irrelevant to them. The consequence, of course, was that their ideas and 'situated knowledge' (Tew 2008: 279) became crucial in determining what research strategy would be most appropriate, as well as what questions would be asked, and how inquiries would be conducted (by way of interviews carried out by service users themselves). In this case, the practitioner researcher involved was quite self-critical about the limited role played by service users in the analysis and 'writing-up' of the study; perhaps, Tew (2008) observes, this is to do with persistent assumptions about the limits of service user 'expertise' and the probability that academics would be 'better at doing' this aspect of the overall task. Nonetheless, there was a substantial degree of engagement with service users as researchers in this particular project, and it is concluded that substantial 'added value' was achieved, especially 'in framing research questions that connected with research participants' experiences . . . and generating findings that . . . could make a very positive difference in terms of how users might experience mental health services' (2008: 285).

Interestingly, this particular project was concerned with promoting change in the interests of service users, but did not take an explicitly 'action research' approach; rather, it could be seen as a form of 'narrative' inquiry which concentrated on 'telling stories' (Tew 2008: 281), and in this way enabling important and distinctive insights to be gained into the experiences of people involved with mental health services. As indicated previously, one of the distinctive characteristics of participative social work research is that it is necessarily change oriented because it involves creating the opportunity for service users to engage with and influence the forms of intervention they experience. However, there are a number of potential models of research practice which can underpin these objectives, including action research, as we have seen, but also incorporating other options, like 'narrative' methods, and other collaborative forms of social investigation. Tew (2008: 285) concludes quite forcefully that 'collaborative . . . partnerships' are 'potentially inspiring and emancipatory . . . and can result in possibilities for change, growth and development for all involved'.

We might perhaps conclude, then, that a proper test of whether participative research designs are genuinely inclusive is the nature of the process itself, rather than whether or not particular methods are utilized. It may be possible to think of user-led research, for example, which utilizes conventional methods (quantitative or qualitative) to explore aspects of the research question, and enables service users in turn to articulate their distinctive perspective on the subject of inquiry. Relations of power and control over the process may, perhaps, be more significant than concerns about the purity of the methodological approach adopted. This consideration may also help to challenge possible tendencies for service users to have to adapt their investigative approach to the preferred methods of academic researchers with whom they become involved.

Participative research: criticisms and concerns

Participative research is always liable to the accusation that it is not 'proper' research precisely because it incorporates the perspectives of research subjects and attempts to be responsive to their views and responses. In other words, the very characteristics which proponents see as real strengths are those which come in for criticism from other (perhaps more conventional) perspectives because they appear to incorporate arbitrary and *ad hoc* elements to the process. This form of criticism can perhaps be differentiated according to whether it is ideologically or methodologically driven. That is to say, there is a distinction to be made between arguments which would effectively devalue service user perspectives, perhaps because they are grounded in well-established paternalistic assumptions, on the one hand and, on the other, those criticisms which question the extent to which participative research is appropriately rigorous or based in legitimate methods. It may be open to challenge, for example, because of its apparently selective use of evidence from service users, or its apparent reification of their expertise: 'The process of involving service users can be beneficial . . . but it does not necessarily mean a better research product' (McLaughlin 2007: 105).

Indeed, one of the primary concerns for conventional research perspectives is that there is, in fact, no way of knowing whether participative research is valid or sound because it does not and cannot meet some of the standards of acceptable practice such as objectivity and replicability. For some, at least, the purity of experimental methods remains the benchmark against which other types of social (work) research should be judged (MacDonald 1999b). We could, it is suggested, use 'non-experimental studies' if we could be sure of 'our understanding of particular problems' (p. 102), but in reality this is not feasible. The task for researchers is thus to improve our empirical 'knowledge-base' and to achieve a 'rigorous, empirically based approach to the evaluation of social work' (p. 103), rather than to accept, perhaps, that this is an unattainable goal. By implication, research which eschews these aims cannot make the same knowledge claims or achieve the necessary degree of certainty to determine the shape of policy or practice interventions.

This may perhaps be associated with a wider set of assumptions which sometimes appears to pervade social research, that is, that certain types of research have their uses but they carry out a subordinate function, preparing the ground for more authoritative forms of investigation. Thus, participative methods may be seen as very useful in exploring problematic issues and marking out the terrain, but they are less appropriate when it comes to the task of 'evaluating' practice and determining the effectiveness of social work interventions. Shaw (2003) associates this with a 'horses for courses' approach, which perhaps quite reasonably takes the view that some research methods are more suited to certain forms of investigation than others. However, he also points out that this might also incorporate an assumed 'hierarchy' which suggests that 'aspects of one methodology are . . . intrinsically superior to the other' (2003: 60). Thus, by extension, service user-led and other forms of participative research are believed to be simply not as good as more 'scientific' means of inquiry. This has had significant consequences on the wider stage, too, with social work research in general being assimilated 'into health research' because of the assumed methodological superiority of the latter (Barnes *et al.* 2007: 192).

Of course, criticisms of participative approaches need not stem only from those who believe that its knowledge claims are insufficiently robust. There may also be rather more technical grounds for concern, arising perhaps from the countervailing assumption that inclusive research involving service users is inherently meritorious, and, in a sense, beyond challenge. However, there are some important reservations to be entered here which should not readily be dismissed. It is not necessarily the case, for example, that research with service users at its centre will avoid partiality of one sort or another; in other words, more powerful interests may still exert an unequal influence on the conduct and outcomes of a particular study. Indeed, even highly positive evaluations of the potential for user involvement raise this kind of concern:

> Service users are a large and diverse group. They do not necessarily have shared experience, understandings or agendas. This can undermine solidarity, give rise to discrimination and create its own inequalities and hierarchies which can limit the potential and effectiveness of user controlled research.
>
> (Turner and Beresford 2005: 6)

It is not possible therefore to make simplistic assumptions about this type of research being any more 'representative' than any other.

The point is also made in this context that there are inherent challenges which are distinctive to user-controlled research, especially where researchers and respondents share similar experiences. User-led research is open to question if it does not adhere to the same kind of ethical and welfare principles to which other forms of inquiry are subject. Nor, too, should we make easy assumptions about the nature and level of service users' 'expertise', or indeed the level of empathy they may have with participants. In fact, the development of specialist skills as a 'researcher' may lead to a sense of detachment from other service users: 'Service users tend to see all researchers and research (and not only service user researchers and research) as reflecting sectional interests' (Turner and Beresford 2005: 5). At the same time, the developing interest among service users in becoming active in the research process is not mirrored by the availability of 'good quality training' (Turner and Beresford 2005: 6), which may consequently impact on the quality of the work undertaken.

This highlights a further area of practical concern regarding the conduct and quality of research with a substantial degree of user involvement; this is the importance of recognizing the time and resource implications. Otherwise, there is the risk that work will have to be done 'on the cheap' with all the consequences that entails:

> User controlled research has particular resource implications. Ensuring equal access, enabling diverse involvement and supporting service users to carry out their own research on equal terms, all have resource implications. User controlled research, for these reasons tends to take longer

and gives rise to additional costs. Both of these issues need to be recognised.

(Turner and Beresford 2005: 8)

This pinpoints a further tension in participative research which needs to be acknowledged. In a nutshell, this concerns the precise purpose of 'participation' itself. Is it perhaps the case that some professional researchers feel the need to incorporate a user perspective because there is increasingly a moral imperative to so, rather than because this will necessarily lead to better research? Might there be an associated risk of 'tokenism', where users are recruited more for their status than because they are seen to have a clear and specific role in the research process? This leads to further potential criticisms: that the 'terms' on which participative research is to be carried out are unclear; that insufficient thought may be given to the need for preparation, training and 'checking-out'; and that the products of the research process may have considerably more value to some of those involved than others.

For instance, it is sometimes assumed that engagement with service users will lead to their involvement in all stages of the research process, for example necessitating provision of training in interview techniques. However, exercising a degree of influence and control over the process does not necessarily imply involvement at all levels and in every stage; service users may, quite reasonably, take the view that those with recognized research expertise should take responsibility for specific aspects of an investigation. There is a tension here between what Tew (2008) believes is a failure of 'academic researchers' to fully involve service users, and the alternative possibility that they might choose which aspects of the process they wish to be directly involved in. I can recall a study in which I was involved into the health needs of socially excluded young people (see above), in which participants in different sites held quite different views about their part in carrying our peer interviews (which, in the end, turned out *not* to be peer interviews in one case for

---

Box 4.2 Keeping your word

It was particularly frustrating to be involved in an evaluation of support for care leavers which produced some powerful video evidence of positive outcomes, resilience and achievement for young people from residential care in one local authority area. As one of the conditions for the production of this material insisted on by participants, it had to be viewed once and then destroyed, so these highly encouraging results could not be communicated more widely.

The initial commitment to the young people had to be honoured, though.

this reason). So, user participation also means having the choice of when not to be involved as well as when to take the lead.

And this perhaps leads to the final area of criticism of user-involved research, which is the problem of research outcomes and the uses to which they are put. Service users may understandably have an array of motives for engaging with and seeking to lead the research process, but some of these are more easily satisfied than others. For example, as Tew (2008) indicates, there may be intrinsic benefits for both user-researchers and user-participants; in the words of one such researcher, the 'experience of them telling their stories and me listening to them was an intensely moving one that both sides connected with' (Glyn 2004, quoted in Tew 2008: 282). Equally, as he also points out, where service users are able to contribute directly to the writing of research reports, 'they might become more effective documents in terms of speaking to a wider readership' (2008: 284). However, this does not entirely resolve concerns about the expectations participants might have of the process, and the sometimes inevitable frustrations of investing a lot of time and emotional commitment into a piece of work which has only a limited impact, in terms of changing lives. Thus, for example, one inquiry into this subject reminds us that

> emancipatory research must lead to changes, not act as an end in itself.
> *'Service users are sick of being asked the same questions over and over again . . . They want payback, a product from all this research, something that would benefit them'*. (Seminar participant).
> (Hanley 2005: 40, emphasis in original)

This report also observes that for those who carry out research as current or ex-service users, they 'find it hard to be taken seriously as researchers' (Hanley 2005: 41). The persistence of this credibility gap remains one of the most fundamental challenges for those engaged in participative research, whatever their starting point.

Making participative research count: final thoughts

Despite the increasingly positive noises on all sides in support of closer and more substantial involvement of service users in the research process, a number of clear challenges remain. Fundamentally, the issue is one of form as opposed to substance. The acknowledged value of engaging service users or even ceding control of investigative activities to them should not encourage us to make either intellectual or practical shortcuts in the name of achieving this goal. We should be wary of the risks of tokenism, unmet expectations and, indeed, exploitation of participants. At the same time, we should not be misled by the assumption that there is a 'gold standard' against which user involvement should be assessed. Indeed, from service users themselves, we can readily draw the conclusion that there are many forms of expertise, and many different perspectives; it is simply unrealistic to think in terms of research processes which encompass all of these effectively. Rather, we should be guided by the underlying principles of user involvement which inform social work more generally while we should also recognize that 'participation' itself does not override the need to be thorough and competent researchers, too, whatever the basis of our involvement or expertise.

Key points

- Participative and user-led research are attractive to the social work discipline because of their commonality with the underlying professional value base.
- Research based on this methodological perspective is rapidly becoming recognized as both legitimate and a powerful source of insight into social work realities.
- Participative methods are not suited to every type of inquiry and models of user involvement must be flexible, not least because their own preferences vary.

5 FROM METHODOLOGY TO METHOD: QUANTITY AND EVIDENCE

Putting it into practice: the search for truth

The previous chapters have considered a number of distinct methodological frameworks which offer different and, to some extent, competing perspectives from which to initiate and conduct research in social work. As we have acknowledged, they can be distinguished for analytical purposes, but the faultlines become rather more uncertain at the point where principles are translated into methods and research practices. The aim in this and the following chapters will be to set out in broad terms some of the methods which can most readily be linked with the different paradigms discussed previously, but it is important to stress at this point that this does not preclude researchers from one perspective drawing on the methods and findings available elsewhere. Indeed, as we have also noted previously, for some the adoption of integrated or multimethod approaches is seen as a positive advantage, which enriches and broadens the scope of their findings.

Despite this caveat, the present chapter will focus on those largely quantitative methods which can most readily be associated with empiricist research traditions and those policy makers and research practitioners who are most concerned with identifying 'what works' in social work and social care.

The assumption is certainly made that there is a clear 'hierarchy' of methods within evidence-based social work research (Qureshi 2004), with the use of pejorative terms to describe methods which do not meet the highest standards of rigour, reliability and validity. This follows from the methodological principles incorporated into this model of social work inquiry, notably that it is possible to classify and quantify individual circumstances and characteristics while also being able to measure and evaluate the impact of social work practices in light of these. Given these pre-conditions, hierarchies have been developed along the following lines:

1 Randomised controlled trials (RCTs)
2 Quasi-experimental studies
3 Cohort studies
4 Case control studies
5 Observational studies (without control groups)
6 Expert opinion, or consensus.

(based on Khan *et al.* 2001)

In the present context, the aim will be to explore what is meant by some of these terms in more detail, and to suggest some of the techniques and strategies necessary to put them into practice. While there are certainly grounds for criticism, as discussed elsewhere the emphasis here is on practicalities. Even so, as Macdonald (1999a: 27) acknowledges, 'a range of technical, political and ethical challenges' do continue to 'present themselves' in the formulation and implementation of specific studies grounded in evidence-based assumptions. Indeed, for the lone researcher it may be these 'technical' issues which prove most problematic in conducting their intended investigation, rather than any great methodological reservations. For example, according to Macdonald (1999a: 27), RCTs can be both very time-consuming and costly because of the numbers involved and the period of time needed to generate 'sufficient statistical power' to achieve meaningful findings. There are other practical problems, too, such as the lack of 'stability' in the 'research context', that is, the messy world of social service provision, and the constantly changing dynamics of relevant policy and organizational initiatives. Researchers who aspire to the most rigorous of these methods may find themselves having to make pragmatic choices in these circumstances.

RCTs: the 'gold standard'?

While some may have questioned the view that randomized controlled trials should be seen as the 'gold standard' for empirical research (Cartwright 2007), the aim here will be to set out the key elements of this model of investigation notwithstanding its possible shortcomings.

RCTs are described as 'the most rigorous way of determining whether a cause-effect relation exists' between an intervention and 'its outcome' (Sibbald and Roland 1998: 201). They incorporate a number of key features which aim to achieve the best possible conditions for making comparative assessments:

- Random allocation to intervention groups
- [Research subjects and researchers] should remain unaware of which [intervention] was given until the study is completed – although such double bind studies are not always feasible or appropriate

- All intervention groups are treated identically except for the experimental treatment
- [Subjects] are normally analysed within the group to which they were allocated, irrespective of whether they experienced the intended intervention . . .
- The analysis is focused on estimating the size of the difference in predefined outcomes between intervention groups.

(Sibbald and Roland 1998: 201)

Even this relatively brief list imposes a series of important requirements on studies which seek to pursue this approach. Critically, the research design must establish clear criteria for determining the characteristics of the target group, the specific constituents of the intended intervention, and the outcome effects to be evaluated; for example, one such study sought to identify the consequences of high-quality 'out-of-home day care' for poor families, in terms of parental employment and educational opportunities, and child health and development (Toroyan *et al.* 2003). Fundamentally, of course, any study based on selective interventions must consider the ethical implications of offering a service to one group but not another (the control group). Toroyan *et al.* (2003) note, for example, that GPs refused to participate in a trial of counselling where patients were to be recruited 'at random'.

Moving beyond this important consideration, it is still necessary to ensure that there is no bias in the allocation of subjects to the comparison groups, albeit selected at random. At this stage of the process, 'minimization' techniques will need to be applied to ensure that possible distorting factors do not intrude – for instance 'size of family [and] lone parenthood' in one study of the effects of early years' provision (Toroyan *et al.* 2003: 2).

Other considerations at the sampling stage include determining the necessary size of the sample to generate 'significant' (in the statistical sense) findings. This calculation depends on the interrelationship between the 'effect size' of the intervention deemed to represent a meaningful impact (Chan 2003), the 'statistical power' or margin for error desired (Toroyan *et al.* 2003), and the type of comparison chosen (Chan 2003). In some cases, contrary to expectations perhaps, this can mean that an acceptable sample size can be quite small. We are helpfully reminded in this respect that this is a process of estimation rather than precision: 'In a research study, there's no such thing as "my results are correct" but rather "how much error I am committing" ' (Chan 2003: 172). It is also worth noting here that even highly influential studies (or series of them) such as the High/Scope Perry Preschool Study (e.g. Schweinhart *et al.* 1993) may be based on samples which do not appear large. In this particular case, the eventual sample size was 123 children overall from 100 families, with 58 children in the 'program group' and 65 in the 'no-program group'.

Once the sample is chosen, the next task is to conduct 'baseline' assessments, to provide a quantifiable basis for comparing outcomes. Given that the groups have been determined randomly, this should also offer confirmation that they are comparable at least in terms of the key measurement criteria. So, in the study quoted, at 'baseline, mothers completed questionnaires on child and family outcomes, and the study paediatricians collected data on child development' using a range of standardised instruments, such as the 'Griffiths mental development scales' (Toroyan *et al*. 2003: 2).

A suitable follow-up period is determined (18 months in this case, although the High/Scope Perry Preschool Study continued to review intervention effects for many yeas; Schweinhart *et al*. 1993), at which point the entire sample or as much of it as possible should be retested using the same (or comparable) instruments. Loss of significant numbers from the original sample ('attrition') may mean either that the level of comparability between groups is compromised, or that the underlying requirements of size are no longer met. RCTs will probably be inappropriate, therefore, for highly mobile or inaccessible groups, which is often a key consideration in social work research.

At the point of follow-up, the data will be subjected to statistical analysis to determine the 'significance' of the findings; the form this will take will depend on the type of data gathered – parametric or non-parametric tests, for example, may be more appropriate depending on the nature and distribution of the data (Blaikie 2003). In the example cited, the study did find evidence of improved employment status and mental development in children from the intervention group than among the control group, but even a study of this size (114 mothers, 137 children) did not provide evidence of large enough effects to meet the 'statistical power' requirement to be able to demonstrate statistical significance.

We should note here, too, the necessary distinction to be made between 'significance', meaning the degree of likelihood that the findings have not arisen by chance, and 'importance', meaning that the findings have real and substantial implications for the subject(s) of study.

RCTs have been used quite regularly in certain areas of intervention such as early years services and youth justice, and they appear to offer some value in specific circumstances (Petticrew and Roberts 2003). For instance, where evidence is sought of the impact of large-scale, standardized programmes of intervention on particular constituencies (socially excluded young children or young offenders, for example), they may well offer insights into the broad direction of change achieved (or not achieved in some cases; e.g. Moore *et al*. 2004). Given that absolute precision cannot be attained, and indeed, is not expected, the systematic framework offered by RCTs can be argued to offer as much certainty as any other approach in determining how services are received and what benefits they provide (Macdonald 1999a). For some, indeed, the real strengths of RCTs are that they offer a 'solution to the implementation of interventions in real-life situations', by providing a vehicle for rationalizing and simplifying complex circumstances, while at the same time their very clarity offers the basis for 'transparency and open communication with the client and other stakeholders' (Soydan 2008: 317).

Quasi-experimental studies: using what is already there

To some, there appear to be distinct but limited differences between RCTs and their nearest equivalent:

> The major distinction between RCTs and quasi-experimental research designs is that the latter does not employ randomization techniques to assign clients to different groups, but makes use of naturally occurring groups that receive differing treatments.
>
> (McNeece and Thyer 2004: 11)

Thus, for example, service users who opt on their own initiative for one form of intervention over another (in this case, individual rather than group therapy) could be compared to determine the relative effectiveness of alternative forms of provision. In such cases, it will not be possible to identify whether or not these groups are similar beforehand, and it may therefore be that there are other prior factors which could affect outcomes unequally between comparison groups. However, where there are good reasons for assuming that groups may be similar in composition, or that the interventions offered are substantially different, then it may be possible to make justifiable comparisons.

In practice, it could be argued that quasi-experimental designs have distinct advantages over RCTs; they are not just a second-best option, although this is sometimes the impression given (Petticrew and Roberts 2003). Quasi-experimental methods certainly provide a degree of flexibility where ethical issues arise which might preclude RCTs (Kellett and Nind 2001), or where there are other practical constraints such as the difficulty of establishing a common baseline, or obtaining access. The fact that research of this type is carried out in more 'natural' settings might be thought an advantage on a number of grounds, not least that it removes one possible distorting factor arising from efforts to control selection decisions and the content of interventions.

Drawing samples from 'real-life' settings also avoids the potential pitfall of applying controls which overlook key characteristics of the research population. However, without control groups, it becomes much more difficult to apply useful and consistent baseline measures, since there may be considerable variation at this point. Some quasi-experimental approaches seem to favour attempts to compensate for this perceived shortcoming by attempting to incorporate the principle of controlled comparisons in creative ways, such as the use of a common baseline and 'staggered' intervention: 'In effect, the participants would become their own controls' (Kellett and Nind 2001: 52).

Other approaches appear to take the opportunity to apply broader or more inclusive approaches than would otherwise have been possible. One evaluation of Sure Start local programmes in England was thus able to include a very large sample of children in both programme (16,502) and comparison

(2,610) areas, thus perhaps adding strength and depth to the findings generated (Belsky *et al.* 2006). In this case, unlike the RCT study of early years services cited previously, a single interview and child assessment formed the basis of the study, so the capacity to test programme effects over time was limited (Moore 2008), but wider variations between sub-groups could be demonstrated perhaps more clearly (and supported statistically).

Similarly, a study of the effects or restorative justice interventions on victims utilized a quasi-experimental design to avoid compromising the data:

> We have been unable to employ a multi-wave before-and –after interview design due to fear of contaminating the RJ treatment itself, and fear of losing victim compliance with the intended treatment as an unintended side effect of discussing their emotions and attitudes with them in great detail prior to the RJ process.
>
> (Strang *et al.* 2006: 284)

This study then relied on interviews carried out very shortly after the restorative justice 'treatment' with 210 crime victims in four distinct cross-national settings. Interviews in this study were clearly 'structured', seeking victims' views as to whether or not they were more or less 'afraid' or 'angry' with the offender, or 'sympathetic' towards her/him following the restorative justice intervention. Although the characteristics of the sites, the participants and the interventions varied, standardizing the interview schedule enabled broad comparisons to be made in relation to these specific outcomes. Although less readily susceptible to powerful statistical tests, the results can be seen as meaningful, to the extent that they illustrate substantial areas of change over time, or variations between sites. In this case, the researchers in fact concluded that

> the victim reaction data presented here reveal that victims of all kinds of backgrounds and circumstances and all kinds of offenses achieve a substantial degree of emotional recovery from RJ. While these effects may be subject to rival alternative interpretations because they lack appropriate controls, the evidence does provide a strong initial indication.
>
> (Strang *et al.* 2006: 302)

What is lost in terms of certainty in comparison to RCTs may, indeed, be made up for in terms of generalizability and relevance of the findings.

Thus, while quasi-experimental research methods may sometimes be seen as a poor relation to RCTs, in widely held assumptions about methodological 'hierarchies' (Gambrill 2006), here it is suggested that they have distinct advantages in their own right. They are particularly appropriate in certain circumstances (Moore 2008), such as when randomization is unethical or impossible because of the likelihood of interaction between comparison groups. Equally, for very large-scale programme comparisons, or where programmes are still 'under development', they may offer useful pointers towards further investigation (as in the case of Strang *et al.* 2006). They may thus provide:

- Descriptive information about the population served
- Information that suggests whether anticipated changes are occurring
- Data that suggest the magnitude of change that is occurring over time
- Information on whether anticipated changes are occurring in some subgroups and not others
- Information on whether some outcomes are changing while others are not.

(Moore 2008: 1)

To achieve any or all of these aims, however, quasi-experimental studies will still need to meet certain criteria in terms of the kinds of data and tools to be utilized. As far as possible, clear, fixed and quantifiable data categories must be specified, findings must meet specified requirements as to their numerical value and statistical significance (sample size is likely to be important, as are measures of variance), and investigative tools such as interview schedules, questionnaires or assessment scales will need to be tightly structured.

Thus, for example, the use of a categorical distinction between teenage/non-teenage mothers (Belsky *et al.* 2006) might generate questions about whether 19-year old mothers have more in common with those aged 13 than those aged 25. This, in turn, suggests that in terms of quasi-experimental social work research, the task of category building will necessitate this kind of difficult and possibly contentious choice. It may thus be important both to seek external validation (from independent sources, perhaps even service users themselves), and to vary categories at the point where detailed calculations are applied to test the robustness of findings.

In many ways, then, the choice of quasi-experimental methods involves a trade-off. Opting, perhaps pragmatically, for a 'real-life' research sample may have ethical and practical advantages, but in order to make justifiable 'knowledge claims', great care must be taken in selecting appropriate measures and research tools, given the specific challenges of finding suitable categories and outcomes which reflect the diverse and changing population of interest. Researchers drawing on this tradition must also acknowledge the implications of the choices they make and 'recognize the limitations of any study in which the researcher has power and the researched are a separate vulnerable group' (Kellett and Nind 2001: 54).

Controlled observational studies: cohort studies

The third and subsequent rungs in this particular version of the research hierarchy (Khan *et al.* 2001) are taken by what are termed 'observational' forms of inquiry, which are more or less strictly controlled. Cohort studies are designed to enable researchers to evaluate simultaneously the impact of specific events or interventions on different groups. Unlike RCTs, these groups are 'naturally occurring' and are therefore not necessarily comparable according to specific baseline characteristics. This kind of study is, though, likely to be highly structured in advance and relies, as might be expected, on detailed observation of interactions and outcomes for those involved. Unlike the methods previously discussed, this kind of approach is highly labour intensive, given that it often depends on the presence, or at least close proximity of the researcher, and on frequent attendance at the research site(s). Equally, detailed and precise recording of data will be important, usually according to a predefined schedule. Some, indeed, would wish to see this type of study as a close approximation to RCTs:

> This perspective asserts that we should first carefully define the science: (a) the units of study; (b) the treatments (i.e., interventions, real or hypothetical) about whose effects we wish to know; (c) the covariates (i.e., background variables) that are assumed to be unaffected by the treatments, and can therefore be used to define subgroups of the units; and (d) the outcome variables that can be affected by the treatments, and all of whose observable values under all possible treatment assignments are represented by the collection of potential outcomes.
>
> (Rubin 2007: 33)

Thus, for example, a recent 'cohort' study commissioned by the Youth Justice Board into the 'effectiveness' of four different intervention programmes (Youth Inclusion Programmes, Youth Inclusion and Support Panels, Anti-Social Behaviour Orders and Individual Support Orders) sets out the following research questions among others:

- What are the characteristics of young people on the programmes and how are they identified?
- What types of contact time and/or interventions do young people targeted as part of prevention programmes receive?
- How well are these matched to their identified needs . . .?
- How strongly are the interventions and/or contact time associated with arrest/(re)conviction or other desired outcomes . . .?

(Youth Justice Board 2008)

Importantly, as this outline recognizes, the strength of this kind of study is that it allows us to follow 'the same subjects' over a period of time, and to evaluate both 'progress' and outcomes, both positive and negative, on a comparative basis.

In some respects, this type of study offers real advantages as compared to other methods (indeed, many of these apply to all types of observational research). For example, there is no intermediary between the researcher and the event or intervention being evaluated; evidence is gathered continuously and progressively; extraneous influences may come to light more readily; and, to an extent, there is an in-built mechanism for checking the suitability and robustness of the research tools in use (i.e. whether or not we are looking for the most appropriate and useful data).

Nonetheless, there are also significant challenges which are not just to do with the absence of comprehensive baseline information, or randomized treatment allocations. As already noted, this type of study is likely to be very labour intensive, and to avoid the risk of sample sizes being too small, this may well necessitate the use of a team of researchers, whose methods of recording must then be validated against each other. Equally, there is the risk that the closer that researchers come to the focus of their investigation, the more likely that they will have a direct effect on it. The challenge of identifying and accounting for the 'Hawthorne Effect', that is, the impact of the researcher on the field of study and its outcomes, has been recognized for a considerable time, but it is of particular significance in observational studies where the researcher's presence may be a constant reminder of what is happening (McCarney et al. 2007).

Ethical challenges arise, too, in this context. The researcher's involvement may risk compromising confidentiality between service users and practitioners, and may also impinge adversely on the quality of the intervention itself. Certain types and stages of intervention will almost certainly be unsuitable or unavailable for direct observation by the researcher. 'Observation' need not be direct, but applying this sort of technique indirectly requires the researcher to specify the content of the intervention or event accurately, and also to build in safeguards as far as possible to ensure that 'like' is indeed being compared with 'like'. It is, for example, a matter of concern in fields such as youth justice that programmes which are ostensibly standardized actually incorporate wide variations in content and process (Moore et al. 2004). It is therefore likely to be problematic if observational studies make assumptions too readily about the comparability of apparently similar programmes delivered in different sites.

Despite these caveats, research of this kind is capable of providing important insights into aspects of health and social care. One study, for example, was able to follow up a substantial sample of breast cancer patients, comparing those who were satisfied with the information provided to them with those who were not, and to relate outcomes on this criterion with the impact of other variables (Kerr et al. 2003). The study concluded that poor communication can be shown to have a significant impact on patients' 'quality of life', irrespective of other issues. In this case, interestingly, and perhaps significantly, the determinant of the quality of the intervention provided (communication) was evaluated by those using the services, rather than based on reports about those services from a provider perspective. Although the research itself utilized a standard 'Quality of Life' instrument, this was deemed appropriate because it had previously demonstrated its value in enabling respondents to express their views in their own terms.

Exercise 5.1

If you were going to carry out a study into the effect of a particular form of intervention on the 'Quality of Life' of service users, what indicators would you use to give meaning and substance to this fairly abstract concept?

Could you consider using the number of 'friends' people say they have as one such indicator, perhaps?

This may have important implications for the type of measures and instruments to be developed even in relatively formalized evidence-based studies of this kind. Clearly, it suggests that the commitment to incorporate a user perspective can (and should) be met in different ways according to the specific research strategy being pursued; this, in turn, may well improve the quality and relevance of the data obtained, rather than diminishing it.

Case control studies: a broader perspective?

In hierarchical terms, the next rung on the ladder is occupied by 'case control studies' (Qureshi 2004). Research carried out according to this design framework typically undertakes a comparative study of the characteristics and experiences of groups with and without particular key features. This kind of study is less concerned with identifying and evaluating the specific impact of defined interventions, but rather what distinguishes processes and outcomes for the groups under comparison. Distinct advantages for this model are identified, including the capacity to capture evidence of 'user satisfaction' (Petticrew and Roberts 2003). In addition, it is noted that case control studies can be 'prospective', contemporaneous or 'retrospective' in design, offering a degree of flexibility not available, say, to RCTs. As a result, it may be possible to incorporate a wider range of measures and to generate findings on aspects of the subject matter which might be excluded by more rigidly defined methods. In other words, case control methods offer a degree of insurance against the risk that critical factors may be overlooked where designs are too narrowly focused.

One example of such a study is an investigation into the health of looked-after children (Williams *et al.* 2001). In this instance, a group of children in care in Wales were matched to an equivalent group of children from the general population, 'matched for gender and date of birth' and living in the same area (129 in each). Clearly, even at this point, researchers had to make a choice about which criteria were most relevant or viable for use in the matching process; other options could have included school attainment, ethnicity, parental employment status, or family composition, for instance.

Both groups were interviewed using the same interview schedule, which was itself derived from the *Looking After Children Assessment and Action*

Records (Department of Health 1995). Interestingly, though, this documentation was used in a rather different way than it would have been in practice: 'Although discussion is encouraged when the questionnaire is used in social work, it was completed without discussion of the answers for the purposes of research' (Williams *et al*. 2001: 281). Although additional comments were invited from parents or carers, it seems that this was essentially a closed interview schedule, and where 'qualitative' material was generated, it was then reanalysed in the binary form of 'presence or absence of conditions' (Williams *et al* 2001: 282).

The findings were thus produced in a form suitable for statistical analysis by means of SPSS (Statistics Package for Social Scientists), and using tests suited to data derived from matched pairs. On this basis, a number of significant findings were generated. While most children in both groups were registered with a GP, the population of children looked after were 'more likely to have changed their GP at least once', they were less likely to be 'fully immunised for their age' (at the older end of the age range); they were less likely to visit a dentist 'regularly'; they were more likely to smoke or use illegal drugs; and they had more interpersonal, behavioural and mental health problems (Williams *et al* 2001: 282).

In this way, this study was able to capture evidence of substantial differences between one population (looked-after children) and another (children in the general population), using a widely accessible research instrument and standard statistical tests. As a 'snapshot', it could not, however, offer any indications as to the causal relationship between the poorer health status of looked-after children and their prior experience or present circumstances. Nor could it offer any indication of the trajectory they are following and whether or not the situation is likely to change, and in which direction. The study could, of course, be repeated to provide this kind of information, although this would still offer little by way of causal indications – indeed, the very fact of carrying out the study is likely to have prompted some action to improve things. In this case, however, this would not invalidate the research; and, in the sense that it might lead to desirable outcomes, it might be felt to offer some justification for it, irrespective of its findings.

Box 5.1 Using key indicators

Reoffending rates are often used as a key indicator of the effectiveness of interventions in youth justice. Kemp *et al*. (2002) carried out a longitudinal comparative study of the relative effects of prosecution and its alternatives on young people's offending in Northamptonshire, which showed that alternatives compared favourably to prosecution, irrespective of young people's offending history.

It is important to emphasize the point that case control studies can offer little by way of causal indicators, although these may sometimes be inferred inappropriately. For instance, the evidence to suggest that children who are looked after are disadvantaged in terms of their health may be taken to suggest that the care system is to blame for this. While this may or may not be the case, strictly in terms of this research model there is no basis for drawing this kind of conclusion, since we have no evidence as to the impact of prior experiences or changes over time.

Retrospective designs of this kind might claim to offer some degree of causal insight, however. Thus, for example, an analysis of compulsory admissions under Section 4 of the Mental Health Act 1983 compared the characteristics of 300 individuals admitted in two London boroughs with different admission rates (Webber and Huxley 2004). By identifying risk factors for admissions under Section 4, the study was then able to conduct a comparison between the groups which demonstrated that there were no significant differences between the boroughs on these variables. As a result of these findings, the plausible conclusion was drawn that the divergence of admission rates was more likely to be attributable to the structures and practices of the two mental health services concerned. Clearly, for this kind of research question a randomized controlled trial would be impractical, and probably unethical, so alternative investigative approaches such as case control studies can be seen as a more suitable option, rather than as second best. In technical terms, they share many of the characteristics with other evidence-based methods such as the construction of suitable data categories, consideration of appropriate sample sizes and application of relevant statistical tests, but they also offer the advantage of being able to draw evidence from existing available sources rather than constructing artificial designs.

Indeed, the examples considered here suggest that this research model offers a fairly powerful tool for gaining an overview of particular service settings and outcomes which might provide the starting point for more detailed and focused inquiry, perhaps drawing on other methods as appropriate. We have also noted that the initiation of such studies opens up important questions about existing policy and practice which might of itself have a subsequent impact. Of course, this, in turn, generates significant ethical considerations in terms of possible consequences for people who use services.

Measuring change? Observational studies without controls

A commonly applied research design takes the form of a 'before-and-after' study, which 'aims to identify the mechanisms through which a programme accomplishes change' (Carpenter 2007: 7). This kind of study is believed to be evidentially weaker than some of the other models discussed here because it does not rely on controlled or comparative tests, but rather tries to elaborate the circumstances and programme elements which are associated with change in the condition under investigation. Many practice initiatives are evaluated in this way, and positive findings are often used to justify substantive changes in policy and practice.

To achieve the maximum possible explanatory power, studies of this kind need to be very carefully constructed. Designs will have to seek to incorporate as wide a range of possible influences as is feasible, both within and external to the programme. It will be necessary, as with RCTs, to establish a very thorough system of baseline measurement. It will be necessary, too, to have specific follow-up periods, and preferably to have more than one point at which subsequent measurements are taken.

It is also important for this research model that attrition (that is, drop-out rates) is kept to a minimum. This is because the loss of too many research subjects from the sample might distort findings. For example, schemes such as the Intensive Supervision and Surveillance Programme in youth justice are reported to have very high non-completion rates (Moore *et al.* 2004). It is difficult on this basis to draw too many strong conclusions about the 'effectiveness' of the programme based on data gained predominantly from those who complete it 'successfully'.

If we are confident that as many relevant variables as possible have been included, that appropriate measures exist for them, that accurate baseline measurements have been taken, and that the integrity of the sample has been maintained throughout the period of investigation, it should be possible to utilize the material generated to begin to articulate explanatory models for the pattern of change (outcomes) enumerated. Typically, this kind of model can be developed using 'regression analysis', which provides a means of linking one or more variables with identified outcomes as well as establishing possible relationships between them ('clusters'; Carpenter 2007).

The outline for one such study of outcomes for 'Mentally Disordered Offenders' offers a helpful illustration (Carpenter 2007). The aim was to identify the possible impact on outcomes of a diversion from custody programme for members of this group, according to a variety of 'contexts' and 'mechanisms' which might be found to be influential. These were identified as:

1. Previous criminal and psychiatric history
2. Socio-demographic factors
3. Sources of referral
4. Assessment and by whom
5. Diagnosis
6. Identification of Needs
7. Actions taken by team.

(Carpenter 2007: 7)

The outcomes considered were:

1. Criminal Convictions
2. Sentences
3. Mental Health Care and Treatment
4. Psychiatric Hospital Admission

(Carpenter 2007: 7)

Evaluation of the outcomes at 3–12 months after initial intervention against the possible predisposing factors utilizing 'cluster analysis', produced a number of model 'careers' which would represent distinctive patterns of prior circumstances, pathways and outcomes for offenders falling into each typical category. As a result, it was possible to identify a range of factors identified with both 'poor' and 'positive' outcomes. Those in the former category typically had a 'significant criminal history, including prison, drug and alcohol misuses', but limited prior histories of psychiatric problems. Those in the latter group were much more likely to have a 'psychiatric history' and continuing involvement with psychiatric services; and they were also much more likely to be women (Carpenter 2007). The development of this kind of typology does not claim to offer proof of causal relationships, but rather to identify patterns and plausible connections between factors which may be of relevance. It might, for example, indicate the potential value of different types of intervention according to the associations identified, as in this example, where 'it looks like the intervention of the custody diversion team is very much more effective with some MDOs than others' (Carpenter 2007: 9).

The advantages of this kind of approach are that it offers the researcher a 'natural' field of study, with investigation being directed to the outcomes of programmes as they are actually delivered, rather than being constructed for research purposes; it is retrospective, so that it is able to incorporate variables which may not have been accounted for in a prospective, controlled study; it is flexible, and so is able to include different types of data (including quite 'soft' information such as the nature of an assessment); and, it is cumulative, so that, to an extent it is able to capture indications of a possible interplay between variables. However, in order to achieve the best possible evidence, rigour is needed in managing diverse and sometimes quite problematic data (for example, socio-demographic information may be fairly general or incomplete), and ensuring that systems for classifying evidence are robust and adequately tested. Otherwise, there is a risk that findings will be seen to reflect researcher expectations rather than generating independently justifiable conclusions.

Two further points should be borne in mind. First, despite Carpenter's (2007: 9) assertion that this type of quantitative research can be 'fun', it is important to recognize that it is likely to necessitate the application of statistical tests of one kind or another. While resources such as SPSS offer a valuable aid in this respect (e.g. Field 2005), these tools cannot be used arbitrarily and require at least some knowledge of their proper use and explanatory potential (Bryman and Cramer 2004, is very helpful on this point).

Box 5.2 Using research software

SPSS is a very useful tool for generating both *descriptive* and *analytical* statistics. When I wanted to discover its value as a package, I drew on officially published statistics on child protection processes in one part of England. Simply by inputting rates of registration of concern about children from one year to the next, it was possible to generate some quite striking visual representations of patterns of change, which in turn represented real changes in behaviour (even if only in the way that data are recorded) among local authorities in quite a compact region.

Second, as Carpenter (2007) again acknowledges, these techniques will almost certainly offer partial but not complete explanations for the influence of alternative factors on outcomes. It is important to recognize that other possible explanations are not ruled out simply because we have gained an idea of some of the factors which may be important in any given context.

It may also seem reasonable at this point to draw the conclusion that, in practical terms, the kind of (partial and tentative) understandings and explanations offered by evidence-based methods in social work are not that dissimilar from many of those generated by the kind of methods to be considered in the following chapters (more likely to be characterized as qualitative than quantitative).

Setting the scene: the use of large-scale surveys

In preceding sections, reference has been made to the need to establish clear baseline information in order to be able to calculate the impact and outcomes of subsequent events and interventions. The work undertaken to establish this kind of starting point is often carried out in the form of surveys, by means of which key characteristics and their level of incidence can be determined across the research population as a whole. It is research of this type which can generate generalizable 'snapshots' of where and how certain problematic issues may be located (prevalence). It does not necessarily (although repetition is possible) seek to determine trends over time but rather sets the terms for subsequent investigation, or for changes in policy and practice.

Researchers working within the empiricist paradigm of evidence-based studies will probably opt for quantitative survey methods, although these may often be supplemented by more detailed qualitative inquiry, too (e.g. Hay *et al* 2007). For this reason, most of the groundwork for this kind of survey will be carried out in advance: 'On designing surveys for quantitative research, most of the hard work is done before you conduct the interviews or mail the questionnaires to the people you are researching' (Alston and Bowles 2003: 96). The research question will have been fixed in advance, which in turn will give an indication of the general population within which the study will be located (sampling 'frame'), and what is the 'unit of study' to be investigated (a family, a child, everyone, or a particular subset of people, for instance). This type of survey will seek certainty as far as possible, and for absolute accuracy, 'every person (or case or event)' within the chosen population would need to the included (Alston and Bowles 2003: 81). This is impossible in most cases, so the need arises to identify a 'representative' group from the wider number who will be included in the survey, and from whose responses conclusions can be drawn about the whole population. An appropriate sampling strategy is therefore essential, for which purpose a number of options are available:

1. Simple random sampling
2. Systematic random sampling
3. Stratified random sampling
4. Cluster random sampling.

(Alston and Bowles 2003: 83)

Whereas the first two of these may be appropriate for populations which are easily accessible, and likely to be randomly distributed, it is quite likely in social work research that this will not be the case (homeless young people, for instance); or, it may be that particular groups will not be sufficiently numerous to enable statistically valid conclusions to be drawn about them (specific minority ethnic groups, perhaps). In these cases, it will be necessary to concentrate sampling efforts in some way, either by specifying a minimum sample number from specific subgroups ('stratified') or by concentrating sampling efforts within specific groups or locations ('cluster').

Whatever approach is taken, it will be necessary to ensure that the eventual participating sample is representative of the wider population it is drawn from, as far as possible. While we know from surveys of voting intentions that it is possible to 'scale up' fairly accurately from relatively small numbers, it is also important to recognize that intervening factors may create distortions such as, notably, response rates. In survey studies, these can usually be expected to be quite low, so it is important to preselect a much larger number of possible respondents.

Sampling is one important consideration in survey research, but it is also crucial to generate questionnaires or interview schedules which are sufficiently specific to produce accurate and meaningful results. Short, clear and unambiguous questions are therefore desirable (Alston and Bowles 2003). Precoded questions using common forms of measurement, such as Likert (1932) scales, may help to provide responses which can be relatively easily aggregated and subjected to statistical analysis. However, the range and specificity of available responses will also need to be sufficiently broad to cover all possibilities and to allow them to be distinguished from each other meaningfully. For closed questions 'three rules must be kept': the range of possible answers must be '*exhaustive*', they should be '*mutually exclusive*' and they must demonstrate '*unidimensionality*', that is, they must all measure the same thing (Alston and Bowles 2003).

It will be important in this context to ensure that questionnaires are properly piloted to ensure that questions meet these criteria consistently across different subgroups, and choices will have to be made about the best medium through which to conduct the survey: the internet, post, telephone, or face-to-face interviews all offer distinct advantages and pitfalls. (Does the use of the internet necessarily exclude those who are less likely to have access to it, for example?)

Surveys, then, offer the potential to generate large-scale and potentially quite powerful findings about issues of interest, such as the impact of crime or patterns of use of particular services such as childcare (Hay *et al.* 2007). However, they also require careful preparation and close management, given the acknowledged problems of response rates and representativeness. They can shed light relatively quickly on a particular topic, but this should be seen for what it is and its limited explanatory value should also be acknowledged. The dangers of interpretation are perhaps illustrated by one recently reported study into the research skills of postgraduate social work students (as reported in *Times Higher Education*, 14 February 2008). Seventy per cent of these were reported to be using qualitative methods, suggesting that there is an imbalance between these and alternative quantitative approaches. Is this a good thing or a bad thing, though, and how would we know? Equally, of course, the direction of change, if any, is not indicated by a 'one-off' survey of this kind, and yet this might be of considerable relevance to any subsequent decisions about what action to take.

Surveys, then, offer us a valuable 'starting point', but they almost certainly generate further questions, whether these are related to the breadth and depth of any problems identified, or their longevity, which perhaps other methods are more suited to address. So, in one study which supplemented initial survey findings with more detailed qualitative interviews,

> it was considered important to include a qualitative element to the overall project in order to place decisions that parents make about childcare in the context of decisions about work and family life, and gather opinions of various aspects of current childcare arrangements within this context.
>
> (Hay *et al.* 2007: 13)

As we shall see subsequently, the value of 'mixed-methods' approaches may be considerable in certain circumstances. This is not an indication of underlying weakness of the survey approach but of the potential added value of complementarity.

Quantitative methods and evidence-based research

This brief summary of a number of strategies available to, and applied by, researchers who are concerned with empirical certainty seems to suggest that it is helpful to consider their value and applicability in different circumstances rather than to think in terms of a distinct 'hierarchy' with RCTs at the apex. Rather, there are a series of trade-offs to be made which are to do with both ethical and practical issues (Qureshi 2004) and the explanatory value of the method used (Cartwright 2007). In fact, at its most basic, *all* social research incorporates both quantitative and qualitative elements, and this suggests that the kind of test to be applied in making methodological choices is one of practical efficacy rather than epistemological purity: ' "Horses for courses" is not a dramatic theoretical insight, but the energy dissipated in debates on methodological primacy could be better used were this aphorism to be accepted' (Petticrew and Roberts 2003: 529). This might in turn suggest that instead of judging particular methods against an assumed hierarchy, and in terms of other approaches, the kind of questions to be asked in determining the quality and value of specific research activities, might be, among others:

1 Is this method likely to generate interesting or important insights into this particular social work research question?
2 Has it been planned, managed and implemented soundly in its own terms?
3 Has it met its own evidence criteria?
4 Does it comply with broader social work values and ethical principles?

Whilst some might believe that this last question presents real challenges for those conducting preplanned and tightly specified 'top-down' studies (Webb 2001), others argue that methodical evidence-based research can lead to improvements in practice which is 'ethical, democratic, sensitive to professional experience [and] faithful to client values and acceptance' (Soydan 2008: 317).

Key points

- Evidence-based social work research is not monolithic and offers a variety of methodological options which can be adapted to different research requirements.
- Ethical considerations remain important, even (perhaps especially) when adopting quite formal and possibly dispassionate methods.
- Decisions about methods are driven both by 'best-fit' considerations and pragmatic choices about the availability of data and access to suitable resources.

6 CRITICAL AND INTERPRETIVE APPROACHES: WHAT'S GOING ON HERE?

Getting under the surface

As we have already seen, researchers operating from a critical perspective take a rather different view to empiricists as to what counts as knowledge, on the one hand, and how to unearth it, on the other. They are less comfortable with the idea that social work and its effects can be straightforwardly measured and evaluated. They have concerns, too, about the meaning and application of concepts such as 'effectiveness' to the field of practice. Indeed, critical researchers would probably take the view that it is essential to subject such notions to detailed inquiry, with a view to unpacking their meaning and implications for those who use services.

Not only should terms such as evaluation be problematized, then, but the focus of inquiry should be shifted from the search for concrete measures of impacts and outcomes to the analysis of complex patterns of ideas, attitudes, feelings and meanings which constitute the lived experiences of service users, and of those who are involved in providing them.

This is not to suggest that the impacts and consequences of social work interventions are of no concern to this perspective; rather, it is argued that such research can provide added depth and subtlety to our understanding of these. At the same time, it will also provide a means of generating ideas and theories about the dynamics of the social networks and relationships which contextualize social work practice and the ways in which it is experienced. It follows from this that the methods and techniques to be applied must be capable of generating explanatory power, rather than offering mere descriptions of events and processes. At the same time, and without the reference points offered by evidence-based approaches, the kind of methods applied must be capable of demonstrating coherence, rigour and credibility, as we have already observed. Interpretive and critical methods may be open to criticism because they do not (and cannot) claim to be scientifically accurate in their measurements and findings, so they must find other ways in which to demonstrate that they are robust and soundly based. We shall explore a number of methodological options here in order to identify their value in specific contexts but the aim will also be to demonstrate that they are capable of achieving the necessary standards of disciplined application to be relied upon as sources of evidence and insight.

Unlike evidence-based approaches, though, there is no sense in which these methods of investigation lay claim to particular places in the research hierarchy; it is more appropriate when judging their potential value to consider their underlying purposes, and the practical and ethical challenges to which they give rise when making choices about which to use and why. There are, nonetheless, some features which they share in common, such as an interest in the words, actions and meanings of research subjects; a preoccupation with depth rather than breadth of inquiry; a reliance on inference and interpretation; and a reluctance to seek out singular sources of truth or unique explanations. This is viewed as an implausible outcome of any attempt to investigate a changing and complex social world, and so it is not sought, deliberately.

A matter of record: using documents and texts

It is possible to undertake critical or interpretive research without necessarily relying on primary data such as observations or interviews. In particular, social work as a field of practice is extremely well endowed with documentary sources of many kinds such as records of case conferences, assessment forms, case records and other 'file' data. Many of these sources are, of course, confidential and may be difficult to access, but others are produced as public documents and thus become more readily available for analysis. The advantage of this sort of research strategy is that it offers the opportunity for systematic inquiry in situations where direct researcher involvement (by way of interviews or observation, for instance) may be impractical or methodologically unsound.

Distinctions are made between 'quantitative' and 'qualitative' approaches to document analysis (Willmott 2008), which suggests that there are different possible approaches to data gathering and the ways in which sources are interrogated. Despite this, there are a number of common features to the raw material in question. The underlying point is that, whatever its origin, documentary material will be a 'secondary source', that is, it represents a construction of social reality, which is then subject to a further process of categorization and interpretation by the researcher. This means that the researcher must incorporate in the design and conduct of the study a way of assessing and accounting for these intermediate processes. This, in turn, will be influenced by both the nature of the original research question and the context and use of the documentary source itself. Thus, for example, social work case files are constructed by practitioners in the knowledge that they are not just a personally held depository for factual evidence, formal assessment and professional judgement in relation to a particular service user, but they will also be available for comment and use by others, including the service user (Horrocks and Goddard 2006), colleagues, supervisors, managers, and service inspectors. In light of this, we must be conscious of the possibility that documents are prepared in the light of the author's beliefs about their possible uses and who will have access to them. For example, personal diaries probably incorporate a greater degree of frankness and willingness to acknowledge one's own shortcomings than formal accounts which may, at some point, form the basis for authoritative and accountable statements, say, in court.

Critical assessment of such material must therefore be designed to take account of its purposes and uses. It is not sufficient, for example, to take formal records at face value; some aspects of the transactions they represent will be omitted on grounds of irrelevance or because they would reveal uncomfortable issues. This suggests a need for the researcher to approach the available evidence with a degree of clarity and certainty about both the research question and the 'partial' (probably in both senses) nature of the material which constitutes the data to be investigated. Based on these prior assumptions, the researcher needs to be aware of the 'totality' of the context in which the documents 'originated' (Kelly 2002: 191). Building on this, there is a need to become attuned to the implicit rules and messages which are embedded in the data:

> This involves immersing oneself in the data, allowing themes or sub-themes to emerge, considering the themes in relation to the overall situation and 'standing' of the documents and a constant reflexivity on the interpretation of the text in relation to other forms of data.
>
> (Kelly 2002: 191)

This suggestion is taken from an account of a study of the impact of 'community and cultural narratives' on decision making in child care cases, which utilized both publicly available documents (inquiry reports) and social work files to explore this question. In this case, the researcher applied a prior decision-making model to provide a coherent frame for analysing these documents (Whyte 1991), which enabled the conclusion to be drawn that there was evidence of 'groupthink' in some aspects of social work processes and record keeping, which reflected an underlying assumption that 'children should be, and are best cared for by their mothers' (Kelly 2002: 196). The important point here is that this study was not designed to test the validity of this assumption, but rather, whether or not the texts themselves revealed a bias in this direction. Given their highly specific nature, the researcher decided to utilize two different document types, and this form of 'triangulation' (Denzin 1970) may help to give greater credibility to the findings. This is likely to have strengthened Kelly's (2002: 196) concluding observation that 'documentary analysis can reveal underlying beliefs and narratives surrounding child protection decision making'. Precisely because they are formal (and sometimes public) records, these accounts may be indicative of prevailing attitudes and assumptions about what views it is legitimate or permissible to express.

Whereas an empiricist investigation might be concerned with the question of whether or not records are accurate or comprehensive, more interpretive modes of inquiry are interested in what these documents represent, in terms of the way people's lives and behaviour are interpreted, and what this might mean, in this case, for the kind of interventions offered to service users. We should perhaps approach documentary analysis not 'to ask whether an account is true, or whether it can be used as "valid" evidence', but rather 'to ask ourselves questions about the form and functions of texts themselves' (Atkinson and Coffey 2004: 73).

For social work as a form of practice with its own internal rules and organizing principles, we can perhaps see how investigating its products in the form of texts and official documents might produce some important insights into how notions of professionalism and best practice are themselves constituted, acting as a crucial reminder too that the implicit assumptions behind these are contestable and may not always be justified (Kelly and Milner 1996; Smith 2005).

Sometimes, of course, interpretive studies will necessarily have to rely on documentary sources as a proxy for the reality they claim to represent, for example in historical accounts of social work (Skehill 2000, 2003). In this instance, too, studies may need to incorporate a number of sources, evaluating 'official' accounts of the past against those which might offer alternative constructions of events. Skehill's accounts of the development of social work in Ireland are constructed in the form of a 'history of the present' which accepts that past accounts of practice are 'constructions' and that the task of the researcher is to incorporate this recognition in analysing their 'archaeological and genealogical' forms (Skehill 2003: 143). The elaboration of 'discourses' of this kind must then be utilized to ascertain their dynamic relationship with practice, rather than taking them at face value.

Box 6.1 Making sense of documents

One evaluative study has drawn on the evidence available from 'Serious Case Reviews' in child protection (Sinclair and Bullock 2002). This overview exercise found persistent tendencies among practitioners and their agencies to view child protection cases according to fixed models of understanding and to frame their interventions around these (questionable) assumptions.

Look and learn: the value of observation

Like documentary analysis, observation studies, too, can be approached from within divergent research paradigms. As such, their shape and implementation can differ significantly. In the present context, we will consider those forms of inquiry that might be considered more 'naturalistic' (Mays and Pope 1995), which aim to account for the experiences and interactions of everyday life. This does not mean that the 'setting' in which the observation takes place cannot be concerned with providing a service or assisting service users in some way, but it does mean that the forms of interaction under scrutiny are not contrived for the purpose of carrying out the study.

Observational studies may be thought of as a particularly useful means for initial exploration of an under-researched area of inquiry, and for trying to account for dynamic social processes in detail. How do people interact and under what circumstances might be one such question, for example? Observational methods also provide a direct view of the subject of inquiry which might be thought of as offering more authenticity than either documentary sources or interview data obtained 'after the event'.

The apparent advantage of being able to get close in place and time to the field of study is offset by a number of significant constraints, however. In some instances outside the field of social work, it has been used covertly to gain access to groups who would not otherwise allow their activities to be observed, such as Fielding's (1981) investigation of the National Front. While researchers might argue that otherwise important subjects would not be opened up for study without such deception, substantial ethical issues arise nonetheless (e.g. Humphreys 1970). It may feel morally more comfortable to carry out observational research 'overtly', 'but this may be offset by the group or individuals reacting to being observed' (Mays and Pope 1995: 182). How can this be reconciled with the aim of obtaining naturalistic evidence? For some, at least, this question can be addressed reasonably well by building a relationship with the individuals or groups who are being researched, so that they resume their normal forms of behaviour, which may, indeed, incorporate the researcher. Corsaro's (1997) work with children in a day-care setting in Italy is perhaps a good example of this. Indeed, the fact that the researcher was not a native Italian speaker actually seemed to ease the children's acceptance of him to some extent. Other examples, though, suggest that researchers may continually negotiate and renegotiate their roles with those they are 'observing'. In one study of interactions between older people in residential care, the research team were at pains to ensure that residents knew that they 'were there to observe, and they kept their notebooks visible and wrote field notes to reinforce the reason' for being there (Hubbard et al. 2003: 103). Sometimes, though, despite this 'the residents drew the researchers into their social worlds' (Hubbard et al. 2003: 103) which in turn provided yet further opportunities for the researchers to obtain a detailed understanding of the residents' views and experiences of social interaction. This is not to gloss over the ethical issues of consent and possible exploitation, of which the researchers were well aware, but it does suggest that this is a feasible strategy, and may well be of real value when seeking to capture something as complex and multifaceted as the nature and meaning of social relationships in a particular setting.

The conduct of observational studies also requires a considerable degree of rigour. It will be necessary to establish a rationale for the choice of setting, as well as clear parameters of time and space, for example (Hubbard *et al.* 2003). In addition, researchers will have to determine from all the available information what they will record and how, as well as what they will not and should not include. Recording in real time is also problematic because it deflects attention from what is going on, and because it draws attention to what the researcher is doing. At the same time, in order to capture the depth and nuances of what is observed, field notes must be very detailed. Of course, video and audio recording are also possible means of capturing data which avoid diverting the researcher's attention but they, too, are potentially compromised by introducing an air of unreality into the setting.

Once data are obtained, researchers will also need to develop mechanisms and processes for undertaking thorough analysis of copious amounts of raw material, deceptively accounted for in just two lines in the study just mentioned: 'Once all the observations had been carried out, each set of field notes was re-iteratively examined for themes. The data software package, *Nud**ist, was used to facilitate analysis' (Hubbard *et al.* 2003: 103). Software packages such as this (now known as Nvivo) can assist but do not by any means obviate the task of detailed re-reading, coding and cross-checking.

Observational methods perhaps run the risk of straying into essentially descriptive accounts of the events or activities under investigation, and they must thus develop a clear and explicit rationale for interpretation and analysis, offering the potential for the development of concepts and theoretical insights. The study described here drew explicitly on 'symbolic interactionism' (Hubbard *et al.* 2003: 102), to provide a theoretical and analytical framework, applying concepts such as 'self', 'role' and 'labelling' to the emergent data. Thus, it was possible to provide an explanatory account of the process by which 'male and female residents who displayed acts of affection' acquired the labels 'girlfriend' and 'boyfriend' (Hubbard *et al.* 2003: 110).

Observational studies thus offer the prospect of being able to identify, record and analyse the behaviour of individuals and groups in 'natural' settings with a view to generating more wide-ranging conceptual and theoretical accounts of their activities and interactions. In some ways, indeed, this might be seen as analogous to some of the methods and approaches utilized by social workers in undertaking assessments and evaluating interventions; perhaps similar ethical and practical issues arise, too. Research of this type, however, need not be so concerned with the immediate implications and applicability of its findings and conclusions. Rather, it may be concerned with generating plausible explanations or exploratory accounts which may inform future work, whether this is further research activity or practice development. Practitioners, for example, may be prompted to think carefully about the positive and negative implications of 'labelling' in particular settings, as the conclusions drawn by Hubbard *et al.* (2003) indicate.

Face-to-face methods (i): the interview

In my experience, the interview very often seems to take a privileged position as the method of choice for qualitative researchers, and it is clearly important to include it as one of the key options for studies which seek to develop a detailed understanding of subjective meanings, attitudes and beliefs. The attractiveness of this method is at least partly attributable to its undeniable strengths, both practical and methodological. It does offer direct first-person access to people's experiences and reflections on the subject under investigation. At the same time, once initial problems of sampling and access are resolved, it also offers a relatively simple and straightforward means of gathering rich and detailed data. Interviewing as a method may also be attractive to researchers from within social work because, like observation, it is closely related to core professional skills and appears to coincide with key values such as enabling service users to speak for themselves.

These obvious points of attraction should not, though, deflect attention from the challenges and necessary requirements of applying the method soundly. Enabling people to talk fully and openly about subject matter which is often intensely personal, sensitive and revealing in a way which also meets the standards of rigour and accuracy required is not straightforward. As the process develops, provisional interview topics will need to be derived from the overarching research question, and the researcher will need to be satisfied that this is the most appropriate means of generating the necessary findings. In parallel with this, full consideration will need to be given to the ethical issues involved, which could revolve around the potential exploitation of respondents, their rights to and the limits of confidentiality, control over the use of the material generated, and the possible consequences of introducing sensitive issues without adequate support available.

The researcher then has a further set of questions to consider about the content of the interview schedule, and the extent to which it incorporates structured, semi-structured or open-ended questions. The more structured the approach, the greater the control over responses will be for the researcher, and as a result data will probably be more easily recorded, coded and analysed. However, removing the option for the respondent to reflect on the topic more widely seems to run counter to the (social work) principles of empowerment and autonomy and it also creates the possibility that key issues will be overlooked because they fall outside the range of responses allowed. A greater degree of openness, by contrast, does offer the respondent

---

Exercise 6.1

What specific factors should be borne in mind when planning to carry out interviews with service users?
    These might include, for instance:

- safety (theirs and yours)
- the possibility of causing stress
- the need to ensure that subsequent support is available, if needed
- The importance of communicating appropriately.

What others can be added?

---

more freedom to answer in her/his own terms, and to introduce new insights. However, this is inevitably more time consuming, and complicates the analytical process. Much research of this nature arrives at the compromise position, utilizing 'semi-structured' interview schedules which enable respondents to answer focused questions in their own way.

Other factors to be considered at the preparatory stage will include the need to pilot the interview schedule, the importance of preparing suitable information and further contacts for participants, as well as consideration of the most suitable medium for the conduct of the interview (in person, by proxy, by telephone, or by internet, for example). Selection of the research sample does not need to be 'representative' and, indeed, in some cases there may be considerable value in recruiting a 'purposive' sample, with specific aims in mind. Thus, one recent study of depression in the social work profession sought to recruit respondents who had previously reported that they had experienced depression (Stanley *et al.* 2007). Given that this was intended as an interpretive study concentrating on this aspect of professionals' experience, this choice was clearly justified, and as a result, the authors conclude, the study 'provides an authentic picture of their [social workers experiencing depression] experiences and perceptions and an account of their attempts to manage their mental health needs in the workplace' (Stanley *et al.* 2007: 285).

Given the sensitive nature of the topic, the decision to conduct the fieldwork for this study over the phone probably also makes sense because it offered a degree of privacy and perhaps greater freedom for respondents to express themselves openly.

Clearly, among its other achievements this particular study was conducted in a way which enabled respondents to speak in depth about matters of intense personal concern, which have a direct bearing on the individual but also wider implications for practice: 'I was working in risky situations where I felt vulnerable with very little support' (practitioner quoted in Stanley *et al.* 2007: 288). Some, indeed, had not felt able to 'disclose their depression' to work colleagues or managers, and so it could be argued that significant aspects of the problem would have remained unacknowledged but for this particular study.

Recording and analysis follow similar lines to those identified in relation to observational studies. Recording methods (manual or electronic) should be as accurate as possible without intruding on the process unduly. Analytical methods will often seek to draw out themes incorporated in the interview structure itself and to build these up into conceptual and theoretical statements based on points of commonality (Strauss and Corbin 1990; Stanley *et al.* 2007).

While interview methods incorporate elements of risk, they also demonstrate a number of distinct advantages, notably the potential to shed light on such unrecognized problems. Respondents sometimes indicate, too, that they welcome the opportunity to discuss an issue which they have previously been unable to share and they are sometimes just pleased that someone else has shown an interest. At the same time, however, it is important for researchers to avoid conveying the impression that the interview will automatically lead to profound changes in policy or practice and risking further disappointment among participants.

As might be expected, then, research based on interviews offers some distinct benefits, which can be encapsulated in the idea of 'depth'. Although they are, inevitably, artificial processes they do offer the opportunity to gather direct evidence of respondents' feelings and the meanings they attribute to aspects of their experience. Given the powerful nature of some of these messages, though, we must be careful not to use these findings inappropriately or to over-claim. As in many other research contexts, participation is likely to be unrepresentative. What about those unreported potential respondents with the same needs or concerns who are not recruited or choose to opt out? What can we say about findings which we have been unable to obtain, like Sherlock Holmes's 'dog that didn't bark'? Nor can we claim that interview data are a pure representation of respondents' views or feelings. What they tell us will be mediated by their perceptions of us, the context, and the potential use of our findings. Reassurance can be offered by way of detailed preparation, creation of a conducive environment, and the offer of the option of withdrawing at any point, however frustrating this may be for the researcher. In the end, however, thorough preparation should lead to richer findings.

Face-to-face methods (ii): focus groups

While interview methods are widely used in social work research, a number of viable alternatives may be attractive in some cases, including focus groups. As previously, the benefits may be seen both in pragmatic and methodological terms. Obviously, carrying out interviews or focused discussions in groups immediately increases the number of research participants significantly. Advantages may also seem to be offered in the sense that group discussions may feel more natural to those involved than the alternative of a one-to-one interview with a stranger. The stranger may still be present, but s/he is not necessarily the main point of attention. In methodological terms, too, this may appear to be a useful gain; the discussion may flow more freely and it may represent more closely what participants *really* think, rather than what they think the researcher wants to hear (or shouldn't hear). Difficult and sensitive topics may be approached in a rather more relaxed manner, and participants will perhaps feel that they can contribute as much or as little as they wish on such issues.

The point is made that the very collective nature of focus groups may enable respondents to feel more comfortable exploring issues relevant to shared identities. One commentator notes, for instance, that the focus group may be viewed as an analogous setting to the kind of group which exists as a matter of course in some cultures, such as those of the Gulf-Arab region:

> A familiar setting in the form of the discussion group 'majlis' can be provided in which relationships can be established and history shared; communality established through, for example, age, gender, religion, ethnicity or profession; and a shared understanding reached through topic discussion.
>
> (Thomas 2008: 86)

This strategy has certainly been employed by one of the present author's students, carrying out research into the caring roles and social status of women in Qatar.

A number of researchers have concluded from their own experience that focus group methods are intrinsically 'empowering' for 'vulnerable populations' (Linhorst 2002: 218); that they promote 'ownership' of the research, and improve 'commitment' and participation levels. Although in some cases 'therapeutic' benefits are also reported, it is clearly difficult to incorporate this as an initial aim of a research study of this kind. Additionally, the possibility that intra-group dynamics will provide additional data for the researcher should be acknowledged, although this may generate some ethical unease, to the extent that it is not explicitly recognized as an objective.

While it appears that focus groups offer significant advantages in terms of empowerment and representing shared ideas and norms more effectively, they are not without potential drawbacks. Clearly, confidentiality cannot be preserved in the same way as in an individual interview, especially where group members 'know each other' (Linhorst 2002). While it may be advisable to agree ground rules at the outset, there are no guarantees that these will be followed by all those present. Participants may be marginalized and effectively disempowered during the course of the group session, and it may be important to guard against the reproduction of inequalities or oppressive relationships imported from the wider milieu. The establishment of the group may itself lead to the expression of views or feelings that participants do not want reported and participation may lead to unrealistic or 'high expectations' (Linhorst 2002), which cannot be met by the researcher.

Despite these reservations, focus groups do offer distinct benefits to critical researchers. They have the capacity to be 'culturally sensitive' (Thomas 2008); to enhance the quality of findings as a result of interactive exchanges (Kitzinger 1995); and to enable vulnerable or marginalized groups to feel more comfortable about expressing their views (Linhorst 2002). It is also quite possible that the group will use the opportunity to set its own agenda, which may be a source of frustration to the researcher but may nonetheless generate new perspectives on the subject matter. This is clearly a calculated risk.

As we have identified previously, preparation and purpose are key considerations. It seems that the kind of research questions this approach could usefully address are those which wish to explore shared meanings, cultural norms and common experiences among identifiable (perhaps marginalized) groups. As the name suggests, discussions are likely to be 'focused' around the core research topics, but they will need to be open enough to prompt free discussion. Participants will need to know in advance what will be recorded and how it will be used, and the value of agreeing explicit mutual ground rules has already been acknowledged. Other considerations may also be important such as the trade-off between using existing 'groups' (family, friends or colleagues, perhaps) with their established internal dynamics, or establishing entirely new groups whose members may be rather less comfortable sharing information with each other. Researchers will also need to consider other criteria for group membership carefully, since the possibility of oppression within the group itself must always be borne in mind.

By their nature, focus groups generate a number of additional practical

---

Box 6.2 Focus groups: a natural setting?

On one occasion, I worked with colleagues to carry out a survey of young people's views on local policy issues, and how their needs might be addressed (Allard *et al.* 1995). We found that focus groups worked well on this occasion, perhaps for several reasons:

- young people felt able to speak in what was probably a more 'natural' setting than one-to-one interviews would have been
- discussions around topics enabled participants to recognize complexity and clarify their own views
- difficult issues, such as fear of crime, could be raised without becoming personalized
- larger numbers could be involved at any one time, improving the breadth and diversity of our sample.

challenges, too. Recording fast-moving and sometimes non-linear discussions can only be achieved effectively by electronic means, but it may not always be possible to attribute comments to identifiable individuals (of course, it may not always be necessary either); the researcher also has other difficult choices to make, for example about the extent to which s/he contributes to or directs the discussion, and whether or not to take active steps to include quieter members. At what point does this introduce a degree of artificiality which impedes conversation or compromises findings?

Kitzinger (1995: 300) argues that 'analysing focus groups is basically the same as analysing any other qualitative self report data'. However, there are some specific considerations, it would seem. For example, groups may express views more or less consensually, and it is important not simply to reflect the opinion of the most eloquent participants; of course, agreement and disagreement may be expressed non-verbally. Groups may change their minds, too, during the course of a conversation, or leave a question unresolved. Analysis of this material may need to be multi-layered, leaving space for differences of emphasis and the emergence of competing ideas as well as consensus. In fact, focus groups may be of particular value in developing nuanced understandings of complex and challenging issues, which do not readily lend themselves to straightforward solutions. In social work terms, this may be of particular value in helping to bring greater clarity to problematic issues, such as the complexities of working with both service users and carers to promote person-centred care (Innes *et al.* 2006), where significant differences of perspective are identified in discussion.

Getting personal: the value of case studies

One of the books which convinced me to pursue a career in social work was *Dibs: In Search of Self* (Axline 1964). This is an account of a prolonged programme of play therapy carried out by the practitioner-researcher with a young boy. The account is effective because it offers a structured and detailed account of the intervention itself and the changes observed in Dibs over time. Although it is essentially descriptive, it also provides the basis for insights and analysis. It seemed that the symbolic aspects of his play enabled the boy to express emotions and gain a sense of personal control which would not otherwise have been accessible to him. He was able to use play and storytelling as a way of addressing his experiences of what appeared to be emotional abuse. As he began to take responsibility for the characters in his own stories, so

> he was building a sense of responsibility for his feelings. His feelings of hate and revenge had been tempered with mercy. Dibs was building a concept of self as he groped through the tangled brambles of his mixed-up feelings.
>
> (Axline 1964: 168)

The use of case studies can be effective to the extent that it provides a level of detail and a sense of an unfolding process of change which could be lost in more generalized accounts. While there are clear risks that this sort of method can become selective and anecdotal, it is certainly arguable that it offers a richness of analysis which would not be available by other means.

To be conducted effectively, case study research has to demonstrate rigour, and must show that it has put safeguards in place to avoid the risks of selective reporting. For example, verbatim accounts of social work inter-actions will probably be necessary (Axline 1964), and careful consideration must be given to the context and framework for the study (e.g. the number, timing and location of interventions) However, this is also a method which can make use of some aspects of the social work relationship which might be seen as potential contaminants in other more formalized research designs. Thus, in one reported study, the nature of the relationship between researchers and participants was viewed as an important element of the process: 'rapport and trust were built with the patients and their families, ensuring a high degree of trustworthiness of the data collected' (Chan and Ma 2004: 180). This particular study sought to work with a number of young women with *anorexia nervosa* to try to understand the origins of their condition, and thus develop suitable 'treatment' strategies. An indication of the thorough-ness of the approach taken in this study is provided by the data-collection strategy adopted, which comprised 'pre- and post-family treatment inter-views, observations of the participants during family treatment sessions and home visits, as well as researchers' field notes'. In this particular instance, further corroboration of the data was offered by the availability of two researchers for each session.

Case studies can thus be designed so as to incorporate a variety of docu-mentary, interactive and observational material, which offers a series of internal checks and balances and mitigates the possibility of relying on partial views or selective recollections. In these examples, is provided first-hand evidence of the subject of study, rather than more distant accounts which might be generated through interviews or documentary analysis alone. It is claimed, too, that drawing on personal experience and accounts in this way lends itself to a 'client-driven approach'. Thus, we are told: 'The participants should play a pivotal role in generating vivid and authentic research data that can enhance the knowledge and practice of social work studies' (Chan and Ma 2004: 184). Where, as in this case, a number of case studies offer divergent accounts and implications this is not seen as an impediment because it prevents generalization, but as an effective way of drawing attention to different aspects of an apparently similar condition (*anorexia nervosa*), perhaps indicating the need for similarly diverse and case-sensitive approaches to intervention. These researchers conclude that a 'symptom-orientated approach is inadequate' (Chan and Ma 2004: 185) and that it is their 'stories' which provide the best clues as to the proper response to service users' needs.

Qualitative case studies, then, appear to offer a number of possible benefits, so long as they are systematically planned and carried out. They offer depth and sensitivity to specific circumstances; they enable individual accounts to be placed in the foreground; and they offer insights which are difficult to extract from aggregated data. In addition, there are certain circumstances where this type of approach might be one of the only strategies available, such as where exploratory research is undertaken in extreme or isolated cases, such as for instance, extreme examples of offending behaviour. In Dibs's case, according to his mother, he had previously been described by a psychiatrist as 'the most rejected and emotionally deprived child he had ever seen' (Axline 1964: 76). Case study research might, then, be of real value in throwing light on the specific issues arising in extreme circumstances, while also enabling us to make links between these and more conventional and routine social processes and outcomes.

Some commentators have suggested, indeed, that case study research is more authentic than other methods because it enables the investigator to elicit 'tacit' knowledge relating to a particular interaction or event (Greenwood and Lowenthal 2005). Recognition of the 'contextual' nature of social work activity 'opens up the possibility that the observation will only ever relate to the situation being observed and provides further inhibition to the concept of generalisation' (Greenwood and Lowenthal 2005: 187). The task of the researcher and co-participants is then to elaborate 'what is going on' through the process of careful description and sense-making, 'so that the meanings that emerge from the different interest groups are represented enabling the experience to facilitate a broad opportunity for learning' (Greenwood and Lowenthal 2005: 192). In support of this claim, Greenwood and Lowenthal cite a specific 'case example' in which a series of meetings between relatives and service providers led to the articulation of a range of very different perceptions about 'risk' and 'vulnerability' of older people, which in turn enabled the participants to reflect on these and make a renewed commitment to collaborative working. In this way, the case study approach is concerned with the depiction and elaboration of key aspects of the situation and the different perspectives brought to bear, but it does not seek to impose a definitive account on what is described:

> This 'tacit' knowledge is not dressed in any claims for truth and certainty, which would be more aligned with a scientific presentation, but is more associated with the messiness of real practice situations; a knowledge that emerges as a consequence of experience rather than from a preoccupation with proof.
>
> (2005: 192)

Case study methods thus appear to offer a particularly good route to the discovery and elaboration of subjective 'meanings' and shared understandings of the social work process.

Learning from life

In the same vein, interpretive research in social work has also developed methods based on recording and documenting people's life experiences, usually over a period of time. In common with other methods discussed here, this will probably resonate with social work practitioners who are used to working with detailed accounts of past life histories, both to inform assessments, and to support interventions (for instance in cases of adoption). As in practice, this type of research is held to be of considerable value in helping to elucidate the meaning and impact of key changes in people's lives, and to relate these to the dynamic contexts around them. As distinct from 'pure' first-person accounts, life story methods rely on the researcher gathering, collating and interpreting accounts from the individuals or groups concerned. This may mean obtaining data from a variety of sources, including oral accounts, written material (letters or diaries, for instance), and sometimes externally compiled 'stories' of someone's life (case files can be very extensive in social work, for example). Part of the reason for carrying out this kind of investigation, though, is to generate 'alternative' versions of the research subject's experience to those which are found in official records or public documents (Lewis 2008). For instance, these accounts offer a means of bringing a sense of coherent 'narrative' to a story which might otherwise appear in formal records as a series of 'events' each of which is accounted for by its own very specific logic. For particular aspects of service users' experiences, then, life stories appear to offer real advantages. People who have undergone repeated processes of classification and institutionalization, and those whose versions of events have been marginalized, may be represented much more fully by this type of research, as Goodley and Tregaskis (2006) have suggested in relation to disability; and as one of these authors also suggests in relation to people with learning difficulties: 'Proponents assert that the major strength of the life history approach lies in its attention to insider perspectives ... life histories do exist as an agency through which historically marginalised individuals may account for their own lives' (Goodley 1996: 334).

Methodological concerns about the accuracy and veracity of these accounts can be addressed in a number of ways. First, we might argue that, by paying attention to people's own words, and other means of communication with which they are comfortable (such as photography or artwork, for example), the source material for investigations gains significantly in 'authenticity', even if it is also selective and relatively narrowly drawn. Second, the likely availability of a number of potential sources, and the ability to return to participants for more detail, or for verification, offer additional safeguards. Third, it has been possible to develop some quite sophisticated techniques for ordering personal histories, using 'life history calendars' or 'cuing individuals with idiosyncratic events from their own past' (Harris and Parisi 2007: 40). And, finally, a case can clearly be made for paying attention to the subjective meanings and impacts participants draw from their experiences, rather than the (apparently) objective representation of a historical event, such as the 'diagnosis' of a child's impairment (Goodley and Tregaskis 2006).

Goodley (1996) also offers cautionary words about possible limitations of life history methods as a helpful counterbalance. Researchers may become 'over-immersed' in dense and moving tales, for example and they run the risk of super-imposing their own 'meanings' on those of their informants. As he points out, personal accounts of exclusion and victimization run the risk of reinforcing 'victim stereotypes'.

Other, more self-evident problems might also be associated with such methods. The researcher must rely to a considerable extent on the genuineness of the informant's account of events in the past which s/he may have 'rehearsed', may not recall clearly, or may simply misrepresent. While it is possible to check for bias to some extent, say, by comparing 'accounts of the same event or experience in different interview settings', it is still important not to use any apparent inaccuracy simply as a means of 'weeding out' unreliable accounts:

> A result of checking the informant's words is that real reasons are revealed for the presence of contradictions and confusion. As trust and rapport develop modification of a story might be expected . . . To ask whether our informants are telling the truth may be irrelevant . . . What is important is to understand why they present their stories like they do.
> (Goodley 1996: 344)

We can see here that from this research perspective, it is not simply enough to present informants' accounts, but to interpret these accounts in the light of wider evidence and prior understandings. Goodley (1996) also argues that it is vital to make connections between personal stories of disability and 'social theories' precisely to avoid the risk of misrepresenting them or pathologizing those concerned yet further.

Another interesting example of this technique in use has explored the 'life experiences' of students training for social work (Christie and Weeks 1998). By inviting informants to reflect on the relationship between key events and their choice of career, this research pinpointed the decisive nature of these experiences for many. This, in turn, suggests that drawing on these events, whether positive or negative, is likely to inform social workers' practice. In this case, again, it should be clear that it is not the absolute accuracy of these accounts or recollections that is important, but what the individuals concerned make of them, and how these interpretations shape their preparation for practice. Their 'life stories' are integral to their professional identity, and thus need to be seen as a potential element in their day-to-day practice: 'Life stories are "social units", to be exchanged between people, an important means through which we communicate and negotiate who we are' (Christie and Weeks 1998: 56).

Box 6.3 Using our own stories in research

A colleague once told me that she also believes that social work practitioners are likely to have been prompted to choose the profession because of specific triggers and events in their own lives. Perhaps this theme is worthy of further 'life story' research.

Research which enables participants to tell their stories thus provides the opportunity to develop an understanding of personal change and the cumulative sense of 'who we are'. Despite its apparent methodological shortcomings, it provides a number of countervailing benefits in terms of the richness and relevance of the accounts and meanings which people generate 'for themselves' – their partiality and inconsistencies thus become an important part of their stories, rather than a reason for excluding them.

Critical approaches to research: widening perspectives

This summary of possible methods available under the broad heading of critical or interpretive research strategies has sought to suggest that there is substantial scope and variety of options available for those who wish to conduct research which gets 'under the surface'. Nonetheless, this is by no means an exhaustive list, and other options such as 'vignettes', visual methods and 'research diaries' can all be seen to offer potential value. These approaches are, however, commonly characterized by their desire to account in some detail for the meanings, attitudes and expectations of participants. In social work terms, these insights are likely to be of particular benefit when we are concerned with questions about defining 'problems' from the perspective of those affected, exploring their use and experiences of services, and considering the nature and quality of their social networks and relationships.

As in the previous chapter, these options are not offered here in any particular order of preference, but rather to illustrate their respective uses in addressing different types of research questions, and dealing with particular practical challenges, such as limited access to groups or individuals who are not readily available to participate. Such methods also seem to be more practical from the point of view of many lone researchers in social work (practitioners and students alike), although this does not mean that we should give them privileged status for this reason alone. The question of the appropriate balance between different methodological approaches is clearly important, and should not be determined either by dogma or pure pragmatism, of course. The concluding observation here should be that we need to think in terms of complementary research methods, rather than hierarchies or exclusivity of approach.

Key points

- Interpretive or critical research methods need to be just as 'systematic' as those carried out from an empiricist perspective.
- Interviews often seem to be the method of choice for research of this kind, but they should not be accorded a privileged position.
- Establishing an appropriate research relationship with service users is not straightforward, because research from a critical perspective is not committed to taking their views or aspirations at face value. It is carried out 'at a distance'.

7 COMMITTED RESEARCH: MODELS AND METHODS

Researching with a goal

In this final summary of research methods, I want to introduce a number of possible ways of operationalizing projects which are explicitly and unashamedly 'committed', either to achieving a particular beneficial outcome, or to representing the viewpoint of particular (service user) interests explicitly. In this context, as we have observed previously, the distinction between 'rigour' and 'objectivity' becomes highly significant. Research carried out from this perspective does not make any claim to be dispassionate or uninvolved, and therefore does not aspire to conventional standards of neutrality or objectivity. However, it takes the view that this is a source of strength, partly because it reflects certain core social work values, such as empowerment, and partly because it enables researchers and co-researchers to develop forms of knowledge and practice *from within* in ways which are not accessible to other approaches.

Clearly, this perspective demands a rather different way of conceptualizing and operationalizing sound and effective research practice, given that its outcome measures, for example, may be quantified in terms of collective change, or enhancements in generalized benefits, such as social capital, according to the perceptions of participants themselves. In some cases, indeed, it may be the process itself rather than the outcomes which is the source of positive gains for participants, who have had the opportunity to 'speak out', and to give an unmodified account of themselves. Research, in this case, becomes a form of social action; it is only through the application of systematic and rigorous methods of articulation and evaluation that it can be distinguished from other related activities such as campaigning and self-advocacy.

At the heart of these forms of research lies the principle of user involvement and participation, which, in some instances, will be realized through service users taking control of some or all of the research process. Effective participation, however, in research as in other forms of practice does not require a uniformity of approach, and the models of inquiry to be considered here tend to adopt different strategies to achieve this aim. Relationships between user-researchers and academic partners may also vary as a result, although it should be possible to discern clear evidence of collaboration and power sharing in the process. Indeed, Oliver (1992: 111) has identified three criteria against which the 'emancipatory' aspirations of committed research can be judged, that is, the extent to which it can be said to have achieved 'reciprocity, gain and empowerment' for participants. Thus, clearly, as much attention must be given to the impact of research *processes* as is paid to the content and implications of research outcomes. As Beresford (2002) has observed, this kind of test is of considerable importance if we are to judge whether or not research from within this paradigm has, indeed, been conducted according to its stated principles and, of course, whether or not it has achieved its objectives. He points out, for example, that user involvement in research is not 'monolithic and uniform' (2002: 102), but has to be assessed in terms of its conduct and achievements, issues 'which all research must address too':

> Any approach to the evaluation of user involvement in research and user-controlled research needs to consider such broader methodological issues as well as narrower ones seen to relate to judgements about the technical merits and demerits of involving service users.
>
> (2002: 103)

Action research: a vehicle for change?

Action research has been developed as a form of 'systematic practice' over a considerable period of time, owing much of its inspiration to the work of Freire (1974) who sought to utilize the power of education to mobilize oppressed groups and communities. Broadly, it utilizes principles of participation and empowerment to inform the entire research process, from the articulation of the initial problem (research question) through implementation and achievement of its primary goals, which are likely to take the form of concrete changes in practice or service provision, rather than written reports or other documentation. Despite this, records of processes and achievements remain important if we are to think of research as contributing to the wider body of relevant knowledge and methodological development.

Action research will thus be oriented towards practical outcomes, and its processes will be participatory and reflective, providing space for participants to review activities and achievements, and to carry out ongoing tasks of evaluation and revision.

Critically, these aspects of the overall project should seek to maintain the same level of participation and engagement as apply at the initial stage of problem definition and at the end point where outcomes are subject to review. Close attention to these internal dynamics of the project are therefore crucial.

Action research typically requires participants to engage in collaborative activities such as:

> identifying their needs, setting up research questions, and using the research findings. The practice involves people reflecting on issues and process during the research . . . and entails an element of risk given that the process and outcomes are in a state of on-going change . . . As the focus becomes redirected, outcomes may not be readily predicted and, for this reason alone, power holders may not be fully at ease with what they are not in control of: the 'knowledge' it produces, the thinking it stimulates, or the action it promotes.
>
> (Todhunter 2001: 2)

In stark contrast to the tightly controlled methods set out in earlier chapters, action research may produce both interventions and 'findings' which are multi-faceted and unpredictable; these, however, are strengths inherent in a method which seeks to engage with participants on their own terms and enable them to address and resolve key questions and issues concerning them.

In my own experience, I have been involved in at least one piece of work which essentially falls within the ambit of action research. This was a project funded by the Department of Health in England which aimed to develop and evaluate a 'training for trainers' package delivered by an organization of people with learning difficulties (Weeks *et al.* 2006). The intention was to draw on the extensive experience of this group as trainers and self-advocates in order to enable others to act as trainers in their own right. As a funded project, clearly there was an expectation that the initiative would be evaluated, so the combined requirement for development and evaluation lent itself quite readily to an action research approach.

The initial phase was the development of a two-day training programme with accompanying materials, which would then be delivered over a number of months in different settings (including a 'care village', a People First group, and several health and social care establishments). The fairly extended timetable enabled those involved to reflect on the programme and revise it over the course of the project; this was supported through my role as an observer on site as the training was delivered, and the ongoing evaluations provided by participants. Action research approaches can thus be seen to utilize a number of techniques which might be based on other methodological strategies such as observation, in this case, or 'in-depth individual and group interviews' in other examples (Todhunter 2001: 2). Crucially, however, these methods are not ends in themselves in this context, but they are applied in order to inform future development and revision of project goals and activities. In the context of this 'training for trainers' initiative, for instance, initial feedback and observations enabled participants to adjust the programme to allow more space for interactive learning.

As the project continued, observation, feedback and reflection enabled the team to ascertain that a number of goals had been achieved. First, it was clear that those attending the training events generally valued them, and in some cases felt that they had acquired the skills and confidence to act as trainers themselves; second, the team felt that their approach and their own expertise had been validated through their experience in designing and delivering the programme; and, finally, the developmental process had resulted in the production of a series of very useful training tools which have been utilized subsequently.[1] We concluded that 'the development of skills and expertise, and the role reversal involved in service users taking the lead in training, are in themselves, both empowering and of practical benefit for people with learning difficulties' (Weeks *et al*. 2006: 53).

In this particular case, the focus and aims of the project ensured that there was a degree of structure and even predictability about the kind of results likely to be generated; however, in other circumstances, this kind of initiative could well lead to volatile and unpredictable consequences. In one such example, concerned with promoting 'drugs prevention', the process of engaging with and empowering participants to articulate their own concerns may have resulted in unproductive conflict between them and local agencies. This degree of unpredictability perhaps indicates that action research strategies need to give careful consideration to the potential ethical difficulties which might arise. The high risk and essentially politicized nature of action research require careful and continuing reflection on the part of those involved, and especially external researchers acting as advisors or consultants who may not have as much to lose from resultant hostility, or refusal to provide continuing services (Todhunter 2001). In this context, the suggestion offered is that the 'groundwork has to be prepared thoroughly', and crucially that those involved on all sides (funders and participants) need to be 'fully aware of the potential pitfalls' (Todhunter 2001: 4). By definition, action research does not lead to comfortable and predictable outcomes, especially where it is (as it should be) committed to 'legitimizing' participants' 'voices and actions', and promoting empowerment and challenge. Ironically, perhaps, an 'uncomfortable ride' might be an indicator of the success of this method rather than an indication of failure or loss of control.

Standpoint research: taking sides in advance

In the same way as action research starts from a position of practical commitment to the interests of service users/participants, so, too, do investigations which come under the heading of 'standpoint research', although this perspective is more likely to be informed by theoretical and principled support for a particular group or interest. This is a research strategy which has close historical links with feminism (Swigonski 1993, 1994). Essentially, the argument is that social work research *must* be explicitly and in all respects committed to challenging the impacts of oppression on specific groups, notably, but by no means exclusively, women.

There is believed to be a substantial overlap between the value-base of feminism and that of social work as a discipline, for example, which provides a principled underpinning for research conducted from this perspective. In addition, the structural location of those engaged in the research process is significant precisely because it offers them distinct and more comprehensive insights into the realities of their lives:

> To survive, subordinate people must be attentive to the perspective of the dominant class as well as their own. As a result they have the potential for 'double vision' or double consciousness – a knowledge of, awareness of, and sensitivity to both the dominant worldview of society and their own perspective.
>
> (Swigonski 1994: 390)

This is not only a necessary 'survival skill' but it offers a particular form of 'expertise' which is not directly available to those in other structural positions. This significantly provides theoretical support for the emerging acknowledgement that service users are, indeed, 'experts by experience'.

Adopting this position also imposes certain requirements on the detailed conduct of investigative activity, which 'must begin from concrete experience, rather than abstract concepts' (Swigonski 1994: 390). Research starts from 'within' a clearly defined group, and builds up a collective view of life experiences for this group. As Swigonski points out, this has meant that certain group-specific subjects have been 'made visible' because of the adoption of this approach, including, from women's perspective, issues of childbirth, domestic violence, prostitution and sexual violence.

In addition, standpoint research will seek to articulate the 'opposed understandings' of the world held by oppressed groups (Swigonski 1994: 391). They have no vested interest in the *status quo*, and so are likely to be able to reflect on it more clearly than those who are committed to it. This may mean, for example, that those who are marginalized or discriminated against on the basis of their sexuality (Fish 2007) are able to account for this process more readily than those who are bound by conventional assumptions about what is 'normal' and acceptable. Thus, it is clear that standpoint studies will encourage participants to elaborate accounts of oppression at first hand. This, in turn, suggests that the subject matter of such inquiries will be the 'daily activities' and encounters of the group in question and the 'appropriate perspective for research activities is everyday life' [Swigonski 1994: 391]. As well as accounts of oppression, this may also enable researchers to focus on those positive aspects of the group's experience, demonstrated through mechanisms of mutual support and valuing of each other.

We can see here that a 'standpoint' perspective provides effective validation for research which seeks to elaborate and acknowledge the importance of service users' experiences and perspectives on their lives, and the services they are provided.

Unrau (2006) suggests that this approach can be applied to specific research questions (the impact of placement moves) on specific service user groups (foster children), but to do so it must meet definite criteria as set out above. In fact, of a large number of studies of placement moves reviewed, she has found that very few effectively represent 'the standpoint of children' (2006: 131). Those that do, rely on detailed interviews with children and young people, either still in care, or at some point after leaving. The areas of concern addressed include their feelings about involvement in the decision-making process (or lack of it), and the number of moves, and their impact on their relationships and feelings of stability and security. Children in these studies may also be asked to rate their placement experience and the process of moving.

As a result, administrative concerns about number and location of placements which largely shape and define foster children's experience are counterposed with the dimensions which seem most important to them, namely feelings and relationships:

> Case record data represent placement moves as an artefact of the system instead of an event experienced by children and other people in the context of the system. Ignoring or overlooking the standpoint of foster children in research on placement moves leaves a major gap in understanding this important dimension of the foster care experience, as well as the impressions or scars left by the move experience. Such gaps in research can also lead to incomplete policy.
>
> (Unrau, 2006: 134)

Articulating children's perspectives in this way also enables another important criterion of standpoint research to be met, namely, that we should use 'the findings of the research to change the lives of groups who are the study subjects' (Swigonski 1994: 392).

Two points of concern emerge in relation to this articulation of standpoint research, however. The first is that it does not, apparently, depend for its authenticity on the direct involvement of service users as commissioners or co-researchers. This may be seen as problematic by those who would argue that failure to secure this level of participation might lead to exploitation or misrepresentation of participants. Standpoint researchers might respond to this by suggesting that the crucial test is whether the conduct and use of material generated is consistent with principles of 'transformation, renewal and empowerment' (Swigonski 1994: 392).

The second problematic aspect of this approach concerns the difficulty of potential or expressed conflict between members of the 'group' which is the subject of study. How is it possible then to represent the findings as the collective experience or views of a particular interest? It is not possible to assume from the outset that common membership of an oppressed group will lead to shared perceptions or aspirations, so researchers may have to consider rather more nuanced tests of the integrity and credibility of their findings. Is it more important to ensure that participants are given a voice and enabled to contribute 'distinctive knowledge' (Swigonski 1994: 392) rather than that this is entirely uniform, or leads to monolithic analyses and conclusions? Unrau (2006: 135) concludes that, rather than overly neat and prescriptive conclusions, the aim of the researcher should be to 'ensure an overall balance of perspective in knowledge building efforts by ensuring that multiple standpoints are represented'.

'Speaking out': service users in the lead

As distinct from standpoint approaches, other strategies to represent service user views and interests start from the assumption that they should play a leading role in the construction and conduct of any investigation. Professional or academic researchers may have a part to play but this is one of advice, consultancy and technical assistance rather than design and direction of the research process. This is not to suggest that there is a pure definition of 'user-controlled' research against which every attempt to implement it should be evaluated (Turner and Beresford 2005). Indeed, it potentially shares common ground with other approaches discussed here, such as action research and participatory inquiry while, at the same time, the mechanisms of user control could be quite different between research projects. However, there does appear to be a degree of agreement that there are some core features to user-controlled research, including the requirement that it must be 'initiated' by the users concerned. Service users also take the view that studies of this kind must seek 'to bring about change and improve the lives of service users' (Turner and Beresford 2005: 22); and they must be underpinned by an explicit set of values which include: 'empowerment, emancipation, participation, equality [and] anti-discrimination' (Turner and Beresford 2005: 27). Turner and Beresford also stress that service user involvement and control should be continuing features of research practice 'and be maintained through to its conclusion' (2005: 27).

Although research may be 'user controlled', this does not mean that there is no place for external input, from academics or other professional researchers, and as we have noted previously this can be an important aspect of the overall project. However, it is problematic (Smith 2004), and requires detailed attention to the establishment and conduct of this outsider–insider relationship. It is possible to conceptualize working arrangements in a number of different ways as 'contractual', 'client' based, or 'supportive', for example (Smith 2004). These all offer some potential benefits but also have drawbacks. How far is it possible, for instance, to offer advice designed to avoid methodological errors ('client' model) without running the risk of imposing an arbitrary model of orthodoxy which undermines the expertise of user-researchers. If, on the other hand, the external advisor simply acts in a 'support' role, enabling users to take whatever approach they wish, is this always possible or desirable, where problematic research practices are apparent? In an earlier article, I suggested that a fourth type of role might be more suitable for the external researcher, that of 'critical friend' (Smith 2004), where advice and criticism can be freely offered, and accepted (or declined) equally freely.

People First Lambeth have produced one study which adopted this strategy (Taylor *et al.* 2007), with a group of people with learning difficulties carrying out and publishing their work, with the support of an external 'supporter' (a doctoral researcher who has spoken elsewhere of the difficulty of 'not taking control'). The research team in Taylor *et al.* set out to find out about 'the problems that people with learning difficulties face' and 'what can be done to change things for the better' (2007: 15). Their account records their collaborative approach to deciding on the initial research question which led to an agreement that they needed to find out 'about daily life' (2007: 20) for people with learning difficulties, 'so that people will know what is going on, how people with learning difficulties are suffering'. This broad framework enabled them to generate an interview schedule, including such questions as 'What do you like in your life?'/'What don't you like in your life?' (2007: 21) – and some more specific questions on bullying and being forced to have sex. These questions originated in the researchers' own experiences of people being 'against us' (2007: 25).

The nature and sensitivity of some of these questions led the research team to decide that they would 'only talk with people we knew' and where they and respondents could 'trust' each other (2007: 22). They believed that this would help people to feel more comfortable about taking part, and that it would improve the chances of positive responses. Interestingly, the positive reasons for making this kind of ethical choice run counter to the assumptions held in other paradigms that researchers and respondents should not be familiar with each other, for fear of 'contaminating' the findings. Here we see that a 'committed' approach means not just identifying with a particular viewpoint but also, in a very practical sense, with those participating in the study.

It is arguable that the very sense of unity between researchers and researched in this instance led to some powerful insights into painful experiences, of bullying and racism, for example, as well as sexual abuse and rape (Taylor *et al.* 2007: 45). For one of those concerned, the research represented a valuable opportunity: 'I was about twelve and it was part of my family that did that to me. When I talked about it with the Research Group it gave me more confidence and put my life back on track' (quoted in Taylor *et al.* 2007: 45). It may not be one of the initial aims of this type of 'social work' research, but its potential to promote individual as well as social benefits may be seen as a distinct advantage.

In any case, these findings and others enabled the research team to draw out some powerful messages for change, including the need for paid work for people with learning difficulties, the need for 'support at night', 'choice' of activities and lifestyle and 'the power and the control over their own lives' (Taylor *et al.* 2007: 96). Not only are these important messages in themselves, but it is also arguable that research undertaken in this way helps us to reconsider the relationship between agencies and 'service users'. Much of the evidence uncovered by these researchers indicates a need to consider people with learning difficulties in a much broader way, as equal citizens, rather than as dependent users of social services.

Once again, we must acknowledge that methods and approaches which have sometimes been criticized from some perspectives actually demonstrate positive advantages in terms of the richness of the material gathered and the capacity to generate alternative views of the subject matter. Equally, these gains can be achieved without compromising on conventional notions of rigour and systematic inquiry, for instance in the way that interview schedules are constructed and responses are recorded and analysed, albeit participatively. Indeed, the very openness of the process builds in its own checks for credibility, authenticity and comprehensiveness, because user researchers are in a sense directly accountable to the participant community, of which they are a part.

Participative inquiry: learning from the inside

In order to be committed, research does not necessarily have to be carried out by members of the population affected, such as service users. Other models are also able to offer an insider perspective; however, these must also adopt alternative strategies to meet the same standards of authenticity. One of these is participative inquiry, which seeks to use processes of dialogue and engagement to achieve a deep understanding of participant perspectives and experience. In this respect, this model can be seen as sharing characteristics with Weber's (1957) notion of 'verstehen', or the social work principle of 'empathy'.

Unlike research practice which is user controlled from the outset, this model tends to the assumption that the research question will be predetermined by an external researcher, although this may yet be subject to negotiation and refocusing as the inquiry progresses. In one such case, although the research processes were clearly constructed to be participatory, the initial subject matter was predetermined, in the form of an evaluation of forensic mental health services (Godin *et al*. 2007). This issue (choice of topic) is linked to wider concerns about the use of 'power' in participatory research and the crucial importance of acknowledging and 'factoring in' established imbalances in status and authority:

> I have witnessed the paradox between the power aversion rhetoric of PAR [participatory action research] and the continuing realities of power played out on many occasions. Repeatedly I have observed researchers claim that participants assumed a primary role in the research process, even in the face of considerable contrary evidence.
> (Healy 2001: 97).

For Healy, then, the methodological challenge is not to find ways of wishing away power imbalances but of incorporating them positively into the participatory framework.

Fenge (2002: 176) argues that the researcher may have a key role to play in 'working with invisible' minority groups who will not even be acknowledged 'unless researchers start to identify and work with them'. She does not believe that being an 'outsider' automatically disqualifies the researcher from initiating participative projects, especially where these involve opening up exploration of the lives and aspirations of under-researched groups, such as 'minority groups of older people' (2002: 177). Once these initial decisions have been made, however, the researcher is obliged to 'acknowledge' this role, while promoting ownership and involvement among the research population. Empowerment remains a running theme of the process, and so participants' feedback must be allowed to influence practice consistently throughout. This is especially important where the aim of the study is to give 'voice' to marginalized groups who are consistently overlooked or dismissed. This is vital, for example, 'when considering the needs' of older people in minority groups who are used to being defined and acted upon 'in light of the dominant discourse' (2002: 177). Research which aims to give such groups a voice will typically be required to adopt methods which enable participants to challenge established 'socially constructed meanings' (2002: 178), and resist their negative consequences.

Fenge (2002) suggests that sampling is a significant issue in this context because the aim of engaging with 'invisible' groups is by definition problematic. It may be necessary to utilise 'snowball' sampling techniques, for instance, whereby contact is made on the basis of personal relationships, and the establishment of trust.

In some instances, too, lack of familiarity with research conventions on the part of participants might necessitate a willingness to adapt analytical tools and processes to their preferences. In one such case, this involved repeatedly filming analytical discussions between service users recruited to the research

---

Box 7.1 Getting too close to the subject

While approaching people you know may appear to offer considerable advantages, it also leads to potential problems. One of my students has recently had some difficulty recruiting participants in a study of South Asian women with depression, because the sensitivity of the topic and the associated fears meant that those she approached in her own community were reluctant to take part.

However, she managed to use links at 'community' level to recruit respondents from another geographical area who were not known to her.

team (Godin *et al.* 2007). In this case, this rethinking of the analytical component of the study reflected the importance attributed to effective engagement between external researchers and participants, as well as the search for an effective way of capturing the research 'outputs' for future use. The use of film as a medium for this aspect of the process provided a natural resource for dissemination which was faithful to the views and interpretations of service users, enabling them to 'have a voice' quite literally. This helped them to convey the key findings directly to important audiences, such as future health professionals:

> The 'take home' message was that although SURs [service user researchers] recognized the relationship between patients and professionals to be qualitatively different to friendship they still expected elements of friendship, such as understanding, empathy, trust, honesty, loyalty, compassion and respect.
>
> (Godin *et al.* 2007: 464)

The collaborative ethos of participative methods suggests that appropriate methods will include focus groups, possibly acting iteratively so that collective understandings can be generated, shared and refined. This kind of approach has been shown to work well in the context of poverty and attempts to articulate the subjective experiences of those on low incomes (Bennett 2004). One such project sought to develop appropriate indicators of poverty in Scotland, for example. A structured approach was used to introduce discussion among participants, but from this they were able to articulate common experiences, such as 'being disregarded' or 'treated with disrespect' (Bennett 2004). Thus, again, we can observe the interplay between structure and empowerment in the research process, with the initial 'framing' of the problem by the researcher actually serving to generate focused discussion which, in turn, gives way to mutually articulated and tested understandings and messages for change.

Despite initial problems of engagement, participatory methods may thus be evaluated in terms of their inclusivity and the nature, extent and quality of the dialogue which they promote. An important methodological question is 'about *who participates*', especially in communities which are subject to fragmenting pressures, and where there remain inequalities of power and access. Participatory researchers need to 'be transparent about the processes used . . . take account of different levels of power and ensure it is not just the more powerful who are included [and] seek out "hidden" groups' (Bennett 2004: 47).

Outputs can likewise be judged to the extent that they enable participants to 'reframe' the problems they encounter and articulate their aspirations and solutions. It is not a question of seeking verifiable truths for participative research, but enabling service users or disadvantaged communities to articulate their perceptions and perspectives, and to present these as alternatives to conventional understandings. This, in turn, creates the opportunity for dialogue and exploration of mutual differences and common ground between 'service providers' and those who use services in the form of 'communicative action' (Godin *et al.* 2007: 468).

Telling stories: meaning and personal experience

Although it may be felt that narrative methods can be categorized along with interpretive or critical research strategies, they are included here because of their commitment to letting service user accounts speak for themselves. They are to be distinguished though from those methods which are explicitly 'user led', since they often arise from the prior interests of researchers who may or may not be part of the population under investigation.

Some researchers argue that the value of narrative methods lies in their ability to bring authenticity to accounts of people's lives and circumstances in ways which are simply not available to other approaches, because they are both subjective and historical: 'We Live in Stories, not Statistics' (Gilbert 2002: 223). Personal accounts are a rich source of evidence in two ways, it is suggested. They provide detailed descriptions of life but they also import-antly illustrate 'the means by which we bring order, that is, we organize our experiences and the information we encounter' (Gilbert 2002: 224). Gilbert (2002) also suggests that narrative methods are appropriate for this kind of purpose because they sit well with a 'natural' predisposition to give accounts of ourselves and events which affect us in the form of stories – in other words, this provides a potential means of ordering and gathering data which accords with day-to-day experience. At the same time, this type of research is freed from the constraint of trying to provide an entirely accurate account of events, because it seeks to incorporate and give explicit voice to the distinctive perspectives of those who are telling their stories. We would not and should not expect these to be uniform or precise and, indeed, their strength lies at least partly in their revelation of different viewpoints and incomplete understandings.

It may be part of the researcher's role to seek out common patterns or underlying themes but these cannot be assumed from the outset and must be allowed to emerge from the data. In this way, for example, shared experiences of the changes (good and bad) associated with a particular form of intervention may be captured, especially as these vary over time.

Box 7.2 The inevitability of a 'viewpoint'

Brian Aldiss's (1973) novel *Report on Probability A* is a very effective illustration of the way even detailed and meticulous accounts of a phenomenon are inevitably constrained by the viewpoint of the observer.

Typically, it is suggested, the notion of a time-ordered sequence is to be found in narrative studies, and the idea of 'stories' implies a probable interest in a number of common elements: 'a beginning, a middle, and an end . . .; events; characters; stance taking or perspective; intentionality, that is, motivation of characters; an underlying time frame; thematic organization, entrance and exit talk; and metacommentary [elements of reflection]' (Gilbert 2002: 227). Researchers need to find both orientations and techniques which allow these stories to emerge, and while they may suggest or draw out common themes, they will not seek to change participants' versions, except insofar as they are ordering and reproducing them.

The researcher cannot remove her/himself entirely from the picture, but the aim is to find ways of capturing participants' stories in ways which are as true to them as possible, and this is the key test of authenticity. Thus, aside from perhaps setting the scene by defining the question, the researcher should play only a minimal part in deciding how and when to gather data. Participants may perhaps be defined only as sharing a broad characteristic such as use of a particular service, being the subject of the same diagnosis, or membership of a particular marginalised group; beyond that, they should be given the freedom as far as possible to recount their experiences in the ways which suit them – these could be by way of interviews, diaries (written, audio or visual), or perhaps even more elaborate visual methods. Although Gilbert has expressed unease about this, the appropriate stance for the researcher is 'essentially as a conduit for the stories of the participants' (2002: 229). While it is undoubtedly the case that the researcher's involvement helps to shape the way in which participants give their accounts, the aim should be to reduce this impact to a minimum; for example, there should be no difficulty in encouraging respondents to amend and add to their version of events on reflection.

Thus, one study of the 'experiences of education' of more than 60 visually impaired people was conducted in different formats (one-to-one interviews and small group discussions) and participants were given the opportunity to review the transcribed versions of these accounts so that they could 'amend their own story before publication, if they felt this was necessary' (French and Swain 2006: 384). The authors of this study stress the importance of seeking out these stories among oppressed groups because their voices should be heard in their own right; they believe that it is possible in this way to reveal 'an oral history that has fundamental personal and political significance' (French and Swain 2006: 385).

This particular study reveals the extent and depth of major unacknowledged aspects of these people's lives in education settings, such as the nature of 'abuse' they experienced, notably in the form of neglect and emotionally cold institutional practices. These personal accounts also give substance to other central features of their treatment such as low expectations, inappropriate preparation for life after school and isolation from family and community. On the other hand, these accounts also enable us to appreciate the positive value attributed to friendships and mutual support. French and Swain make the final point that this is not just a matter of telling stories and revealing negative experiences, but that this very process may contribute to a broader process of empowerment and liberation and a 'politics of hope'. Their stories enable these visually impaired people and others to 'reclaim' their own history (2006: 394), and also demonstrate their own achievements and experiences of 'survival, collective empowerment and resistance'. The study's initiators argue that 'storytelling' is not simply a matter of retelling what is already known or agreed upon but it is, from the participants' viewpoint, 'a creative process of reformulation and reflection'. Thus, the process itself demanded close attention to ensure that all involved could 'get it right' (2006: 395). The researchers acknowledge that they had to reflect on their own part in the process and how to remain true to its underlying purposes. This gave them 'considerable food for thought'.

Perhaps because of their concerns to give proper recognition to participants' perspective, the written account of this study appropriately devotes a very large amount of space to the testimonies of participants in their own words. The authors conclude: 'We believe that oral history and insider perspectives, from the past and the present, are essential . . . A wide range of views and experiences are necessary so that both commonality and diversity can be explored' (2006: 395).

Autobiographical research: a legitimate method?

At the opposite end of the spectrum in methodological terms from the randomized controlled trial lies autobiographical research, which deliberately highlights the value of subjectivity in the most direct sense. The researcher's own attributes and experience become the subject of investigation, and it is precisely the capacity to draw on one's own internal feelings and perceptions that give this approach its explanatory power, according to its proponents. There is no problem, for instance, of imposing external data definitions or analytical categories and thereby failing to capture the precise nature of individual experiences. Rather, the researcher has direct access to these, although this does mean that interpretation and explanation for others may become more problematic as a result.

As in the case of other methods based on 'telling stories', autobiographical research may be based on a range of initial points of inquiry, including a service-based research question (Plakhotnik *et al.* 2006), a common identity (MacDonald and MacDonald 2007), or a specific experience (MacDonald 2003). These prompts may lead to different ways of organizing investigations but in each case the researcher is clearly identified as being directly implicated in the subject of inquiry.

Distinguishing autobiographical research from other forms of first-person account is an important task if we are to expect it to be accorded credibility. Thus, for example, we might expect a degree of forward planning, so that the field of study is clearly articulated in advance, research questions specified and perhaps even data recording and analysis techniques developed (such as structured diary keeping, or reflexive conversations): 'I start with my personal life. I pay attention to my physical feelings, thoughts, and emotions. I use what I call systematic sociological introspection and emotional recall to try to understand an experience I've lived through' (Ellis and Bochner 2000: 737)

Because of this, it is acknowledged, the task of carrying out autobiographical research can be stressful and demanding, involving as it does close 'self-questioning' and a focus on issues of experience or identity which might be stressful or painful. One example, which is almost literally so, is provided by MacDonald (2003) in her first-person account of the meaning of 'chronic pain' and the problem of being on the receiving end of pathologizing and labelling processes. This individual account, she argues, not only helps to illuminate the specific experience, but also provides the basis for arguing that research and practice should pay attention more widely to 'women's stories' and the 'proclamation of their own voices' (2003: 17).

In other examples, it is apparent that an autobiographical approach offers a distinctive understanding of culture, identity and oppression (MacDonald and Macdonald 2007). In this case, the researcher describes her journey as an iterative and reflective process, whereby her personal perspective was interwoven with the external influences which shaped the cultural context of her own practice as a social worker:

> Through detailed reflection I wrote and thought about my early work experiences; I researched the literature and current practices, hence returning to the reflection process with new insights. Subsequently, an iterative . . . process of analysis emerged . . . Finally . . . new insights and understandings surfaced.
>
> (MacDonald and MacDonald 2007: 35)

In her role as a Mi'kmaq social worker, the researcher was able to gain an immediate empathic sense of the depth of alienation experienced by First Nations children coming into the welfare system, and was able to recount the implications of historical and structural discrimination for present-day use of services. Evidence of mistrust and suspicion of statutory services was perhaps easier to come by for the researcher who shared a common identity and cultural background with these service users. This sense of exclusion and oppression was thus found to resonate with the researcher's own experience as a practitioner and educator, where, for instance, 'courses on child welfare with Aboriginal populations . . . are not offered on a continuous basis and are usually classified as an elective course' (MacDonald and MacDonald 2007: 43). For her, this merely reinforced the recognition that there is no such thing as a neutral approach to such fundamental issues and that it is necessary to adopt a committed approach 'to challenge and to change the system that continues to colonialize First Nations people' (MacDonald and MacDonald 2007: 44).

Exercise 7.1

How important do you think 'empathy' is when carrying out autobiographical research of this kind?

Does this mean that the researcher must share essential characteristics with other research subjects in order to establish authenticity?

Does this requirement always apply; for example, must one have experienced alcoholism to be able to research 'alongside' alcoholics?

Clearly, this is not the only means by which such evidence could be generated or similar conclusions drawn, so the advantages must be seen in terms of the power and depth of the messages conveyed and the particular kind of authenticity which is associated with embedded personal experiences. Nor would we expect these benefits in terms of immediacy and direct access to override the requirement for any research to be systematic, transparent and honest. In some cases, too, additional ethical considerations apply, such as the possibility of identifying others (colleagues, service users or family members) known to be associated with the researcher. Thus, in some ways the apparent advantages of adopting a method which is above all else 'true to life' may be offset by additional risks arising for this very reason. Stories which might not otherwise be told and which need to be told may also expose the teller and others around her/him to further problems (Giri 2006).

Demonstrating its value and rigour somehow seems to be a particular problem for autobiographical research or 'self-study', as 'one topic invariably enters discussion: . . . "How can we tell whether a study is a good one?" ' (Bullough and Pinnegar 2001: 14). Bullough and Pinnegar offer some suggestions for assuring the quality of this form of investigation, such as the necessity of demonstrating that one has interrogated 'the relationships, contradictions and limits of the views presented' (2001: 20), providing reference points in terms of 'context or setting' (2001: 18) and that one has taken 'an honest stand' (2001: 16), incorporating one's own relationship to the material presented.

In the end, though, the very nature of partial accounts of this kind is that there are alternative views, and so the quest is not for claims of absolute truth, but originality, 'insight and interpretation' (2001: 16) and 'fresh perspectives on established truths' (2001: 18). In the same way as social work practice advocates the importance of empathy and depth of understanding, so does autobiographical research offer this quality in particular and, in the same way that postmodernism espouses the value of individual accounts and multiple truths, so perhaps subjective methods of this kind provide a particular form of valid knowledge. So it is that a former child worker asks, as an autobiographical researcher: 'is it right that it should be labelled as "abusive" or "exploitative" if parents expect their children to perform adult tasks?' (Giri 2006: 18).

Committed research: true to social work values?

All research from whatever tradition starts from a particular 'standpoint'. Research which claims to be 'committed' therefore might justifiably argue that it is simply being honest about this and factoring in its particular aims and objectives. In this sense, it may even lay greater claim to authenticity than research which claims to be 'objective' in some formal sense. Nonetheless, this does not mean that 'anything goes' and the various methods discussed here can all be shown to adopt some criteria of quality and rigour against which they can be judged. Most important, perhaps, is the need for transparency, so that, as far as ethically and practically possible, observers are able to identify and track the processes by which investigations are undertaken, findings generated and conclusions drawn. In other words, the need to be 'evidence based', in the broadest sense, remains compelling.

However, the additional advantage offered by committed research is that it can claim readily to align itself with key social work values such as empathy, empowerment and advocacy. It is important to recognize that this does not amount to a claim that it is only people who belong to a particular group or share a common experience whose knowledge of this is accurate or authentic – indeed, neither may be the case. No one has an exclusive claim to truth or wisdom, and it is clear that some research questions do not easily lend themselves to participatory or user-led modes of investigation. Corby (2006: 178), for instance, citing the dangers of relying only on a 'consumer perspective' on child protection, argues that 'despite the clear need to give voice to service users in research, there are some dangers in over-reliance on their views'.

Despite this, the apparent flaws in the processes of inquiry and evidence gathering of these strategies are revealed to be no more than methodological challenges of the kind encountered by any research method. Once addressed, there are no further obstacles to seeing committed approaches as a source of real value and benefit in extending our understanding and, at the same time, supporting the underlying social work objective of achieving social justice.

Key points

- Carrying out research which is 'committed' does not mean that 'anything goes'; indeed, preparation and planning may be all the more important where participants are not experienced researchers.
- The questions of ownership and control need to be addressed openly where service user researchers are working alongside professional colleagues.
- In this model of research practice, the uses of research, and questions such as 'what comes next?' are always of major importance.

Note

1. Unfortunately, however, the funder, the Department of Health showed absolutely no interest in the findings when the final evaluation report was submitted!

8   MAKING IT HAPPEN

Turning ideas into action

In previous chapters we considered the principles and processes available to those intending to conduct research in social work. At this point, though, I want to change the focus, moving from these essential preparatory considerations to take a practical view of how to go about carrying out the task. However well prepared the intending researcher is, there is something a little daunting about taking the plunge, making irreversible choices, and actually carrying out one's intended project. The sense of apprehension at this point is widespread, apparently, according to the observations of two Australian academics, who are concerned about 'the fears and misconceptions that exist among many social work students and also practitioners with regard to research. The general aversion to social work research is almost a standing joke' (D'Cruz and Jones 2004: 1). They go on to suggest that similar 'attitudes' have been observed among social work students in the United States, too. This partly reflects the wider feeling in the world of social work that, as an essentially practical task, there is no great value in carrying out research which very rarely offers unequivocal messages for practice. At the same time, there may be a sense that research represents a body of knowledge and skills which are beyond students' level of competence, perhaps because it is associated with mathematics or statistical techniques (D'Cruz and Jones 2004). However, as we have already seen this need not be the case, and there are many options available, at least some of which are very close in ethos or substance to the values and methods of social work practice itself.

At the same time, I hope that previous chapters have demonstrated the considerable potential offered by well-conducted and properly framed investigations in the broad domain of social work. Research findings have contributed significantly to important developments in policy domains, such as prevention in children's services, and research has had direct impacts, too. Thus, for example the adoption of participative methods has offered an additional and sometimes effective means of validating and 'listening to' the views of service users (Turner and Beresford 2005). D'Cruz and Jones (2004: 3) also agree on this point, arguing that research in social work 'can play a significant part in social change by focusing on personal and collective experiences of structural inequality and recommending strategies for change'. Clearly this suggests that there is something to be gained from being 'research aware', at least. This, in turn, can effectively be achieved in practice, just as other relevant knowledge and skills are gained. Our appreciation and evaluation of research messages are likely to be significantly strengthened if we have a clear and practical knowledge of how they have been generated.

Social workers and social work students should not feel daunted because applied research is an essentially practical task just like the 'day job'. Not only is this the case, but many of the skills they apply in their day-to-day work have clear analogies in the research context. The interview, for instance, which is a core feature of much social work assessment, is also a major component in many research studies; in this respect, social workers with interview skills should, in fact, feel themselves to be better equipped than many other intending researchers. So, we should turn with a degree of confidence to consider the distinctive components of the task of 'doing social work research'.

Deciding on the research topic: what makes you tick?

The first practical decision to be made is the subject of study itself. For many researchers, this is a constrained choice because they will be carrying out a commissioned piece of work on behalf of funders, or perhaps for their employing agency. Nevertheless, even if this is the case, clarity is important, given that this initial focus will have a fundamental bearing on what follows.

For others, though, including qualifying and research students in social work, the field may be much more open. The choice of topic may therefore be guided by interest, motivation and practical considerations. I recall a former colleague expressing the view that most people involved in social work had chosen this career path because of critical events or experiences in their own lives (see above). While this may be a contentious assertion, it does suggest that many people involved in the discipline are motivated by specific concerns and a commitment to achieve certain goals. In one case, for example, a qualifying student was definitely influenced in her choice of topic by her personal knowledge of domestic violence and its meaning for women from South Asian communities (Chana 2005). As we have discussed previously, there is no inherent problem in undertaking a study in an area with which the researcher is already well acquainted or even personally involved, since properly conducted 'subjective' accounts have no less value than those which are provided from a more dispassionate position. On the other hand, there are risks in adopting this sort of approach. Revisiting difficult contexts from one's own past can clearly be uncomfortable and emotionally demanding and it may be difficult not to impose one's own prior assumptions on participants, as well as findings.

Equally, as in the example mentioned, to put one's own experience at the centre of the project may mean revealing certain information about oneself (and possibly also family and friends) which may be problematic. This is not to discourage intending researchers from taking on subjects which matter to them for intensely personal reasons; rather, the intention is to suggest that the resultant challenges are not, as commonly supposed, predominantly methodological, but they are more likely to be practical and emotional.

Other possible 'triggers' for inquiries might well include our involvement in a particular area of practice, and our views of it, positive or otherwise. In my own case, an early study was inspired by my participation in a particular innovative project (Smith 1987). The study was prompted by a view, shared with others, that this was a successful and significant initiative which should be documented and disseminated. Naturally, this highly optimistic view of the work being undertaken had the potential to influence the research process and findings. In this case, again, the responsibility of the researcher was to construct a study which provided safeguards against this possibility, but this did not automatically invalidate the project. For many intending researchers in social work this will be an important issue, because both their existing interests and the practical demands of resources and access often limit their capacity to go far beyond their immediate practice environment to seek out subjects of inquiry. Choices of this kind, and the safeguards built in, need to be explained and 'accounted for' certainly, but they are not precluded.

A further consideration to be applied at this stage concerns the question of whether the chosen topic is relevant as well as valid. That is to say, is it 'social work' research? What is it, for example, about a study of poverty which determines whether or not it should be seen as falling under this subject heading, especially in view of the recognition that most service users will live in disadvantaged circumstances? We might conclude perhaps that an investigation which seeks at a societal level to quantify poverty and determine its prevalence among certain groups does not fall into the category of social work research, even though its findings might be highly pertinent for decisions about service user needs, resource allocation and delivery strategies. A study of this kind would not meet several of the criteria used by Dominelli (2005) to define the nature and objects of social work research, for example:

- a change orientation
- more egalitarian relationships between researchers and researcher
- accountability to 'clients'/service users
- a holistic approach to the problems of those who are the subjects of study.

Nor, of course, is such research concerned with the interaction between people and the systems which impact upon them. On the other hand, a study which considers social workers' attitudes towards and use of welfare benefits on behalf of service users could well meet these criteria, even though it does not directly involve service users as participants.

It is, of course, too simplistic to state simply that social work research is defined by its subject matter, so the choice of topic must be guided by reference to both this and the manner in which the research is conducted. Social work research can include, for example, investigations of

- the determinants of practice (e.g. Jones 2001)
- the construction of social work knowledge (Hall *et al.* 2003)
- the needs and experiences of service users (Broad 1998)
- the rights, wishes and feelings of service users (Taylor *et al.* 2007)
- the impact and outcomes of social work interventions (MacDonald 2002)
- the organization and management of social work delivery systems (Parton 2006)
- the education and training of social work practitioners (Smith and Anderson 2008).

Thus, it is possible to conduct research in a number of spheres of activity, including the context, the nature of practice, the service user experience and practice outcomes under the heading of social work research but, in order to qualify as such, it must also incorporate those features which give it its distinctive quality. As McLaughlin (2007: 13) observes, none of the features specified by Dominelli (2005) 'exclusively characterises social work research, but combined [they] can be seen to typify its nature and scope'. In his view, these qualities should also be supplemented by a commitment to promoting empowerment and participation, challenging social injustice and 'transforming' practice.

This does mean that the remit of 'social work research' may extend into other areas of practice such as social care, community work and youth work, but it is important here to distinguish between the subject matter (informal care, for example), and the methodological orientation of the research itself. There is thus a potential mismatch between social work as a 'discipline' and social work as a 'profession', which in itself is probably an appropriate topic of inquiry. Because what social work is and what it claims to be are contested, then, it is not surprising that this should become an important research domain in its own right. Indeed, because it is about the interface between people and social systems, and because it is based on notions of challenge and change, it is perhaps inevitable that one other essential feature of social work research is that it is *contested*. Whereas in some contexts this might be viewed as a drawback, this is not the case in a discipline which is concerned with the nature and dynamics of interactive processes. It means, too, that where the researcher is faced with a choice of topic, the key question is the extent to which the approach to the subject matter can be justified in the methodological terms we have discussed here, rather than its substantive nature. Thus, for example, it would be feasible to carry out a specifically 'social work' research investigation into the claim sometimes attributed to police officers that they regularly have to act as frontline social workers.

From research topic to research question: making it 'do-able'

The exercise of choosing a topic should ensure that the intending researcher has identified an area for investigation which is subject-specific and in which s/he has a degree of interest and commitment. However, refining this choice to the point where it is converted into a practical and achievable task is not always straightforward. Once again, there are important questions to be considered, both methodological and practical. This is a critical stage in the process because it largely determines the substance of the inquiry to be carried out. Often, even at this point, assumptions about what is achievable may threaten to override key considerations as to the importance and relevance of the question to be addressed. Of course, it is important to distinguish between the issue of whether a particular question is researchable at all, whether it is researchable in the circumstances, whether it will produce relevant and usable insights and whether it is actually what the researcher wants to know about. Small differences in the formulation of questions have substantial implications for the conduct of the subsequent study. One word can have major implications as in these alternatives:

1 'Do people from minority ethnic groups make proportionally less use of mental health services?'; or
2 'Why do people from minority ethnic groups make proportionally less use of mental health services?'

As can be imagined, the nature of the investigations following from these two options will be radically different in methodological terms. Framing one's question accurately and appropriately is thus a matter of considerable importance.

At the same time, close attention to the formulation of the research question should enable us to avoid incorporating impossible aims or unsuitable assumptions into our investigation. For instance, it may be very difficult to arrive at a judgement about whether or not a particular intervention achieves 'better' results than another, unless we can reach a clear and specific agreement beforehand about what this means. Better for whom? Better in what way? Better overall, or in specific respects? Better in whose opinion? Equally, it may be important to consider what other types of assumptions may underpin our questions. Should we, for instance, consider the impact of domestic violence in terms of 'the effect on victims', or 'the experience of survivors', and how this choice of words would affect the investigation subsequently?

Punch (1998: 38) suggests that the formulation of the research question offers clear benefits in terms of helping to orientate the investigator and staying on track. It will help to:

- organize the project and give it direction and coherence
- delimit the project, showing its boundaries
- keep the researcher focused during the project

- provide a framework for writing up the project
- point to the data that will be needed.

Whatever the researcher's methodological preferences, the conduct of a study is necessarily a methodical and disciplined exercise, which means deciding what s/he will *not* attempt to do and sticking to this, as much as it does focusing on what will be done (see Figure 8.1).

In applying these principles, it may be useful to think in terms of a selection process, whereby the initial aim is to generate 'a list of possible questions', to decide what sort of questions they are, and then to differentiate them 'and put them in some kind of order' (D'Cruz and Jones 2004: 20). Even at this stage it is worth checking out with others (colleagues or supervisors, perhaps) whether the meaning of these draft questions is sufficiently clear and consistent. D'Cruz and Jones (2004) also suggest four criteria to enable choices to be made between alternatives: relevance, researchability, feasibility and ethical requirements. They point out, too, that this is not an abstract process, but typically occurs in a complex social environment:

> These criteria once again underline how research occurs in a social context that has to be taken into account if one wishes to see potential topics for enquiry progress from ideas to actions. They highlight, too, how the formation of a research project, while driven by what one hopes is a well-formulated question(s), is inescapably bound up with the political processes of gaining financial, organizational and ethical approval to proceed.
>
> (2004: 21)

From this point on, the research project is shaped by an unfolding process of compromise and adjustment between what the investigator sets out to achieve and the slippery but sometimes intractable nature of the real world with which s/he is engaging.

In terms of the suggested criteria, the issue of 'relevance' may be con-

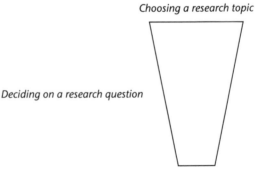

Choosing a research topic

Deciding on a research question

Drawing up a research design

Figure 8.1 Narrowing down the field of study

sidered in terms of the need for a particular type of study, its topicality and perhaps its potential applications. The researcher is likely to be influenced from the start by considerations of the potential uses and audience for the findings, while it is also worth considering the ways in which the intended subject area has been studied on previous occasions. Thus, for instance, in the field of youth justice, much greater attention has been given to the impact of interventions on male than on female offenders, and this may influence the specific focus of the study. Of course, the question of relevance is not the same as that of coverage. Even if the research question only concerns a relatively small subgroup of the population, this does not mean that it is not worth doing, as in the case of one student who chose to try to find out about the experience of disabled women subject to domestic violence. Sometimes, indeed, it is this kind of question that a small-scale single investigator study is best suited to addressing.

Researchability, too, is a crucial consideration. In some cases, questions which are complex or multi-faceted may not lend themselves easily to translation into coherent research processes; some may incorporate problematic assumptions (for example, the word 'Black' has contested meanings and is therefore difficult to operationalize in research terms); and sometimes questions may be too imprecise ('quality' is a difficult word to give meaning to, for example). In some cases, it may be possible to reduce the scale of the task by reducing its range in straightforward practical terms, perhaps by restricting geographical coverage, or the age range to be included. Given the specific importance in social work research of adopting a collaborative approach, it is also important to consider whether or not service users themselves will be willing to participate, for instance in those circumstances where they can see little immediate benefit accruing to them.

In the same vein, the matter of feasibility has to be considered, especially where the researcher has limited resources or constraints on access to the intended subject matter. Studies of institutional settings, for example, clearly depend on the ability to get over the threshold and carry out work on the 'inside'. It may be possible to make compromises in this particular situation by shifting the focus to ex-residents, although then the feasibility issue becomes one of locating them. More generally, at this early stage, the researcher must give serious thought to the practical challenges of carrying out the study. Such questions of access, permissions, resources and time need to be considered as early as possible to avoid subsequent problems.

And, finally, ethical issues run throughout the process; at this early stage, though, broad questions arise such as the level of intrusion into people's lives likely to occur, what its impacts might be and whether these are justifiable in light of the project's aims. This is particularly challenging in the social work field, given that much of our research will inevitably concentrate on problematic subject matter which might trigger painful memories or risk exposing sensitive material in public. Equally, there are likely to be ethical concerns about comparative studies which offer (supposedly) beneficial interventions to some service users and withhold them from control groups. At present, these considerations will also be influenced by the issue of whether or not the proposed study will be the subject of formal ethical review procedures which can be intensely frustrating and time consuming.

Having stressed the importance of gaining as much clarity and precision about the intended research question at the outset, it is also important to acknowledge two ways in which it should not necessarily be seen as fixed and non-negotiable for the duration of the project. First, both contingent events and also the changing nature of the study as it unfolds are likely to prompt reflection and possible revision of the initial question. This is clearly easier in the early stages, but it may be helpful to try to build in a little leeway for this and perhaps to identify fixed points at which it will be possible to reconsider one's starting point (on 'completion' of an initial literature survey, for instance). And, second, especially in those projects which have an explicitly participatory or exploratory aspect (or both), it can be expected that the initial question will be subject to debate and revision as service users and others negotiate and shape the direction of the study itself. The possibility of amendment and adaptation should not be seen as problematic necessarily, and may be a positive commitment in any case, but it is better to acknowledge the need for contingency plans from the outset. I always suggest to intending researchers that they should have a 'Plan B'.

Scoping the project: the literature and beyond

Deciding on the research question should give the researcher a fair indication of the type of preparatory work that will be needed before decisions are made about how to implement the project. An exploratory exercise at this stage will help in a number of ways, and as well as reading, it may well include discussions with others involved in the field of study and drawing on other material that may appear relevant, such as media reports, even if they are not 'academic'. Some texts offer an array of reasons for carrying out this work (20 in one case; Blaxter et al. 1996), and it is likely that a substantial number of these will apply to each study.

Clearly background reading will help to address basic questions such as what we know already about the topic, and if and how it has been researched previously. It will also help the researcher to clarify her/his own prior assumptions and identify other possible perspectives. This process should also help to crystallize key issues and assist in the formulation of suitable methods and research tools. In a tactical sense, the literature review will also enable the researcher to justify knowledge claims and demonstrate a detailed understanding of the subject. Sometimes in research, specific subjects are so closely identified with particular 'experts' that the researcher must demonstrate familiarity with these in order to be able to claim credibility, although it is not necessary to agree with them, naturally. Where the research project is to be part (or all) of an assessed piece of work demonstrating this kind of knowledge of the field will be seen as a central requirement.

These observations prompt further thought about the necessary breadth and depth of reading, and what counts as a legitimate source. In social work, for example, much 'literature' takes the form of policy documents and guidance, internal agency evaluations or small-scale studies which may not be reported in conventional academic outlets. It is also important in the present day to be aware of, and willing to draw on other sources, such as the media (written, visual and electronic) which may offer distinctive opinions and insights. If, say, we are interested in researching service user views of social workers, it is clearly helpful to have some idea about the way the profession is represented in the public arena. Increasingly, it is recognized that 'grey' literature is a valid source of background material, and should not be discounted (Berman 1994; Coad *et al.* 2006; Hartman 2006).

It may seem that this only adds to the problem of deciding what to include in this exercise (and what to leave out). In some subject areas, though, there is relatively little published work. As I write this, in the past few minutes, for instance, a student visiting my office commented that there is not much research available on social work and visual impairment. On the other hand, there are aspects of practice which have been thoroughly researched over many years – the aspirations and needs of young people leaving care, for example. Davies (2007) agrees that these two opposing concerns may well affect researchers, depending on their choice of question. Where there appears to be too much material, he suggests reducing 'the focus of your research question' so that it is possible to narrow the range of literature which could be relevant. It may be necessary, too, to develop a checklist which enables the researcher to apply reasonably strict tests of 'relevance'; thus, it may be helpful to consider whether or not the material is sufficiently recent, in some cases, or whether it is culturally or geographically local enough to the intended research population.

In the opposite case, Davies (2007: 41) suggests that 'the fear that nobody has ever written anything about the chosen topic' is frequently even greater for intending researchers. But, he stresses, this perception is not often justified. However, it may be necessary to 'venture away from familiar academic tracks' and draw on other non-academic sources as suggested earlier. Sometimes, too, a subject which is relatively under-researched in one's own discipline may have had much greater attention from others. A quick search in relation to visual impairment suggests that there may be relevant material to social work practice obtainable from opthalmological research, for instance. Of course, we are in the contemporary era able to draw on a vast range of internet-based material which should offer reassurance that there will be some useful material 'out there' somewhere. In my experience, Google is as useful as the specialized academic search facilities, not least because it offers ready access to both the 'grey' literature and the websites of relevant organizations with knowledge of the subject in question.

While 'browsing' of this kind is helpful to get things started, Davies (2007) also reminds us that it is not sufficient because of the need to provide structure and coherence to the material obtained and to ensure that it relates to the research question. He does suggest, however, as long as we retain this kind of focus that, just as in recruiting research participants, in seeking out relevant literature 'snowballing as a technique is standard practice: that is, find one useful article or book [or report], and it is virtually certain that scanning the references or the bibliography will lead you to others, then do it again with each of them' (2007: 40). Not only does this offer access to a range of sources, but it will also probably offer an indication of which sources are cited more frequently by others, and which are seen as particularly authoritative (this does not mean that they are 'right', of course).

New or additional material may come to light throughout the research process but it will be necessary at some point to carry out two further preparatory tasks based on what is already available: a critical evaluation, and an assessment of the most appropriate method(s) for the task in hand. There is sometimes a tendency for inexperienced researchers or those who are unfamiliar with the specific field to take earlier work at face value; however, it must be considered critically. Indeed, it can be judged against the sort of criteria we have discussed in earlier chapters: is it credible, consistent and authoritative, say? Where there are differences in the evidence or analysis between previous accounts, where does the weight of opinion lie, which seems more plausible, and why? While it is difficult not to react against material which we disagree with, it is important to test out whether this is purely a 'gut reaction' or is based on more substantial grounds. At this point, too, it is important to try and draw out the theoretical and methodological assumptions incorporated in the material under review. These may not be made explicit, as in social work practice itself, but there will always be an underlying body of ideas or prior assumptions of some kind.

At the conclusion of this exercise, the researcher should be able to draw together this evidence in the form of a focused literature review, which explores the key themes to be addressed in the study, and which offers

---

Box 8.1 Theoretical saturation

The idea of 'theoretical saturation' can usefully be borrowed from Glaser and Strauss (1967) to assist you with the decision of when to stop trawling the available literature. If new material is no longer contributing any additional insights, either theoretically or substantively, then it is probably a good time to stop searching.

clear indications as to the specific fieldwork strategy to be adopted. Researchers sometimes find it difficult to make connections between different phases of the overall project, particularly at the point of linking the essentially analytical task of reviewing the existing literature to the practical task of articulating and applying methods and research tools. Nonetheless, it is important to seek to make these links effectively, in order to maintain the justification for the approach taken and the coherence of the whole. We might conclude the literature review, for instance, by summarizing what is known about the subject, what questions have been addressed and answered (and how well), and what remains to be known. This will, in turn, provide the rationale for our research question and the practical steps we plan to take to address it. From this, our methods should follow, seamlessly.

Methods, techniques and skills: putting it into practice

When you have decided on a topic, refined it and specified objectives, you will be in a position to consider how to collect the evidence you require. The initial question is not 'Which methodology?' but 'What do I need to know and why?' Only then do you ask 'What is the best way to collect information?' and 'When I have this information, what shall I do with it?'

(Bell 2005: 115)

At this point, the researcher is faced with a crucial choice, of course: which method(s) to adopt. Although the scoping exercise described earlier will almost certainly point in a certain direction, the range of methods identified previously indicates that there will almost certainly be alternatives available. Davies (2007: 168) perhaps oversimplifies when he suggests that 'you should always choose the method most likely to throw the most light on your research question'. One method may not always stand out as the most obvious. For example, if we wished to investigate the impact of a particular form of intervention on service users, we could carry out follow-up interviews, apply before-and-after behavioural scales, conduct a file analysis or undertake an observational study of the intervention as it happens. In fact, we might conclude that it would be most appropriate to carry out a 'mixed-methods' study in this case.

Our decisions might also be made clearer here by taking the intermediate step of subdividing the research question. We might, for instance, choose to operationalize the term 'impact' by reference to a number of components of the term, such as user satisfaction, reduction in assessed need and reduction in levels of vulnerability and risk.

The second part of Davies's (2007: 168) observation in this context *is* pertinent, though: 'your choice may be constrained by what is feasible, given the limitations of time and other resources' (see also Bell 2005: 116). This does not mean, however, that we should allow concerns about the suitability or practicality of certain methods to override what we have already decided is the best way to construct the research question itself. We should still be guided by the options that this generates. It is only at this point that we can allow room for pragmatism. Nevertheless researchers in social work may well have a preference for methods which coincide with their own professional skills, such as using interviews or carrying out practice observations. And why not? Certainly, it seems to me that social work students sometimes underestimate their own aptitude for aspects of the research task, and there seems no good reason not to apply skills acquired as part of their professional portfolio in the research environment, so long as they are clear about the different role requirements involved.

On the other hand, the easy way is not always the best way, and it is perhaps unfortunate that for many lone researchers conducting small-scale studies out of necessity, the interview becomes the default method of choice. It is Davies, again, who reminds us that there 'is more to qualitative research than interviewing' (2007: 168). It is perhaps not surprising that the interview is such a popular option for social work researchers, given the coincidence between the method, recognized professional skills and practical considerations such as ease of access and the availability of respondents. Interviews are relatively easy to conduct and record; they enable a dialogue to develop which allows for clarification and checking-out; and they follow a format with which both parties are likely to feel comfortable – both are able to exercise a degree of control over proceedings. They are also flexible, in the sense that they allow for the incorporation of structured, semi-structured and open-ended questions, thereby facilitating different methods of analysis, even within the same interview schedule.

Despite these apparent advantages, it is worth spending a little time considering the advantages of other options, for both pragmatic and methodological reasons. Might 'focus groups' be better, for instance, where they represent a more 'natural' way of interacting, perhaps with friendship groups or professional teams?

There are other essentially pragmatic reasons, too, for having a number of possible methods at one's disposal. One, at least, is the explanatory potential of combining methods: 'if possible, efforts should be made to cross-check findings, and in a more extensive study, to use more than one method of data collecting' (Bell 2005: 116). In this way, the benefits of 'triangulation' can be

---

Exercise 8.1

Draw up a comparison chart for interviews and focus groups identifying the advantages and disadvantages of each option. This should help to determine when and in what circumstances each is most appropriately used.

incorporated in the study and this may be done relatively easily, even where time and capacity are limited. How difficult would it be, say, to supplement an interview-based study of service users' experience of their initial contact with a statutory agency by spending a few afternoons sitting in the front office carrying out a structured observation of these encounters? (Of course, there are also challenging ethical issues to be considered here, even if this does all take place in a public space.)

The other reason for having alternative methods in place is that it cuts down on the cost of failure. If one option becomes impractical, or does not generate 'good' data, the availability of a back-up becomes all the more important. Questionnaires often seem to be a good source of a reasonable quantity of data, and may be an attractive way of attempting to measure service use and satisfaction. The pervasiveness of electronic forms of communication (email, text, blogs) may seem to increase their attractiveness, since they can be fairly widely accessed. However, as they have become more prevalent, it has increasingly been recognized that response rates are now very low; to achieve a satisfactory sample, considerable work has to be put into preparation, targeting and follow-up (Bell 2005).

Some methods which might seem attractive in the social work domain seem to be relatively under-used, too. Sometimes, it seems that this is partly attributable to a degree of uncertainty about what 'counts' as data, but there is no reason not to utilize readily available published material where appropriate (Davies 2007). Content analysis, for example, can provide a relatively unproblematic approach to the analysis of the meaning and interpretation of policy and practice guidance. We might use this to address the question of Leicester's distinctive approach to the issue of 'heritage' in its materials on assessing children's needs, perhaps (Leicester City Council 2005).

Another option which is perhaps under-used in social work research is the 'vignette', which provides an opportunity to gain access to practitioners' attitudes and intervention strategies without encountering the ethical problem of discussing real-life examples. By this means, it is possible to construct plausible 'scenarios' which might be encountered in their actual practice, in order to generate evidence about underpinning beliefs and predispositions. Taylor (2006), for example, offers a detailed account of the potential value of constructing and utilizing vignettes incorporating a number of variables in order to determine the 'factors' which influence social work decision-making.

Choice of methods, then, is a tactical matter, combining elements of pragmatism with the need to think creatively and systematically about the most appropriate *and* the most convenient way(s) of obtaining the findings we need. However, it is usually possible to find a practical means of approaching the task, as long as the research question is formulated clearly and specifically enough. Indeed, the ability to specify a suitable and practical method is a good test of the 'researchability' of the original question – but only in extreme circumstances should it be necessary to rethink this at this point.

Ethical and practical considerations: governance and management

The very nature of social work means that research into the subject is bound
to be fraught with ethical and practical challenges. In one sense, this is merely
a reflection of wider research dilemmas concerning the balance between
present risks of harm, however slight, and future gains, which are uncertain.
These are the kind of challenges encountered by scientists involved in animal
research, drug testing, or the use of human tissue. In fact, it is social work's
concern with human welfare and its close association with health care in
particular which has led to some of the contemporary procedural challenges
encountered by would-be-researchers in today's 'risk society' (Beck 1992).

Research governance has become the subject of a considerable regulatory
framework in recent years, largely because of prior ethical breaches such
as the misuse of children's body parts in the Alder Hey case which came to
light in 1999 (Department of Health 2005). Most research conducted in
statutory settings will now be subject to a preapproval process and will
require authorization by the relevant local health or local authority body.
Recent experience suggests that even some large and well-organized research
teams have found it very time consuming, and in some cases impossible,
to negotiate the demands of these procedures, however well intentioned they
are (Elwyn *et al.* 2005; Cook *et al.* 2007). Even more problematically, the need
to negotiate these labyrinthine processes may have an unhelpful impact on
the aims and practices of the researchers themselves: 'at times, the team were
aware that seeking approval to carry out research had become both the means
and the end of our work' (Cook *et al.* 2007: 64). Formal compliance of this
kind should not become more important than the underlying professional
principles of establishing and maintaining good ethical practices, although
this does appear to reflect wider social trends towards a preoccupation
with form rather than substance. In any case, the time and effort involved
in securing this kind of formal approval will have an effect in terms of
researchers' project planning. It is not just a matter of securing willing
participants in the field but also recognizing the necessity of negotiating
permissions from a completely different set of people within agencies,
especially where statutory services are concerned.

Aside from these external expectations, research carried out from an
academic base will also be subject to internal ethical approval, under the
aegis of the relevant research committee. This is an important opportunity to
test one's own perceptions of the risks and safeguards in place for all concerned (including the researcher her/himself) against the considered views of
others who are also committed to ensuring that good, effective and ethically
sound research is produced for wider benefit. While it must be acknowledged
that there is an inevitable element of organizational self-interest involved,
researchers can expect such consideration to be driven by a concern to
facilitate their work rather than to obstruct it. Despite this, research projects
should incorporate some allowance of time for the preparation of the

necessary documentation and formal completion of the approval process; prior planning, though, should ensure that other parallel tasks can be completed during this period (further work on the literature or fieldwork tools, for instance).

McLaughlin (2007) offers a number of useful headings under which ethical considerations can be addressed at different phases of the overall project:

1 Before the Research Starts
   • Research Governance
   • Informed Consent
   • (Use of) Covert Methods
   • Anonymity and Confidentiality
2 During the Research Process
   • Right of Withdrawal of Participants
   • Protection from Harm (of Participants and Others)
   • Protection of Researchers (from Harm)
3 On Completion of the Research
   • Sharing of Findings
   • (Control over) Publication of Results
   • Authorship
   • Confidentiality and Consequences.

This provides a useful checklist for intending researchers to consider at the point where they are seeking ethical approval for projects. It is important, too, that these procedural considerations are clearly located within a meaningful substantive framework which is specific to the discipline. Social work research is informed by a concern with practice and its impacts in this field and so 'the ethics of social work research must be at least compatible if not coterminous with the ethics of social work generally' (Butler 2002: 241).

This recognition has inspired an attempt to set out an acceptable ethical statement for the discipline, which has gained a broad measure of support. For the UK, the Joint University Council Social Work Education Committee has formally adopted the 14-point code originally developed by Butler (2002) as the basis for social work research practice (JUC SWEC 2008). These principles are substantially similar to those set out by other disciplines, especially those in the social sciences (British Sociological Association 2004; ESRC 2005), but there are several areas where it is clear that they have been adapted to reflect wider aspirations for the discipline itself. Thus, for example: 'social work and social care researchers should seek to promote emancipatory research and work together with disempowered groups . . . towards social justice'; they 'must not tolerate any form of discrimination'; they should 'retain a primary concern for subjects' welfare and they have a 'duty to report results which reflect unfavourably on agencies of the central or local state [or] vested interests' (JUC SWEC 2008). They should also try to avoid publication of their work leading to 'damaging representations of service users'. In this way, clearly, there is an explicit attempt to ensure that researchers from and of social work reflect the profession's committed value base in their own practice.

Aside from the ethical approval process, there are a number of other practical details to be dealt with at the preparation stage. My preferred analogy here is with decorating, where a very large proportion of one's time seems to be taken up with 'getting ready' – stripping wallpaper, filling holes, sanding woodwork and so on – relative to the task of decorating itself. So it is with research. Recruiting participating sites and individuals, planning for attrition (some will drop out, almost certainly), preparing and testing research 'tools' (piloting interview schedules, for example), testing equipment (visual or audio recording hardware, perhaps) and making time for site visits, say, are all essential preparatory tasks in most projects. Other ongoing practical steps are also strongly advised in order to be prepared for unpredictable events, such as keeping a spare copy of everything, subject to any ethical constraints which may apply. I know at least one student who lost most of her master's dissertation because of a computer failure with no back-up, and I also know of another student who was conducting his fieldwork in another country and flying back and forth with the only copy of his very substantial findings in his luggage.

Carrying out a successful research project often seems to be a matter of good management as much as anything, because it involves bringing together a range of project skills as well as those associated with the specifically 'research' task of conducting some form of 'systematic inquiry'. Time and resource management, good communication and negotiation skills and effective contingency planning all feature as elements of the portfolio of competences required. In the end, 'managing a research project from start to finish is very different from writing an essay . . . it will . . . have a number of strands to it, and for a successful end-result, you will need to handle each of them competently' (Davies 2007: 11).

Of course, to some extent this also mirrors the social work task, with its

---

Box 8.2 Mapping a 'critical path'

It may help to draw up a 'critical path' map of the research process, identifying all the essential elements (e.g. literature review, research design, fieldwork, analysis, 'writing-up', dissemination), and perhaps subdivisions of these where it is helpful (different phases of fieldwork, for instance). By calculating the length of time each will take and assessing what tasks can be carried out in parallel, and which must be undertaken sequentially, it is possible to come up with a rough estimate of timescales, and the requirements to be met to comply with any in-built deadlines along the way.

many requirements spanning 'competences' such as communication, assessment and planning skills, supported by a set of demanding core values focusing on the promotion of social justice. Much of what is good about good research is not due to highly skilled or sophisticated techniques of inquiry and analysis, but it is about being well prepared, identifying what is needed at the outset and setting out tasks and timescales which are sustainable yet flexible enough to accommodate unforeseen events.

Are you ready?

At about this point, the researcher should feel equipped to start gathering data. What we have seen is a progressive process of formulating general topics of interest, refining these and then operationalizing the questions which emerge so that it is possible to carry out some sort of fieldwork investigation. This process is broadly followed irrespective of the researcher's methodological orientation or chosen subject matter. There will be variations depending on the site and sources of data – ethical issues are much more straightforward where the potential data are already in the public domain, for example – but the stages and direction of the process will be more or less the same in every case.

Careful documentation of these preparatory stages will also provide the researcher with material which will, in the end, generate content for the final report of the study, and importantly, it will assist in the necessary task of offering a methodological critique, without which any account is less than comprehensive, in my view.

Therefore, keeping a research log, of events as well as findings, is another practical option which will almost certainly pay dividends and enrich the final product.

Key points

- Research is like decorating. A considerable part of the task involves preparation; it will probably not be seen (although it may be reported), but if done well, it ensures that the finished product is more easily accomplished.
- Researchers should always start with a topic of study which interests them and fires enthusiasm. When things get tough, as they probably will, this will provide a large part of the necessary motivation to continue.
- Always have a 'Plan B'.

9 PUTTING IT ALL TOGETHER

Producing the goods

Having completed the preparation phase, it is now time to move on to the production of our original research. As the project progresses, the findings and insights it produces take on unique qualities, which are in one sense exciting but also leave the researcher with some very distinctive challenges and decisions to be made, such as how to make sense of or classify ambiguous responses, or how to deal with the practical problems of data management in less than ideal circumstances.

It will certainly help intending researchers to subdivide this part of the project and break it into 'bite-size chunks'. The different aspects of the production process do, in fact, represent very different tasks with their own demands and timescales, so it clearly helps to be able to address these separately. However, as before, the aim is also to ensure that each element connects seamlessly to the next one, so that the internal logic of the overall project is maintained, and it can be presented in this way to the intended audience on completion. It is far better and easier to be able to account for variations and unpredictable events (which are bound to occur) within a sound and coherent overall framework than to have to make last-minute or contrived changes because 'something happens' (Heller 1974).

In this chapter, we will cover five stages of the process: data gathering, making sense of the data, discussing and drawing conclusions from the findings, self-critical reflection, and the dissemination and use of the study. Taken together, these components can be identified as the critical phase of the research process, whereby we give substance to our initial ideas and preparatory work, and turn these into credible and (hopefully) valuable observations on key aspects of the social work terrain. Because social work is an action-oriented discipline, I believe that it is important to demonstrate a degree of consistency between aims, processes and outcomes. Rooting our research practices in social work values and principles also, it seems to me, means that we should reflect on what this means for the uses and consequences of this activity. Even at the preparation and planning stage, it is important therefore to have some idea in mind of possible audiences, applications and impacts of a study. In this way, hopefully, a trail can be followed from the researcher's initial thoughts and motivations through the research journey to its eventual conclusions and dissemination.

The ground should now be prepared, but one final task remains before starting for real, and this is to iron out any kinks in research tools, to test facilities, settings, equipment and recording methods, and to reassure oneself that one has the necessary investigative skills. Piloting is an important opportunity to make this kind of adjustment, but it need not always be carried out in 'live' situations; recording skills can be assessed, for example, in informal settings with friends or colleagues. Equally, when testing tools such as interview schedules or behaviour scales, the kind of feedback that is helpful relates to the meaning and content of the questions, and so these do not always have to be tested with respondents from the intended sample. In some cases, though, this may be more important, such as where service users employ specific means of communication. In any case, the central aim is to reassure ourselves about the strength and reliability of our chosen tools as far as possible, and to make necessary changes at this point.

Data gathering

Whatever data-collection methods are chosen, there will be some common considerations which apply, and which will need to be addressed in order to ensure that the most reliable evidence possible is obtained. There are three questions, in particular, which tend to arise:

1 What counts as data and how do I record it?
2 How do I classify this piece of evidence?
3 How can I check this finding out?

In the first case, irrespective of the rigour or flexibility with which the researcher has imbued the tools and techniques to be applied, there is likely to be a degree of uncertainty at the margin as to whether certain types of material count as data or not. This is partly dealt with by way of prior specification, but as Mason (1996: 68) reminds us, this still leaves us with the need to make 'situated yet strategic decisions – for example, about what to look for next, whom to speak to next, what to record in some way and follow up'. Although this point is made specifically in relation to observational methods, similar choices will arise in most data-collection settings.

For those carrying out interviews, for instance, the process almost inevitably means making a number of 'trade-offs'. Taking detailed notes guards against the failure of electrical recording equipment but it may inhibit conversational flow and make respondents self-conscious. On the other hand, some respondents may not want their answers to be recorded, so note taking is the only option. There may also be choices to be made here about noting additional evidence such as facial expressions and gestures, and how that evidence is weighted against the spoken word. How do we account at this point for other complicating factors such as gender and cultural differences? In one case I am familiar with, the research student concerned had to recruit and prepare female interviewers to act on his behalf because he was not permitted to meet female respondents alone on religious grounds. This was a necessary adaptation but it also meant putting in place ways of ensuring that evidence was collected in comparable ways by different interviewers.

These challenges do not just apply to predominantly qualitative methods of the kind described earlier. Any method which relies on accounts of behaviour or feelings, or the researcher's judgement will involve an element of selection and the question here revolves around the need for care when applying apparently definitive categories to material which is rooted in human experience or personal testimony.

This leads us to our second key data-collection question which relates to the process of making instant judgements *in situ* about what sort of data have been uncovered and how they should be classified. Sometimes this may involve decisions about authenticity or reliability of the information obtained. We know that in some cases research subjects will respond in ways which are influenced by the situation, and we may need to make allowances for this. It may be possible to base judgements on the consistency or depth of responses or relevant material. Mason (1996: 75) suggests that it is useful to consider what 'level of detail or fullness is provided' by the data. In some cases, it is possible to incorporate reliability or validity checks in the data-collection instruments (such as asking the same question in different ways in interviews or questionnaires, or using similar mechanisms in social functioning scales). However, this can also lead to problems of conflicting findings and the necessity of making decisions about which version or variation is more reliable (if any). Mason additionally suggests, in relation to the use of documents or observational material, that it is important to consider the circumstances and the possible ways in which evidence is shaped: 'Do I need other forms of data, or other contextual information to make sense of' the findings (1996: 75)?

There is no certain way of ensuring that the data-collection process is pure, even if we try to develop highly structured and more or less impersonal ways of 'finding out'. As we are reminded: 'The researcher and informants' positionings and subjectivities influence even the most structured methods of data generation and their outcomes' (D'Cruz and Jones 2004: 110). Even those methods which we have discussed previously that rely on commonality of experience and interest between researchers and researched cannot entirely dispense with concerns about the reliability and value of the evidence gathered. Shared assumptions and belief systems do not necessarily result in common experiences or perceptions, and these cannot simply be inferred from a sense of mutual solidarity.

How then can we begin to establish a degree of confidence in the evidence we uncover? There are several strategies which are of some use, although none offer absolute guarantees, of course. The first of these is to establish a consistent basis for our own processes of recording and verification, as far as possible. This is, to some extent, easier to achieve when there is a predetermined structure to the method being used, but even here it is necessary to pay attention to those regularities which are to be incorporated such as measuring behaviour over a standard timescale or in similar circumstances. Common forms of classification are important, but alongside this, we may also need to provide an account of our own interpretive processes when making decisions on which category applies. The evidence can never stand entirely alone, and the researcher will need to 'factor in' her or his own influence, both at the point where information is obtained and in subsequently contextualizing and making sense of it. This 'reflective' element of the research strategy finds echoes in social work practice which also necessitates a degree of self-awareness among practitioners (Wilson *et al.* 2008).

Additionally, the researcher will probably find it helpful (and appropriate) to develop ways of 'checking out' findings. In the most straightforward terms, this may involve sharing recordings, observations or transcripts with research participants to enable them to verify both the substance and meaning of the evidence they have provided. In some cases, too, this offers an important opportunity to clarify and to enable those involved to make sure that their accounts are as intended. This process is not exactly the same as changing the evidence, rather it enables a process of reflection which may well enhance the quality of the data. It seems appropriate, too, to the extent that it fits with social work's participative ethos.

Within the bounds of ethical constraints, it makes sense, as well, for researchers to seek clarification and confirmation from colleagues and supervisors, who may well be very familiar with the subject matter. In larger projects, where researchers work in teams, it is common practice to establish mechanisms to ensure consistency of practice and interpretation, but even where the researcher is working alone, there are opportunities to test assumptions with others who may bring relevant knowledge and expertise. This process may help to bring a sense of coherence and order to research findings, but it should not be assumed that any remaining partial, incomplete or inexplicable data should be excluded from consideration. This runs the risk of over-simplification and imposing certainty where it does not belong. Research may aspire to be a rational exercise but it cannot account for everything, and indeed, apparently exceptional observations may indicate the direction for further investigation and practice innovation.

Making sense of the findings

Although it is set out here as a separate stage in the process, interpretation and analysis will in fact run throughout the research project. It is impossible to avoid bringing one's own prior understandings and practice wisdom to the inquiry and, indeed, as we have already observed, some methodologies celebrate this fact. Others suggest the use of techniques such as epoche (see Chapter 3), which essentially means 'bracketing off' the researcher's prior attitudes, characteristics and 'usual assumptions' in order to develop a sense of distance from the object of study (Butt and Parton 2005), or at least to provide a basis for others to account for the researcher's influence on the process (Gearing 2004). At best, though, this does not exclude the researcher's perspective from the picture, but it can offer us a means of taking account of it in our own interpretation of the material.

So, analysis is neither pure nor context specific. Nonetheless, we may find it helpful to try to sketch out some approaches to the task of making sense of data which help in the practical sense of generating understanding. Mason (1996: 107, 135) suggests that the process of analysis, in qualitative research, involves two stages: 'sorting, organizing and indexing' findings and 'producing analyses and explanations'. The first of these will involve rather different processes depending on the initial methodology adopted. Some studies will specify in advance the categories and themes under which data will be grouped for analysis, especially where they are concerned with the identifiable effects of certain actions or interventions. Others, though, may be more interested in a process of 'discovery', whereby essential themes and categories are allowed to emerge from the data, perhaps based on their regularity or prominence. As Mason (1996: 120) puts it: 'some researchers will wish to generate indexing categories in a fairly grounded way on the basis of their ongoing interpretation of the data, whilst others may be less concerned with this', because their categories are already predetermined. Nonetheless, in both cases, researchers must evaluate their findings in terms of common characteristics which enable them to identify patterns and interconnections. Where categories are predetermined, this means also deciding what criteria to apply to enable one to assign a particular piece of data to one or other of these. What level of increased use of a service might be taken to indicate improved rates of satisfaction amongst service users, for instance?

Where we are engaged in the process of exploring data to identify patterns and themes, there are a number of questions to consider such as the relevance and significance of these in relation to the original research question. As Mason puts it, this involves an iterative process, whereby the data, the emerging themes and your central question act as a set of checks and balances:

> Essentially, you need to create for yourself a mechanism for moving back and forth between your intellectual puzzle, your research questions and your data, so that you develop your indexing categories through this process of interaction.
>
> (1996: 120)

As the researcher undertakes this task, the relative strengths of the categories may also become clearer, and they should also become richer and more detailed.

Where the project generates large amount of data, analysis can now be streamlined by the use of relevant software packages, such as SPSS and Nvivo. The former is used essentially with quantitative data in order to establish statistical correlations and frequencies whereas the latter has the capacity to organize conceptual themes and make connections between them. In both cases, there are a number of user-friendly but effective guides to their use and relevance (for SPSS, see Bryman and Cramer 2008; Field 2005; for Nvivo, see Bazeley 2007). However, at least three notes of caution must be sounded here. First, these packages only add real value where there is a considerable amount of material to analyse. Otherwise, it is usually quicker and, in fact, more reliable to use manual or visual means of coding and collating findings. Second, where sample sizes, or particular analytical categories are small, using software may give a greater sense of certainty than the numbers really allow – in the same way as small numbers expressed as percentages or proportions can be somewhat misleading ('8 out of 10 cats', for example). And finally, the introduction of technical aids of this kind may be exclusive of some of those engaged in the research process; this is a particular concern where research seeks to apply participative principles throughout the process.

Once the data have been interrogated thoroughly to produce patterns of evidence, to group findings together and to demonstrate connections between these groupings, the next task is to develop explanations for what has emerged. Mason (1996, 2005), again, is helpful here. As she points out, what constitutes an 'explanation' is linked to the researcher's methodological starting point:

> For example, your view may be that empirical observations, or events, or patterns can demonstrate connections, causal correlations, explanations or even laws in and of themselves . . .
>
> Alternatively, you may consider that such empirical patterns are not useful so much in themselves, as because they can provide circumstantial evidence for *underlying processes* or causal mechanisms . . .
>
> Or, you may consider that interpretations of meanings, experiences, accounts, actions, events, can be developed into explanations and understandings . . .
>
> (1996: 139)

Interestingly, though, these forms of explanation are not necessarily linked exclusively to underlying methodological assumptions or objectives. Although Mason associates the first of these with a 'classic positivist version of social science research', whereby factual evidence is taken at face value to prove or disprove prior hypotheses, it is equally the case that those producing highly personal narrative accounts also want findings as far as possible to speak for themselves, and to be 'self-explanatory'.

Explanatory strategies can also be distinguished in other ways, for example, according to whether they are intended to be: comparative, developmental, descriptive, predictive or theoretical (Mason 1996). These are not necessarily exclusive but may provide useful pegs on which to hang accounts of the connections and disparities between data, categories and themes. A developmental account may, for example, include elements of comparison between intervention strategies in different geographical locations, such as exemplified by Packman's series of studies of child care practices in contrasting local authority areas (Packman 1981; Packman et al. 1986; Packman and Hall 1998).

At this point, researchers may feel a degree of pressure, either self-imposed or from external sources, to achieve certainty and closure in their explanations. It is most likely however that they will face conflicting possibilities or only partial accounts of what has emerged. Claiming causal connections between events even where they are strongly associated is problematic, as Hodgson and Webb (2005) have demonstrated in the case of the assumed link between school exclusion and offending. There is a risk, too, that in seeking comprehensive explanations, exceptional findings may be excluded. In some circumstances, there may be justification for ignoring 'outliers', but in other cases this may simply result in a level of neatness and order which is illusory. Frustratingly, explanatory accounts in social work research will almost inevitably leave room for uncertainty, and for further investigation. The aim should be to achieve 'best fit' between the evidence and the explanation rather than absolute certainty.

Researchers also struggle on occasion to make links between evidence, analysis and theory. For Mason (1996) theory is implicit in all forms of explanation, but this rather underestimates the challenges of relating the minutiae of unique findings in practice with the broad and generalized accounts which operate at the level of macro-theoretical constructs. The example offered by 'grounded theory' (Glaser and Strauss 1967) suggests that this is a progressive exercise, whereby common themes and conceptual categories are generated, leading to the potential for mid-range theory generation, as in, say, characterizing the range of strategies employed to deal with chronic illness (Hardiker et al. 1986). From this, it may be possible, perhaps by linking studies, to generate substantive theories about the meanings of

---

Box 9.1 Doing exploratory research

On a number of occasions, I have carried out 'developmental evaluations' of community projects which have not sought to account for what has happened, even though past events have to be described in some way, but rather have attempted to provide possible options for future development.

These have not been concerned with finding explanations, but with exploring views and relationships and identifying a plausible basis for mutual understanding and developing common agendas for change.

and responses to disease in western societies. For those concerned with theory testing, on the other hand, this process needs to be seen in reverse, and the challenge is to find plausible means of operationalizing broad theoretical positions in the initial phase of research so that it can be subject to empirical examination. Of potential relevance to social work in this respect might be Blauner's (1964) attempt to substantiate and test out the Marxist concept of 'alienation' among the workforce (see Jones 2001, for example).

Accounting for what we have found

It may seem that once we have organized our material in such a way as it offers a justifiable explanatory account the task is complete. There are, however, a number of loose ends remaining. Based as it is in an applied discipline, social work research needs to account for itself in terms of practice implications and consequences on the ground, and we need to connect the explanations generated to the wider context and existing knowledge and assumptions. We can perhaps agree here with Corby's personal statement of principle: 'I hold to the value position that research-based knowledge should be one of the key underpinnings of social work practice' (2006: 173). If we are to ensure that research is used to inform practice, we must, of course, demonstrate its relevance to practice. In light of this, the completion of the task of generating our own evidence and ideas requires us also to complete the circle and reconnect this work with its starting point, and its original impetus. In a very practical sense, this is the point at which everything needs to be brought together to complete a systematic account of the research project, too (Bell 2005; Davies 2007).

As we saw at the beginning of the process, it is sometimes difficult to make clear and coherent connections between the different elements of the research project, and I have certainly encountered on a number of occasions draft reports which only make limited reference to the contextual material introduced and discussed in the review of the literature. There may be pragmatic reasons for this, such as lack of time, but this is an important opportunity to build on prior understandings, to challenge conventional wisdom where necessary, and to take ideas and practice a step further.

Often the 'writing-up stage' of a research project is represented in a fairly linear and formulaic fashion. Davies (2007: 211), for example, offers the following prescriptive framework:

> The primary requirement for success is a report that, within the limits of the word length specified, follows a predictable pattern:
>
> 1. Prelims
> 2. Introduction of the topic
> 3. Literature review
> 4. Research aim(s)

5. The methods used
6. Research findings
7. Discussion
8. Conclusion
9. References.

However, as he himself acknowledges, this can be somewhat misleading if we interpret this as a sequential process. Themes and connections will need to be interwoven between the different elements, and so this also means remaining alert to these throughout. It may help, for instance, to start building up notes and references (and cross-references) under each of the intended elements of the whole so that thematic relationships can be identified and developed as the project develops. Equally, it is important not to close the door on one element, such as the literature review, at the point where fieldwork begins. Some elements are more fixed than others (interview schedules, for instance, cannot easily be revised part-way through the fieldwork), but it is always helpful to retain as much flexibility as possible, and to continue building up the available resources as long as possible. Davies also stresses the value of what I call 'hoovering', although he describes it rather more elegantly:

> If you are actively thinking about your project all the time (as most researchers say they do), you will find that you stumble across pertinent quotations in books, magazines, journals and newspapers. Write them down and keep the reference carefully.
>
> (2007: 210)

Two further points appear important to me at this point, where researchers are thinking in all probability in terms of tidying up loose ends and accounting neatly for all they have observed. These are largely concerned with the different ways in which the project should, in fact, be left 'unfinished'. It is sometimes frustrating to read lengthy research reports which conclude with, among others, a recommendation for more research in the subject area. One is inclined to wonder why these additional questions could not have been resolved in the existing piece of work but, of course, life is not like that. We have already considered the kind of choices researchers have to make to ensure that their intended studies are manageable and we also know, especially in the field of social work, that we are dealing with shifting and unpredictable terrain. The rapidly changing relationship between new technologies and the lives of older people, for instance, is a subject needing regular reinvestigation as a matter of course. While our discussion and conclusion should consider the key empirical and theoretical messages from the immediate project, they should also be seen as an opportunity to reflect on those findings which do not sit easily with these explanations, or the indications of further unanswered questions. For those concerned, in particular, with completing a piece of work which will be assessed, at whatever level, it is not an admission of failure or incompetence to recognize that more (or different) work could have been done.

It is also at this point in written research reports that researchers should feel that they have a bit of latitude to express their own views and aspirations about the subject in question. This helps the reader to understand where the 'researcher is coming from', but it also helps potential audiences to consider the further implications of the study itself. In some cases, of course, such recommendations may be expected as part of the negotiated arrangements between the researcher and participating interests. We might expect, too, that social work research has a responsibility grounded in its value base to make findings known, to inform service users, to improve practice or to assist agencies to develop better policies.

Thus, the second point to reflect on here is that academic considerations should not unduly overshadow the other 'outputs' of research. It may be more appropriate to see written accounts as ancillary in some cases to the major objectives, perhaps of developing an assessment tool, enabling service users to have a voice or changing practice. In this respect, then, research is not a linear process with fixed timelines and narrowly defined 'products'. As well as being an investigative activity, it is inevitably a creative process, whether this is intentional or otherwise. This is one of the reasons, of course, that researchers are expected to reflect on the ethical implications of their involvement. What they do will change things. In some cases, these aims are, indeed, the reason for their involvement; action research will be shaped primarily by the intended impact of the research activity 'on the ground'. For research students, whose key definition of 'success' (Davies 2007) is almost inevitably the achievement of an academic award, these other dimensions should not be overlooked. In terms of the documentation of outcomes, it may be helpful to include in research reports additional material (such as practice guidance) which demonstrates these aspects of the project in the form of appendices. These outputs represent concrete gains from successful research and therefore also provide a form of validation for the exercise overall.

In this way, accounts of the research process and outcomes are not simply static and self-contained documents, but also provide the basis for a continued dialogue between exploration and understanding on the one hand, and practice learning and development on the other. Individual studies may be seen as falling on a continuum, linking what we already know with new evidence and insights which, in turn, point towards future developments, both in practice and its evaluation. As we have known for some time:

> Research in the social work field will almost always be in some sense 'applied'; which is to say that, if sensibly conceived and successfully carried out, it will contain some truths which have a purchase at some level of policy, management or practice.
>
> (Cheetham et al. 1992: 120)

Its products, then, may be quite varied and wide-ranging in both presentation and application.

Reflection and critique

Much is made of the importance of 'reflection' in social work (Taylor and White 2000; Fook 2002; Wilson *et al.* 2008) because it offers the practitioner a means of understanding her/his own part in and influence on the intervention process. In the same way, and drawing on essentially the same skills, research activity is enhanced through the exercise of a self-critical awareness through-out. The account of a completed project will be strengthened by the inclusion of a section on its possible limitations and areas in which it could have been improved. Researchers are perhaps understandably a little reluctant to turn the spotlight on possible shortcomings in their methods or analysis, but an honest appraisal of this kind is capable of providing reassurance to the reader; in particular, it helps to demonstrate that the researcher has remained open to other possibilities, and has tested the findings thoroughly against alternative explanatory frameworks.

It is important that we apply these principles throughout the process and that we can demonstrate this:

> we should be reflexive about every decision we take, and . . . we should not take any decisions without actively recognising that we are taking them. This casts (qualitative) researchers in a very active role . . . as *practitioners* who think and act in ways which are situated and contextual but also strategic.
>
> (Mason, 1996: 165)

Although Mason addresses this 'message' to qualitative researchers alone, there is no reason to restrict it to this group. The point that we should constantly be reviewing our strategies and practice seems legitimately applic-able to all aspects of the research process, whatever the methodological basis for it.

There are a number of ways in which the researcher may usefully reflect on the research process. First, of course, there are the different implications of her/his own characteristics and influence on the process. For example: 'our own ways of knowing may reflect bodies of knowledge that are taken for granted as legitimate in our society, such as professional, organizational and cultural assumptions' (D'Cruz and Jones 2004: 43). The question to be con-sidered here is whether these initial orientations have impacted on the ways in which we think about *and* engage in the field of study. Could we have started from a different point, or based the investigation on different assumptions, for instance?

Not only is it a matter of our own prior assumptions, but the process is also likely to be influenced by perceptions of us held by other participants,

---

Box 9.2 The value of checklists

It may be a good idea to draw up a checklist to enable yourself to carry out a self-evaluation of your research project. For instance:

1. Did I do what I set out to do? How can I account for any deviations from the original plan?
2. Have I applied my methods and analytical techniques properly?
3. Did I check things out with participants in the right way?
4. Could I have approached the task differently? In what ways might that have changed the result?
5. What is missing?
6. How might any omissions have been rectified?
7. Does this piece of work comply with ethical principles and social work values?
8. What have I achieved?
9. How can this research be put to good use?

---

especially if they attribute to us a certain kind of expertise, or identify us with formal sources of 'power' (Smith 2008). Obviously, characteristics such as gender, ethnicity, culture, age, disability or sexuality may be viewed on both sides as significant and affect the process of engagement. Other factors, too, including demeanour and perceived status may be less clear cut but still influential. Even in participative studies, there is a risk that others involved may defer to the researcher, possibly.

In addition to these issues to do with the characteristics of the researcher/ researched, and the research relationships, critical reflection also involves a thorough review of the conduct of the inquiry. Very often practical decisions about sample sizes or representativeness are enforced by circumstances and pressure of time, so the researcher will need to evaluate the possible consequences of these. I have just been speaking to a student who found that her intended interview sample had all been drawn from the same faith group, although this was not what she intended. We have agreed that she will consider the implications of this in her evaluation of the study. In my view it limits the scope of the study in some ways, but is beneficial in others; the findings may well have greater depth than they would have done, and additional insights may be gained because the student actually shares the same background as the respondents, historically.

As well as considering the effect of pragmatic choices such as this, the critique of the research should also cover other aspects of the implementation of the study, such as the choice of methods and tools, and how well they were used. Clearly, the use of more or less formal methods such as Likert Scales may generate different types of data than more naturalistic methods of observation or conversational analysis. In each case, there are likely to be gains and losses and it is probably helpful to show that these have been weighed against each other. At the same time, the suitability and application of the chosen method is also something which should be evaluated in retrospect. In the example just cited, the unexpected concentration of the sample also brought the influence of religious belief and practice to the fore, and the student had not, in fact, incorporated questions or prompts on this aspect of the subject in her interview schedule. In reflecting on her work, she might well make the observation that it would have been better to have prepared for this possibility while, at the same time, she may also be able to show how she has adapted her data coding and analytical strategy to incorporate this dimension effectively.

Of course, it is impossible to anticipate or account for every eventuality at the start, although it is always useful to have alternative options available at crucial points, such as the recruitment of respondents in difficult circumstances. But it is just this observation which indicates the importance of keeping the process and outputs under constant review; where pragmatic choices have to be made, they should still be determined within the overarching structure and logical framework of the study, and it will help to document the thinking behind such choices as and when they have to be made.

It is worth bearing in mind, where research is to be communicated to an intended audience that, for different reasons, openness about problematic aspects of the process will be valuable. For those who are not familiar with the uncertainties of the research process, it will be important not to give a misleading picture of the ease and simplicity with which it has been carried out. And for those who are familiar with the ups and downs of carrying out a study, and the need to make adjustments and running repairs, there is a likely to be a degree of scepticism about the study overall if there is no evidence of any problems or challenges encountered. Smooth and trouble-free research studies are a rarity, so readers are more likely to expect reports of problems and pragmatic choices than of straightforward processes and routine outputs.

Again, if we think of the research project as something more than a self-contained exercise, then the lessons learned from carrying out a through project evaluation may be valuable sources of guidance for future studies, too. The completion of a research study does not exhaust the possibilities to draw lessons from it, and to inform future work. Indeed, accounts of difficulties and how they are (or are not) resolved are often extremely valuable in their own right, offering important insights to those carrying out similar projects subsequently.

Critical reflection and accounting for our work thus serves a number of potential purposes. For those who intend to carry out further studies, it offers the opportunity to learn from experience and improve skills. Lessons learnt in this way can also be made available to others intending to carry out similar projects. Explicit accounts of self-evaluation may help to give greater confidence in the findings; and, clearly, it enables readers to contextualize the evidence and to make a more rounded appraisal of the material presented.

Getting the message across: dissemination and use of research

For a number of reasons, it sometimes seems as if the research process ends with the completion and submission of a written account. This is perhaps understandable in the very large number of cases where the researcher is a qualifying student, whose priority is to ensure that this piece of work achieves a 'pass'. On the other hand, though, there are a number of very good reasons for seeking to do a bit more and making use of findings to influence the social work environment in some way. Very often, for example, although they may be small-scale projects, research studies carried out as part of a student assignment may be part of a very limited body of knowledge about a particular subject. I can recall one study of the experience of disabled women survivors of domestic violence which deserved wider attention, for example. In another case, a student went to great lengths to document and do justice to the experiences of parents with learning difficulties (but see also Booth and Booth 2004).

In addition, expectations may have been raised due to the investigation itself, and there is thus almost a moral obligation to 'do something' with the eventual product. This is especially so where the chosen method is participatory and action oriented. Research users will perhaps anticipate that some of their concerns will be articulated as a result of their involvement and change (or the possibility of change) achieved.

Even where this is not the case, formal or informal feedback to participants is a concrete demonstration of appreciation for their involvement and may contribute to greater understanding of the specific subject matter for them. At the very least, it offers some reassurance that they have been 'heard'. It may also provide them with additional resources to support attempts to negotiate service change.

In the same vein, as we have already noted, there may be a more or less formal understanding between the researcher and participants or organizations that the outcomes of the inquiry will be fed back, in the form of reports or presentations perhaps. This may have been the subject of a prior agreement to facilitate the study; even if this is not the case, the opportunity to deliver key research messages in this way is probably worth seeking out. For small organizations, indeed, small-scale student projects may be the only source of evaluation and analysis of their practice available to them. Even for researchers who are not very confident or lacking experience, it is important not to underestimate the potential contribution their knowledge can make.

In service settings, the possible benefits to practice of small-scale studies should be acknowledged, too. Practitioner research has an important role to play here, drawing on the concerns and aspirations of those who have an 'insider' view of what may or may not work in the field. My first substantial research project was carried out from a practitioner perspective (Smith, 1987, 2007) and it was grounded in a belief that the lessons from a specific innovative project should not be lost, good or bad. Although I was confident that my investigation could and would validate this particular form of practice, obviously this cannot be taken for granted; despite this, the value of practitioners feeding back their findings (positive or not) *as* practitioners should be acknowledged more widely.

Indeed, this draws attention implicitly to one of the systemic difficulties in gaining an audience for research in social work, and this is what I see as a relative lack of interest historically on the part of agencies and policy makers in taking account of evidence from the field (especially when it does not provide the answers they want). This may be culturally specific, and it is noteworthy that in other jurisdictions not too far away from here (England), there seems to be a much greater valuing of research among service providers. The Irish Probation Board, for example, gives over part of its own website to dissertations from research students. More encouraging evidence recently is to be found at the Children's Workforce Development Council which has initiated and funded a programme of practitioner research.

Although there may be practical challenges to be overcome in sharing messages from research, we should perhaps also take note of the underlying potential for social work research to make a contribution to the overarching professional objectives of giving service users a voice and promoting empowerment:

> The expectation that research be disseminated is associated with an agenda for research that it has an impact and assumes a significance beyond research communities themselves, that it exerts some agency in social change and development.
>
> (D'Cruz and Jones 2004: 173)

Wherever possible, then, researchers will need to seek out opportunities to make unacknowledged experiences public and to ensure that their evidence is acknowledged and appreciated. Of course, there may be ethical issues and

---

Box 9.3 Applying (and misapplying) the messages from research

The diversion project in which I worked in the 1980s was the subject of a considerable number of positive evaluations yet the lessons were never incorporated into mainstream practice in youth justice, and where they were acknowledged (Audit Commission 1996) they were misapplied by policy makers with a prior agenda.

Nonetheless, research still provides a key opportunity to identify and publicize positive developments.

constraints on using material freely to be considered, but the underlying principle of shedding light on often unrecognized concerns remains of great significance.

Where it is possible that research findings will be published, or gain considerable attention in other ways, it is important to consider the implications for participants who may not have thought through the possible consequences of their highly personal issues being aired widely. Even where permission to use material is given, it may not be unconditional, and researchers will need to take this into account. It may be necessary, for example, to 'renew' permissions if the outcomes of a study are to be used in new ways, especially where this may lead to significant public exposure.

Of course, there is also a well-established 'academic' route for the dissemination of research through print and (increasingly) online journals (such as *Practice* and the *British Journal of Social Work*). These options offer advantages and disadvantages, but they should not necessarily be dismissed by researchers who may think that their work is not 'good enough'. While academic conventions apply to publication in these outlets, they are usually geared to encouraging submissions from new sources, and it is the originality and value of contributions which should determine whether they are considered for publication. Indeed, a recent edition of *Social Work Education* was specifically dedicated to the inclusion of service users as contributors and editors in order to promote the inclusion of original insights and ideas from non-traditional sources.

Those involved in social work research may be a bit cautious and hesitant about promoting their work for a variety of reasons: it may feel a bit like self-promotion; it may seem as if no one is interested; we may not think that what we have done is original; we may think that it is not much good; we may encounter a degree of institutional indifference; we may not have the time or energy; we may be wary of creating controversy; and there may be little encouragement from colleagues and supervisors. Despite all these possible deterrents there are powerful reasons for seeking to share the messages from our investigations, not least that they may otherwise go unacknowledged despite their capacity to promote the interests of people who use services and achieve positive change in practice. Not only are substantive findings worth sharing, but most research incorporates a methodological journey which is worth sharing. Future students can benefit, for example, from a successful (or unsuccessful) account of attempts to recruit participants from marginalized groups, in ways which are both respectful and meet the needs of the study (Allen 2008).

In many cases, then, thinking about the dissemination and use of social work research may not be *necessary* in order to achieve immediate goals (such as meeting course requirements); however, the nature and values of the discipline itself do make it *desirable*. Research is historically undervalued and underutilized in social work, but it is and should be capable of informing ideas and practice in both small-scale and local, and large-scale and generalized ways. Researchers should, therefore, approach their intended projects with these possibilities in mind.

Coming full circle: completing the research task

In these two chapters, I have attempted to present a (necessarily) linear view of the key elements and stages in the research process. This at least gives some idea of the overall structure and organization of a social work research project.

Exercise 9.1

Make a list of the things that most concern you about undertaking a (or, if you've been down this road before, this) research project. Take this list into your first session with your research supervisor.

It should not be assumed that the research process is a series of sequential or mutually exclusive tasks, even if it helps to retain some degree of separation in your mind. New and emerging literature sources, for example, are likely to come to light throughout the study, and will need to be incorporated and accounted for. Similarly, as we have just observed, obtaining permissions may not be a 'one-off' exercise, but these may need to be revised and renewed in light of either the findings that emerge or the intended uses of the outputs from the study. It is thus somewhat misleading to think of research in terms of a logical and predictable sequence of events; indeed, even on completion it may be important to carry lessons learned and key messages forward, as we have just observed.

Perhaps two considerations are helpful at this point. First, it is important not to present one's completed research project as a neat and tidy, 'finished' piece of work. There will certainly be questions left unanswered, equivocal findings, groups left unrepresented at the sampling stage, or mixed messages which need further investigation. It is both realistic and reasonable to incorporate these 'loose ends' into the conclusions of a research report.

Second, to complete the circle, it is important to make full use of the introduction to the research report. The explanatory and contextual value of an 'introduction' is perhaps sometimes underestimated. It should always be written last, because it tells the story of the project from beginning to end, and prepares the ground for the reader. It enables the investigator to explain and begin to account for the actual path taken in light of what was intended. It also gives a sense of overall shape and logic to the study, linking different elements and brining coherence to what may be a disparate whole. The introduction is also a suitable context for the researcher(s) to introduce and account for her/his/their own aims and motivations in undertaking the specific study to follow. This helps us as readers to 'situate' the study in relation to the researcher's own perspective and assumptions.

Key points

- Remember that social work skills have much in common with aspects of the research task.
- Some parts of the research process come more easily to us than others. Try to retain a sense of where you are in relation to the overall project when you feel 'bogged down'.
- Close attention needs to be paid to the task of 'linking' different elements of the study, both as it is carried out and in writing it up.
- Keep a research diary.

---

10 THE VALUE OF SOCIAL

WORK RESEARCH

What's so special about social work research?

This attempt to conceptualize and then operationalize social work research practice has been highly condensed and has been organized around the intention of making it 'doable'. However, in adopting this approach, it sometimes feels as if I have not given enough space to discussing the justification for pursuing this as a discrete form of inquiry. Why is it distinctive, and what does it or can it achieve that meets the underlying aims and aspirations of the profession as a whole? So, in conclusion, I want to devote a bit of space to reflecting on these questions, partly, of course, to offer some mutual reassurance that this is a worthwhile and productive activity. This discussion is partly guided by the emerging recognition that there is some merit in considering questions such as this, as well as some hope of offering constructive answers to them. Others, too, have raised similar questions:

> is it possible to identify ways to categorize the kinds of research in social work in a form that recognizes and respects the aims and values of social work? [And] assuming that we ought to do so, in what ways should the quality of social work research be assessed.
>
> (Shaw and Norton 2008: 953)

Earlier chapters suggested that there is a very wide range of methodological assumptions and strategies which claim to address key subjects of inquiry in social work research. These, in turn, clearly draw on an even wider body of social scientific knowledge and investigative practices. We might perhaps be tempted to conclude that the only truly distinctive feature of social work research is its eclecticism; this, in turn, seems to offer a very limited basis for claims of disciplinary distinctiveness or a common subject identity.

As we observed earlier (see Introduction), some, such as Humphries (2008) appear to argue that diversity of approach is a necessary consequence of the challenge of having to answer very different types of question about what is itself a complex and multi-faceted subject area. Finding out what is the impact of a particular intervention, for example, feels like a very different kind of task to identifying the number of children who are at risk of 'significant harm' at a particular point in time, although there may well be a relationship between the two, of course. If this is so, it may prove difficult to move much beyond circular definitions in the search for common ground:

> we defined social work research as consisting of any empirical or scholarly inquiry (research, evaluation or analysis), conducted by researchers, practitioners, service users/carers, and others within the social work community, that is intended, wholly or to a significant degree, to address the purposes of social work.
>
> (Shaw and Norton 2008: 954)

Nonetheless, it may be useful to spend a little time here considering just a few of the common features of social work research which may be held to give it a particular identity. What, indeed, are the shared 'purposes of social work' around which both practice and research can be said to cohere?

Social work research is action oriented

In this context, I want to concentrate on three attributes of social work research which I believe to be of particular importance, and perhaps go some way to offering a justification for this form of activity.

First of these is the notion that it is a particular approach to 'finding out' and knowing which is not and cannot be satisfied with producing knowledge for its own sake. Clearly this is not a research orientation which is exclusive to the discipline of social work, as we shall see, but it is nonetheless a key feature of it. While the distinction between 'pure' and 'applied' research (Shaw and Norton 2008) may not always be very well defined, it is still used to distinguish between forms of inquiry which have practical applications and relevance, and those which may do so but are not carried out with this intention. Furlong and Oancea (2005), for instance, suggest that 'historical research' is a purely academic form of inquiry with no necessary relevance to practice, although this is something Skehill (2003) would probably dispute in relation to social work itself. In contrast to this, it is suggested that

> applied and practice-based research [is] an area situated between academia-led theoretical pursuits . . . and research-informed practice, and consisting of a multitude of models of research explicitly conducted in, with, and/or for practice.
>
> (Furlong and Oancea 2005: 9)

Although this definition was initially formulated in respect of educational research, it has a number of features which may be attractive to those concerned with social work research, as Shaw and Norton (2008) acknowledge. It, in turn, is derived in part from an earlier formulation, known as Pasteur's Quadrant, which is based on the principle that types of research can be distinguished according to whether or not they incorporate 'considerations of use', on the one hand and whether they aspire to achieve 'fundamental understanding' or not, on the other (Furlong and Oncea 2005: 7).

These definitional distinctions are very helpful, in that they enable us to recognize the diversity of potential social work research methods and methodologies (see earlier chapters), while also identifying common grounds in terms of aims and orientation. The further differentiation between 'applied and practice-based research' (Furlong and Oancea 2005: 7) may also be useful. Some types of social work research are self-evidently *about* practice: how it is carried out, whether it 'works', or how it is experienced, perhaps. Other investigative strategies may be more concerned with the conditions and contexts in which practice takes place: the backgrounds and experiences of service users; the socio-economic influences on practice; or maybe the preparation and training of social work practitioners. The latter appear to comply with the definition of 'use-inspired basic' research while the former are associated rather with the notion of 'pure applied' research (Furlong and Oancea 2005).

As these authors are quick to point out though, this does not mean that there is no overlap or exchange between these categories. Intensely 'practical' methodologies can offer a great deal in terms of insight and 'basic' understanding:

> Action research and reflective practice, for example, are models that offer arguments against the idea that applied research is only focused on use and that it does not and cannot contribute to more theoretical knowledge production while at the same time achieving changed practice.
>
> (Furlong and Oancea 2005: 8)

Furlong and Oancea believe that this also legitimates the idea that there should be a two-way dialogue between research and practice. These are 'integrated activities that borrow from each other, inform each other and support each other' (2005: 8). As we have already observed, this principle can be seen to operate even in the overlapping skills of investigation and analysis which are to be found in both social work practice and research activity. These observations lead Furlong and Oancea to conclude that practice-oriented research should not be seen as 'methodologically depleted' (2005: 9) in relation to those modes of inquiry which are concerned only with producing knowledge and theory. In practice, they cannot easily be distinguished, and there are signs of a productive interplay between them. Many of those involved in participative and user-led research would undoubtedly argue that their insights have contributed hugely to our understanding and ability to conceptualize power and discrimination in the social work field and beyond (Beresford 1999, 2002).

Shaw and Norton (2008: 954) have addressed similar questions directly to the 'social work community' as well as other relevant interests. Their examination of current practice in the field, as well as aspirations for social work research led them to a number of 'provisional conclusions', exemplifying common ground across a fairly diverse body of activity:

Social work research should be conceptualized in such a way that:

- 'pure' and 'applied' are not in conflict;
- applied research is not seen in deficit terms as a methodologically lesser form of research.

(2008: 955)

Indeed, far from constructing a hierarchy of research orientations and methods, they argue for 'a dialectical relationship between different methodologies' (2008: 956) which does not see them as incompatible alternatives, but as sharing common aims and perspectives. This, in turn, leads to an argument for 'quality standards' which are equally and equitably applicable to all forms of social work research. It is no good aspiring to dialogue on an equal footing if our means of evaluating what is best implicitly favours certain approaches. Thus, for example, judgements about the *usefulness* of research should not be concerned solely with its direct impact along one dimension. We should take account of 'the different ways' in which social work research may be used, how far a study *aims* to be useful' irrespective of its actual applications, and whether 'use' should be judged in terms of short-term or longer-term outcomes (2008: 968). These authors go on to stress that this does not offer a licence for 'free-for-all relativism' and that we should still attempt to evaluate research against the criterion of usefulness among others. It is the applicability of the product of investigations which is crucial, rather than how and in what context they have direct practical implications.

We can perhaps draw the conclusion that social work research is action oriented and concerned with practical consequences, but that these are broadly drawn and not necessarily immediate in their manifestations. Equally, this does not mean that it is only about practice and has no wider strategic or theoretical implications. Perhaps we can say that social work research must be about, with or for practice but it should not be restricted to this; it is capable also of generating broader and deeper insights which enables it to engage effectively with other disciplines, too.

Individual research projects in social work can therefore also be evaluated against a broad but specific range of criteria relating to their practice relevance and impact, without needing to demonstrate immediate and concrete outcomes or changes. As we shall see later, though, there are also important considerations in terms of the nature of change to which our inquiries aspire and their relationship to social work values.

The relationship between social work research, learning and practice is unbreakable

> What is the point of doing research that is stuck in a dusty journal on a library shelf and nobody ever sees it?
>
> (social work academic, quoted in Shaw and Norton 2008: 961)

In a sense, the previous section prefigures this one, in that it emphasizes the essential nature of the research-action relationship in social work. However, it is important to go on and consider the nature of this relationship in more detail, as it is played out in the process of learning from and applying what we find.

In one sense, of course, it seems an entirely rational process to explore the field (research), to make available the evidence from this activity (learning) and to apply the lessons from this (practice); and, then to recommence the process by repeating our initial investigation and evaluating the impact of what we have done. However, things are not that simple. The reasons for this are both mundane and more fundamental. At the level of the everyday, there is only limited space for engagement between the three facets of this triangle. As we have already observed, opportunities for practitioners to undertake research are limited, as are those for researchers to engage in practice, for that matter. In structural terms, there is little apparent enthusiasm from agencies and policy makers to establish a more dynamic relationship, at least in the English context.

Not only is there a relative lack of interest in the research contribution in this respect, but at the place where it might have a stronger foothold, in social work training, there are other adverse influences such as the demands of an already crowded curriculum incorporating practice learning, subject-specific knowledge and skills development. These, of course, are all likely to be research informed, but this may not be sufficient to achieve recognition of the value of research as an active element in developing expertise and understanding.

Research tends not to come neatly packaged with straightforward and easily applicable solutions to intractable problems. Rather, it deals in tendencies, probabilities and alternative options, leaving room for uncertainty and competing interpretations. It may be unsettling too, if it challenges existing practice conventions, or, sometimes confronts us with uncomfortable 'truths'. It took the profession some time, for example, to absorb the lesson that we do not always know best, and that sometimes our interventions are resented by service users (Mayer and Timms 1970; Fisher et al. 1986). Researchers might argue, too, that there is a tendency to turn away from difficult issues and challenging findings, so that funding is more likely to be available for studies that produce 'acceptable' results.

In any case, the combined effect of these various adverse factors is that research as an activity and as a source of understanding often appears to be marginalized in social work. Despite this, there are powerful reasons for asserting its place in the three-way relationship described earlier. As a reflective activity, for example, social work practitioners need to be able to engage with and make sense of their own interventions in order to improve outcomes for service users. Research may be seen as an additional means by which such 'reflection' can take place, systematically. It offers a vehicle for checking out what we do, for identifying whether we are having the impact we think we are, and for offering insights into the potential benefits of alternative approaches. In this sense, it is reflective practice 'writ large'. Not only does it offer a means of reflecting on what we do directly, but it also gives us access to a wide range of other perspectives, including those of service users. It is, in this respect, a way of formalizing processes of evaluation and feedback. To the extent that this is systematized, too, it offers some assurance that we are not simply receiving partial or 'off the cuff' messages.

Research, then, should be seen as having a direct role in informing practice as well as supporting learning and teaching in social work. At the same time, there is a reverse logic which suggests that practitioners, teachers and learners should themselves be engaged in research activities. As I have already stressed, this is at least partly because there are some very similar skills involved in carrying out investigations, whether in research or in practice. Additionally, direct involvement in research of those currently or about to be involved in practice offers further benefits, not just to the individuals concerned, but because their distinctive perspective offers a particular kind of insight, as well as opening up areas for study which may otherwise go unscrutinized. It is not just a matter of completing assignments or passing courses, but also a powerful opportunity to add substantially to the pool of knowledge and understanding to which all involved in social work should have access.

The problems we face in gaining recognition of the contribution of research, both as a learning resource and a direct influence on practice, arise from a collective undervaluing of it. In order to change this prevailing mood, a number of practical steps can be taken. First, we should incorporate the principle that research *should* be in dialogue with practice at the design stage. This means considering a number of issues in preparation for the investigation which might not always be accorded priority, such as the possible audiences and intended uses, the direct implications for service users as well as longer-term gains, building in feedback mechanisms, and taking a proactive approach to promoting and publicizing messages from research. This is not something that social work researchers necessarily feel comfortable with, but if we value what we are seeking to achieve, then speaking out about it is a necessary part of the process.

While research practitioners thus have some obligations to take an active role in promoting their work, there are wider responsibilities here, too. We cannot expect researchers on their own to resolve deep-seated historical and structural forms of resistance. There is a responsibility for social work education programmes (pre- and post-qualifying) to be research aware and to ensure that social work students and practitioners share this, both by critically engaging with existing findings, and by developing the skills and insights necessary to undertake their own investigations. This is not a luxury; not only does this offer an opportunity to supplement social work skills of inquiry, analysis and reflection, but it also enables practitioners to appreciate the continuing value of dialogue between their day-to-day activities and the processes of inquiry which inform and underpin professional knowledge and understanding.

Finally, an increased emphasis on the value and potential uses of research in the context of social work education should provide a stronger base for the substantial task of developing a more positive attitude to its applications and worth among organisations and policy makers. This is crucially important if we are to avoid repeating mistakes from the past, 'reinventing the wheel', or simply reducing practice to a routinized set of tasks which will become increasingly detached from changing needs and circumstances. In this sense, interest in the messages of research should be a given, rather than something which has to be repeatedly sought out or stimulated.

Social work research is rooted in social work values

Finally, and most crucially, it is important to re-emphasize the connection between the practical task of asserting the importance of social work research and the underlying values which give meaning and purpose to this exercise. We need to be clear that processes of inquiry and evaluation share the same overarching aims and objectives as direct work in the field and offer another means to achieve them, acting as a sounding board and facilitator to empowering practice.

For these reasons, we will need to reassure ourselves that research in, about and for social work complies with the same expectations that we would apply to practice. Research needs to be carried out to the appropriate standards, but it also needs to meet certain normative requirements as well, if it is to achieve its underlying objectives of contributing to better practice and better outcomes for people who use services:

> Good social work research means doing social work research with a confident and robust understanding of the values on which social work itself is predicated. One important way in which to pursue this in the current scientistic and managerialist context is by mapping those values into the research process itself; seeing social work research as a continuation of social work practice by other means.
>
> (Butler 2003: 25)

This aspirational statement is immediately qualified with an acknowledgement of the 'problematical' nature of applying normative 'codes' to the complex and sometimes contradictory settings for practice. Butler does, however, go on to suggest a number of questions applicable to social work research in general, and to specific studies:

- What is social work research for?
- How will data be used?
- Whose interests is the research likely to serve?
- How far will the research 'further social work's broader transformatory ambitions'? (2003: 26)

Other questions could also usefully be added to this list, which both offers a basis for critical review of previous research and a form of self-evaluation at the planning and design stage of a proposed investigation:

- What changes could reasonably be anticipated as a result of this research?
- Can the research demonstrate that it has taken account of the service user perspective?
- What might be the 'unintended' negative consequences of the research?
- Is the inquiry carried out according to social work principles?
- What action can be taken to ensure that the research will be acknowledged and used in the interests of service users?

Butler recognizes, rightly, that he is promoting an explicitly committed view of social work research, which is effectively to be carried out from within the discipline, necessitating 'a personal engagement on the part of researchers' (2003: 27).

This does not mean, however, that any one methodological approach is accorded privileged status. The key question for any research study is whether or not it passes these tests, which integrate quality standards with ownership and articulation of the appropriate values. Thus, for example, neither randomized controlled trials nor user-led research studies can claim to be more authoritative than other methodological approaches. As we have seen, both have distinctive strengths in terms of their ability to uncover substantive evidence, but neither can claim to be necessarily more ethically grounded than alternative approaches.

These key features of social work research thus set it apart from other disciplines. Although it draws on a wide range of methodological traditions, and utilizes methods associated with other subject domains, none of them can claim to incorporate it. Its practice-based nature and its very eclecticism set it apart from other 'pure' disciplines, while its focus on the specific territory of practice associated with social work distinguishes it from other 'applied' forms of research such as educational or nursing studies. This aspect of the discipline ensures that it will be concerned with the needs, rights and aspirations of individuals, groups and communities who are disadvantaged and discriminated against. This, in turn, requires it to demonstrate a level of commitment to these interests and a willingness to 'take sides'. As we have seen in previous chapters pure objectivity is unattainable in practice; but, equally, it is an undesirable aspiration for a body of research which is committed to achieving change and social justice on behalf of a particular group of interests, who are, by definition, structurally and personally disempowered. Just as 'diversity' is at the heart of social work practice, so it should be a key feature of the 'kinds and quality' (Shaw and Norton 2008) of knowledge that serves as a resource and a driver for practice: 'The concept of social work knowledge needs to be inclusive and to incorporate all the principles of diversity that are so central to the contemporary vision of the profession' (Trevillion 2008: 449).

Of course, in undertaking any given research inquiry it is impossible to be certain that it will generate positive outcomes. It would not be necessary to carry out an investigation of any kind if we knew the answer beforehand. We must also be prepared for the possibility of uncovering findings which are not what we expect, or which may suggest negative conclusions. Indeed, there is clearly value in obtaining evidence that something will not 'work' as intended. It is important to distinguish between this sort of finding and those research practices or outcomes which may be harmful to the interests of service users. So, we should be prepared to unearth and engage with results which are awkward and difficult to assimilate, such as the ambiguous responses of the 'partners of child sex offenders' (Philpott 2008); and we should accept that sometimes research is about generating better questions rather than obtaining conclusive answers. In a very real sense, knowledge is empowerment; by the very act of focusing on disadvantaged groups and posing previously unconsidered problems, social work research can require established interests and powerful agencies to take notice and respond accordingly.

Of course, it would be presumptuous to claim that it is only social work research which can contribute towards emancipatory knowledge and improvements in well-being. Clearly, other disciplines such as social policy, education and medicine would be likely to make similar claims; the distinction is that social work is more or less exclusively concerned with issues relating to disadvantaged, oppressed or socially excluded groups rather than the general population. Thus, its unique character lies in the recognition that research in

---

Box 10.1 Research making a difference

Research has played an integral part in the introduction and development of the Duluth Model for tackling domestic violence, which has now gained international recognition as a leading model programme (e.g. Shepard and Pence 1999).

this disciplinary area *must* be concerned with the problems arising from inequality, unfairness and abusive experiences. From this, it follows logically, that social work research has an obligation to consider and prioritize the service user perspective both in the conduct of inquiries and the production of its findings. As Butler (2003: 27) reminds us, though, this is to give 'the user of services an important, but not decisive role in the process of knowledge building'. Nonetheless, what we must do, in carrying out, disseminating and applying the lessons of social work research, is to consider and then demonstrate how we have gone about reflecting the service user perspective, and issues of rights and social justice, at the heart of the process.

The last word: making a difference

My aim here has been to try to weave together a number of strands which collectively demonstrate both the underlying need for research in social work, and a range of strategies to enable intending researchers to undertake this task. This overview has spanned the conceptual, the technical and the normative issues involved in order to try to link underlying principles with the very practical and often seemingly mundane demands of actually delivering (and applying) a good piece of investigative work.

In taking this approach, I have tried to avoid privileging any one strategy or method; although I have preferences, I think it is important to recognize that the fundamental issue is the suitability of a particular method for the research question to be addressed, rather than its degree of compliance with a predetermined set of methodological or epistemological assumptions. In this respect, at least, I think there is much to be said for those who argue for a non-hierarchical, 'horses for courses' approach (Shaw 2000; Petticrew and Roberts 2003). Furthermore, there is an increasing recognition that combining methods and methodologies, that is, full-scale 'triangulation' (Denzin 1970) offers real benefits in terms of the breadth and depth of understanding to be gained. It would be unhelpful, in light of this, to ascribe preferred status to any given method/methodology.

Indeed, as this final chapter has sought to demonstrate, it is the degree of consistency between the chosen method and processes and the essential values of social work which is the most important criterion to apply. It is only then that the issue of how well the chosen strategy has been implemented comes into play. Ensuring that our core values are reflected in our actions as well as our aims and products is a necessary requirement, of course, and this, in turn, may necessitate methodological compromises; but this is as it should be, in this respect our 'means' and 'ends' are indistinguishable. Demonstrating our respect and commitment to participants' interests throughout the process is a fundamental requirement if we are to claim authority in representing these same interests in the production and dissemination of our findings. If we can justify this claim, then we will have gone a long way towards producing research which can legitimately be seen as promoting the essential aspirations of social work towards improving peoples' lives.

Key points

- Social work research *is* distinctive by virtue of its values, context, action focus and 'holistic' frame of reference.
- Social work research makes an essential contribution to improving practice, enhancing knowledge and promoting service user interests.
- Social work research can 'make a difference'.

REFERENCES

Aldiss, B. (1973) *Report on Probability A*. London: Sphere.

Allard, A., Brown, G. and Smith, R. (1995) *The Way It Is*. London: The Children's Society.

Allen, D. (2008) *Researching the Lives of Gypsies and Travellers*. MRes Dissertation, De Montfort University.

Alston, M. and Bowles, W. (2003) *Research for Social Workers*. London: Routledge.

Atkinson, P. and Coffey, A. (2004) Analysing documentary realities, in D. Silverman (ed.) *Qualitative Research: Theory, Method and Practice*. London: Sage.

Audit Commission (1996) *Misspent Youth*. London: Audit Commission.

Axline, V. (1964) *Dibs: In Search of Self*. Harmondsworth: Penguin.

Baker, K., Jones, S., Merrington, S. and Roberts, C. (2005) *Further Development of ASSET*. London: Youth Justice Board.

Banks, S. (2006) *Ethics and Values in Social Work*. Basingstoke: Palgrave.

Barnes, H., Green, L. and Hopton, J. (2007) Guest editorial: social work theory, research, policy and practice – challenges and opportunities in health and social care integration in the UK, *Health and Social Care in the Community*, 15(3): 191–4.

Bazeley, P. (2007) *Qualitative Data Analysis with Nvivo*. London: Sage.

Bebbington, A. and Miles, J. (1989) The background of children who enter local authority care, *British Journal of Social Work*, 19: 349–68.

Beck, U. (1992) *Risk Society*. London: Sage.

Bell, J. (2005) *Doing your Research Project*. Maidenhead: Open University Press.

Belsky, J., Melhuish, E., Barnes, J., Leyland, A., Romaniuk, H. and National Evaluation of Sure Start Research Team (2006) Effects of Sure Start local programmes on children and families: early findings from a quasi-experimental, cross sectional study, *British Medical Journal*, 322: 1476.

Bennett, F. with Roberts, M. (2004) *From Input to Influence*. York: Joseph Rowntree Foundation.

Beresford, P. (1999) Social work: what kinds of knowledge?, ESRC Seminar Series, *Theorising Social Work Research*, 26th May, available at: http://www.scie.org.uk/publications/misc/tswr/seminar1/beresford.asp.

Beresford, P. (2002) User involvement in research and evaluation: liberation or regulation?, *Social Policy & Society*, 1(2): 95–105.

Beresford, P. (2007) *The Changing Roles and Tasks of Social Work from Service Users' Perspectives: A Literature Informed Discussion Paper.* London: Shaping Our Lives.

Berman, Y. (1994) Grey documentation as a knowledge base in social work *Science Communication*, 15(3): 307–20.

Biesetck, F. (1961) *The Casework Relationship.* London: Allen & Unwin.

Blaikie, N. (2003) *Analysing Quantitative Data.* London: Sage.

Blauner, P. (1964) *Alienation and Freedom.* Chicago, IL: University of Chicago Press.

Blaxter, L., Hughes, C. and Tight, M. (1996) *How to Research.* Buckingham: Open University Press.

Booth, W. and Booth, T. (2004) A family at risk: multiple perspectives on parenting and child protection. *British Journal of Learning Difficulties*, 32(1): 9–15.

British Sociological Association (2004) Statement of ethical practice for the British Sociological Association, available at: http://www.britsoc.co.uk/NR/rdonlyres/468F236C-FFD9-4791-A0BD-4DF73F10BA43/0/StatementofEthicalPractice.doc.

Broad, B. (1998) *Young People Leaving Care: Life After the Children Act 1998.* London: Jessica Kingsley.

Bryman, A. (1988) *Quantity and Quality in Social Research.* London: Unwin Hyman.

Bryman, A. and Cramer, D. (2004) *Quantitative Data Analysis with SPSS 12 and 13: A Guide for Social Scientists.* London: Routledge.

Bryman, A. and Cramer, D. (2008) *Quantitative Data Analysis with SPSS 14, 15 and 16: A Guide for Social Scientists.* London: Routledge.

Buchanan, A. (2002) Family support, in D. McNeish, T. Newman and H. Roberts (eds) *What Works for Children?* Buckingham: Open University Press.

Bullough, R. and Pinnegar, S. (2001) Guidelines for quality in autobiographical forms of self-study research, *Educational Researcher*, 30(3): 13–21.

Burnett, R. and Appleton, C. (2004) *Joined-up Youth Justice.* Lyme Regis: Russell House.

Butler, I. (2002) A code of ethics for social work and social care research, *British Journal of Social Work*, 32(2): 239–48.

Butler, I. (2003) Doing good research and doing it well: ethical awareness and the production of social work research, *Social Work Education*, 22(1): 19–30.

Butler, I. and Drakeford, M. (2005) *Scandal, Social Policy and Social Welfare.* Bristol: Policy Press.

Butler, I. and Pugh, R. (2004) The politics of social work research, in R. Lovelock, K. Lyons and J. Powell (eds) *Reflecting on Social Work: Discipline and Profession.* Aldershot: Ashgate.

Butt, T. and Parton, N. (2005) Constructive social work and personal construct theory: the case of psychological trauma, *British Journal of Social Work*, 35: 793–806.

Carpenter, J. (2007) Social work counts, *SWoRD – Social Work Researcher Development Workshop*, 22 June, Cardiff University, available at: http://swap.ac.uk/docs/eventreports/220607sword_jcarpenter.pdf.

Cartwright, N. (2007) Are RCTs the gold standard?, *Biosocieties*, 2: 11–20.

Chan, Y. (2003) Randomised Controlled Trials (RCTs) – sample size: the magic number?, *Singapore Medical Journal*, 44(4): 172–4.

Chan, Z. and Ma, J. (2004) Aetiology of *anorexia nervosa* in Hong Kong: a social work qualitative inquiry, *Child and Family Social Work*, 9: 177–86.

Chana, P. (2005) *Domestic Violence: Impact of Culture on Experiences of Asian Women*, Norwich: University of East Anglia (Social Work Monographs).

Cheetham, J., Fuller, R., McIvor, G. and Petch, A. (1982) *Evaluating Social Work Effectiveness*. Buckingham: Open University Press.

Christie, A. and Weeks, J. (1998) Life experience: a neglected form of knowledge in social work education and practice, *Practice*, 10(1): 55–68.

Cicourel, A. (1968) *The Social Organisation of Juvenile Justice*. London: Heinemann.

Coad, J., Hardicre, J. and Devitt, P. (2006) Searching for and using 'grey' literature, *Nursing Times*: 35–6.

Cohen, R., Ferres, G., Hollins, C., Long, G. and Smith, R. (1996) *Out of Pocket: The Failure of the Social Fund*. London: The Children's Society.

Cohen, S. (1985) *Visions of Social Control*. Cambridge: Polity Press.

Cole, A. and Williams, V. (2007) *Having a Good Day? A Study of Community-based Day Activities for People with Learning Disabilities*. London: SCIE.

Cook, M., Cook, G., Hodgson, P., Reed, J., Clarke, C. and Inglis, P. (2007) The impact of research governance in the United Kingdom on research involving a national survey, *Journal of Health Organization and Management*, 21(1): 59–67.

Corby, B. (2006) *Applying Research in Social Work Practice*. Maidenhead: Open University Press.

Corsaro, W. (1997) *The Sociology of Childhood*. Thousand Oaks, CA: Forge Press.

Cox, P. and Hardwick, L. (2002) Research and critical theory: their contribution to social work education and practice, *Social Work Education*, 21(1): 35–47.

Critcher, C., Waddington, D. and Dicks, B. (1999) Qualitative methods and welfare research, in F. Williams, J. Popay and A. Oakley (eds) *Welfare Research: A Critical Review*. London: UCL Press.

D'Cruz, H. and Jones, M. (2004) *Social Work Research: Ethical and Political Contexts*. London: Sage.

Davies, M. (1981) *The Essential Social Worker*. Aldershot: Arena.

Davies, M. (2007) *Doing a Successful Research Project*. Basingstoke: Palgrave.

Denzin, N. (1970) *The Research Act*. Chicago, IL: Aldine.

Denzin, N. and Lincoln, Y. (eds) (2000) *Handbook of Qualitative Research*. Thousand Oaks, CA: Sage.

Department of Health (1995) *Child Protection: Messages from Research*. London: HMSO.

Department of Health (2001a) *The Children Act Now: Messages from Research*. London: The Stationery Office.

Department of Health (2001b) *Valuing People*. London, The Stationery Office.

Department of Health (2005) *Research Governance Framework for Health and Social Care*. Available at: http://www.dh.gov.uk/en/Publicationsandstatistics/Publications/PublicationsPolicyAndGuidance/DH_4108962.

Department of Health and Social Security (1985) *Social Work Decisions in Child Care*. London: HMSO.

Department for Education and Skills (2003) *Every Child Matters*. London: The Stationery Office.

Dominelli, L. (2005) Social work research: contested knowledge for practice, in R. Adams, L. Dominelli and M. Payne (eds) *Social Work Futures*. Basingstoke: Palgrave.

Dyson, S. and Brown, B. (2006) *Social Theory and Applied Health Research*. Maidenhead: Open University Press.

Economic and Social Research Council (2005) *Research Ethics Framework*. Swindon: ESRC.

Elliott, J. (1990) Educational research in crisis: performance indicators and the decline in excellence, *British Educational Research Journal*, 16(1): 3–18.

Ellis, C. and Bochner, A. (2000) Autoethnography, personal narrative, reflexivity: researcher as subject, in N. Denzin and Y. Lincoln (eds) *Handbook of Qualitative Research*. Thousand Oaks, CA: Sage.

Elwyn, G., Seagrove, A., Thorne, K. and Cheung, W. (2005) Ethics and research governance in a multicentre study: add 150 days to your study protocol, *British Medical Journal*, 330: 847, Letter.

Everitt, A. and Hardiker, P. (1996) *Evaluating for Good Practice*. Basingstoke, Palgrave.

Fenge, L-A. (2002) Practising partnership: participative inquiry with older people, *Social Work Education*, 21(2): 171–81.

Field, A. (2005) *Discovering Statistics Using SPSS*. London: Sage.

Fielding N. (1981) *The National Front*. London: Routledge and Kegan Paul.

Fish, J. (2007) *Heterosexism in Health and Social Care*. Basingstoke: Palgrave.

Fisher, M., Marsh, P. and Phillips, D. with Sainsbury, E. (1986) *In and Out of Care*. London: Batsford.

Fook, J. (2002) *Critical Social Work*. London: Sage.

Foucault, M. (1980) *Power/Knowledge*. New York: Pantheon Books.

Freire, P. (1970) *Pedagogy of the Oppressed*. Harmondsworth: Penguin.

Freire, P. (1974) *Cultural Action for Freedom*. Harmondsworth: Penguin.

French, S. and Swain, J. (2006) Telling stories for a politics of hope, *Disability & Society*, 21(5): 383–96.

Furlong, J. and Oancea, A. (2005) *Assessing Quality in Applied and Practice-based Educational Research*. University of Oxford, Department of Educational Studies, available at: http://64.233.183.104/search?q=cache:lz1CTUH-ukgJ:www.bera.ac.uk/pdfs/Qualitycriteria.pdf+John+Furlong+assessing+quality&hl=en&client=firefox-a.

Gambrill, E. (2006) Evidence-based practice and policy: choices ahead, *Research on Social Work Practice*, 16: 338–57.

Gearing, R. (2004) Bracketing in research: a typology, *Qualitative Health Research*, 14: 1429–52.

General Social Care Council (GSCC) (2003) *Codes of Practice for Social Work*. London: GSCC.

Giddens, A. (ed.) (1974) *Positivism and Sociology*. London: Heinemann.

Gilbert, K. (2002) Taking a narrative approach to grief research: finding meaning in stories, *Death Studies*, 26: 223–39.

Gilbody, S., House, A. and Sheldon, T. (2002) Outcomes research in mental health, *British Journal of Psychiatry*, 181: 8–16.

Giri, B. (2006) An autobiography of child work: a reflexive account, available at: http://www.childhoodtoday.org/downloadphp?id=11.

Giuliano, K. (2003) Expanding the use of empiricism in nursing: can we bridge the gap between knowledge and clinical practice?, *Nursing Philosophy*, 4: 44–50.

Glaser, B. and Strauss, A. (1967) *The Discovery of Grounded Theory*. Chicago, IL: Aldine.

Glynn, T. (2004) There is a better way, in S. Cochrane (ed.) *Where You Stand Affects Your Point of View: Emancipatory Approaches to Mental Health Research*. Available at: http://www.spn.org.uk/fileadmin/SPN_uploads/Documents/Papers/SPN_Papers/SPN_Paper_4.pdf.

Godin, P., Davies, J., Heyman, B., Reynolds, L., Simpson, A. and Floyd, M. (2007) Opening communicative space: a Habermasian understanding of a user-led participatory research project, *Journal of Forensic Psychiatry & Psychology*, 18(4): 452–69.

Goodley, D. (1996) Tales of hidden lives: a critical examination of life history research with people who have learning difficulties, *Disability & Society*, 11(3): 333–48.

Goodley, D. and Tregaskis, C. (2006) Storying disability and impairment: retrospective accounts of disabled family life, *Qualitative Health Research*, 16(5): 430–46.

Gould, N. (2004) Qualitative research and social work: the methodological repertoire in a practice-oriented discipline, in R. Lovelock, K. Lyons and J. Powell (eds) *Reflecting on Social Work: Discipline and Profession.* Aldershot: Ashgate.

Gramsci, A. (1971) *Selections from Prison Notebooks.* London: Lawrence & Wishart.

Gray, J. (2007) (Re)considering voice, *Qualitative Social Work*, 6: 411–30.

Greenwood, D. and Lowenthal, D. (2005) Case study as a means of researching social work and improving practitioner education, *Journal of Social Work Practice*, 19(2): 181–93.

Hall, C., Juhila, K., Parton, N. and Poso, T. (eds) (2003) *Constructing Clienthood in Social Work and Human Services.* London: Jessica Kingsley.

Hammersley, M. (1995) *The Politics of Social Research.* London: Sage.

Hanley, B. (2005) *Research as Empowerment.* York: Joseph Rowntree Foundation.

Hardiker, P., Pedley, J., Littlewood, J. and Olley, D. (1986) Coping with chronic renal failure, *British Journal of Social Work*, 16: 203–22.

Harris, D. and Parisi, D. (2007) Adapting life history calendars for qualitative research on welfare transitions, *Field Methods*, 19(1): 40–58.

Hartman, K. (2006) Social policy resources for social work: grey literature and the internet, *Behavioral & Social Sciences Librarian*, 25(1): 1–11.

Hay, J., Boyle, J. and Patterson, K. (2007) *Parents' Access to and Demand for Childcare Survey 2006: Final Report.* Edinburgh: Office of Chief Researcher, Scotland.

Healy, K. (2001) Participatory action research and social work, *International Social Work*, 44(1): 93–105.

Heller, J. (1974) *Something Happened.* London: Jonathan Cape.

Hodgson, P. and Webb, D. (2005) Young people crime and school exclusion: a case of some surprises, *Howard Journal of Criminal Justice*, 44(1): 12–28.

Holdaway, S., Davidson, N., Dignan, J., Hammersley, R., Hine, J. and Marsh, P. (2001) *New Strategies to Address Youth Offending: The National Evaluation of the Pilot Youth Offending Teams.* London: Home Office.

Holman, B. (1987) Research from the underside, *British Journal of Social Work*, 17(6): 669–83.

Horrocks, C. and Goddard, J. (2006) Adults who grew up in care: constructing the self and accessing care files, *Child and Family Social Work*, 11: 264–72.

Howe, D., Brandon, M., Hinings, D. and Schofield, G. (1999) *Attachment Theory, Child Maltreatment and Family Support: A Practice and Assessment Model.* Basingstoke: Palgrave Macmillan.

Hubbard, G., Tester, S. and Downs, M. (2003) Meaningful social interaction between older people in institutional care settings, *Ageing & Society*, 23: 99–114.

Hudson, A. (1985) Feminism and social work: resistance or dialogue?, *British Journal of Social Work* 15: 635–55.

Humphreys, L. (1970) *Tea-room Trade*. London: Duckworths.

Humphries, B. (2008) *Social Work Research for Social Justice*. Basingstoke: Palgrave.

Innes, A., Macpherson, S. and McCabe, L. (2006) *Promoting person-centred care at the front line*. York: Joseph Rowntree Foundation.

Janesick, V. (2000) The choreography of qualitative research design: minuets, improvisations, and crystallization, in N. Denzin and Y. Lincoln (eds) *Handbook of Qualitative Research*. Thousand Oaks, CA: Sage.

Johnson, T., Dandeker, C. and Ashworth, C. (1984) *The Structure of Social Theory*. Basingstoke: Macmillan.

Jones, C. (2001) Voices from the front line: state social workers and New Labour, *British Journal of Social Work*, 31(4): 547–62.

Jordan, B. (1987) Counselling, advocacy and negotiation, *British Journal of Social Work*, 17: 135–46.

JUC SWEC (2008) *JUC Social Work Education Committee: Code of Ethics for Social Work and Social Care Research*. Available at: http://www.juc.ac.uk/swec-res-code.aspx.

Kellett, M. and Nind, M. (2001) Ethics in quasi-experimental research on people with severe learning disabilities: dilemmas and compromises, *British Journal of Learning Disabilities*, 29: 51–5.

Kelly, N. (2002) Using documentary sources to reveal narratives of mothering, in C., Horrocks, K., Milnes, B. Roberts and D. Robinson (eds) *Narrative, Memory and Life Transitions*. Huddersfield: University of Huddersfield Press.

Kelly, N. and Milner, J. (1996) Child protection decision making, *Child Abuse Review*, 5: 91–102.

Kemp, V., Sorsby, A., Liddle, M. and Merrington, S. (2002) *Assessing Responses to Youth Offending in Northamptonshire*. London: Nacro.

Kerr, J., Engel, J., Schlesinger-Raab, A., Sauer, H. and Holzel, D. (2003) Communication, quality of life and age: results of a 5-year prospective study in breast cancer patients, *Annals of Oncology*, 14(3): 421–7.

Khan, S., ter Riet, G., Popay, J., Nixon, J. and Kleijnen, J. (2001) Study quality assessment, in S., Khan, G., ter Riet, J., Glanville, A. Sowden and J. Kleijnen (eds) *Understanding Systematic Reviews of Research on Effectiveness, CRD Report No4*. York: University of York.

Kitzinger, J. (1995) Qualitative research: introducing focus groups, *British Medical Journal*, 311: 299–302.

Kurri, K. and Wahlstrom, J. (2003) Negotiating clienthood and the moral order of a relationship in couple therapy, in C., Hall, K., Juhila, N. Parton and T. Poso (eds) *Constructing Clienthood in Social Work and Human Services*. London: Jessica Kingsley.

Leicester City Council (2005) 'The Heritage Model,' http://www.leicester.gov.uk/your-council-services/social-care-health/young-peoplefamilies/support-services/leypsp/key-information/the-heritage-model, accessed 8th June 2009.

Lewis, D. (2008) Using life histories in social policy research: the case of third sector/public sector boundary crossing, *Journal of Social Policy*, 37(4): 559–78.

Likert, R. (1932) A technique for the measurement of attitudes, *Archives of Psychology*, 140: 3–55.

Linhorst, D. (2002) A review of the use and potential of focus groups in social work research, *Qualitative Social Work*, 1(2): 208–28.

Lishman, J. (2000) Evidence for practice: the contribution of competing research methodologies, ESRC Seminar Series, *Theorising Social Work Research*, 27 April, available at: http://www.scie.org.uk/publications/misc/tswr/seminar5/lishman.asp.

Little, M. (1998) Whispers in the library: a response to Liz Trinder's article on the state of social work research, *Child and Family Social Work*, 3(1): 49–56.

Lorenz, W. (2000) Contentious identities: social work research and the search for professional and personal identities, ESRC Seminar Series, *Theorising Social Work Research*, 6 March, available at: http://www.scie.org.uk/publications/misc/tswr/seminar4/lorenz.asp.

McCarney, R., Warner, J., Iliffe, S., van Haselen, R., Griffin, M. and Fisher, P. (2007) The Hawthorne Effect: a randomised, controlled trial, *BMC Medical Research Methodology*, 7: 30.

McNeece, A. and Thyer, B. (2004) Evidence-based practice and social work, *Journal of Evidence-based Social Work*, 1(1): 7–23.

McCord, W. and McCord, J. with Zola, I. (1969) *Origins of Crime*. Montclair, NJ: Patterson Smith.

MacDonald, G. (1999a) Evidence-based social care: wheels off the runway?, *Public Money & Management*, 19(1): 25–32.

MacDonald, G. (1999b) Social work and its evaluation: a methodological dilemma?, in F., Williams, J. Popay and A. Oakley (eds) *Welfare Research: A Critical Review*. London: UCL Press.

MacDonald, G. (2002) Child protection, in D., McNeish, T. Newman and H. Roberts (eds) *What Works for Children?* Buckingham: Open University Press.

MacDonald, J. (2003) One woman's experience of living with chronic pain: the proclamation of voice, *Journal of Social Work in Disability & Rehabilitation*, 3(2): 17–35.

MacDonald, N. and MacDonald, J. (2007) Reflections of a Mi'kmaq social worker on a quarter of a century work in First Nations child welfare, *First Peoples Child & Family Review*, 3(1): 34–45.

McLaughlin, H. (2007) *Understanding Social Work Research*. London: Sage.

McLaughlin, H., Young, A. and Hunt, R. (2007) Edging the change, *Journal of Social Work*, 7: 288–306.

Marsh, P. and Fisher, M. (2005) *Developing the Evidence Base for Social Work and Social Care Practice*. London: SCIE.

Mason, J. (1996) *Qualitative Researching*. London: Sage.

Mason, J. (2005) *Qualitative Researching* (2nd edition). London: Sage.

Mayer, J. and Timms, N. (1970) *The Client Speaks*. London: Routledge & Kegan Paul.

Mays, N. and Pope, C. (1995) Qualitative research: observational methods in health care settings, *British Medical Journal*, 311: 182–84.

Metcalfe, F. and Humphreys, C. (2002) Fostering action research and action research in fostering, *Qualitative Social Work*, 4: 435–50.

Moore, K. (2008) Quasi-experimental evaluations, *Research-to-Results Brief: Child Trends*, available at: http://www.childtrends.org/Files/Child_Trends-2008_01_16_Evaluation6.pdf.

Moore, R., Gray, E., Roberts, C., Merrington, S., Waters, I., Fernandez, R., Hayward, G. and Rogers, R. (2004) *ISSP: The Initial Report*. London: Youth Justice Board.

Mullender, A., Hague, G., Imam, U., Kelly, L., Malos, E. and Regan, L. (2002) *Children's Perspectives on Domestic Violence*. London: Sage.

Newman, T., Moseley, A., Tierney, S. and Ellis, A. (2005) *Evidence-based Social Work: A Guide for the Perplexed*. Lyme Regis: Russell House.

Oliver, M. (1990) *The Politics of Disablement*. Basingstoke: Macmillan.

Oliver, M. (1992) Changing the social relations of research production?, *Disability, Handicap & Society*, 7(2): 101–14.

Orme, J. (2003) It's feminist because I say so!, *Qualitative Social Work*, 2: 131–53.

Packman, J. (1981) *The Child's Generation*. Oxford: Blackwell and Martin Robertson.

Packman, J. and Hall, C. (1998) *From Care to Accommodation*. London: The Stationery Office.

Packman, J. with Randall, J. and Jacques, N. (1986) *Who Needs Care?* Oxford: Blackwell.

Parton, N. (1999) Some thoughts on the relationship between theory and practice in and for social work, ESRC Seminar Series, *Theorising Social Work Research*, 26 May, available at: http://scie.org.uk/publications/misc/tswr/seminar1/parton.asp.

Parton, N. (2006) *Safeguarding Childhood*. Basingstoke: Palgrave.

Parton, N. and O'Byrne, P. (2000) *Constructive Social Work: Towards a New Practice*. Basingstoke: Palgrave.

Pawson, R. (2006) *Evidence-based Policy: A Realist Perspective*. London: Sage.

Pease, B. (2002) Rethinking empowerment: a postmodern reappraisal for emancipatory practice, *British Journal of Social Work*, 32: 135–47.

Petticrew, M. and Roberts, H. (2003) Evidence, hierarchies, and typologies: horses for courses, *Journal of Epidemiology and Community Health*, 57: 527–9.

Philpott, T. (2008) *Understanding Child Abuse*. London: Routledge.

Pinkerton, J. (1998) The impact of research on policy and practice: a systemic perspective, in D. Iwaniec and J. Pinkerton (eds) *Making Research Work: Promoting Child Care Policy and Practice*. Chichester: Wiley.

Pinkerton, J. (1999) The research system as site of negotiation, ESRC Seminar Series, *Theorising Social Work Research*, 20 September, available at: http://scie.org.uk/publications/misc/tswr/seminar2/pinkerton.asp.

Plakhotnik, M., Delgado, A. and Seepersad, R. (2006) Autobiographical exploration of selves as adult learners and adult educators, paper presented at *Midwest Research-to-Practice Conference in Adult, Continuing, and Community Education*, University of Missouri-St. Louis, 4–6 October.

Popper, K. (1980) *The Logic of Scientific Discovery*. London: Routledge.

Poulantzas, N. (1975) *Classes in Contemporary Capitalism*. London: New Left Books.

Powell, J. (2002) The changing conditions of social work research, *British Journal of Social Work*, 32: 17–33.

Punch, K. (1998) *Introduction to Social Research: Quantitative and Qualitative Approaches*. London: Sage.

Qureshi, H. (2004) Evidence in policy and practice: what kinds of research designs?, *Journal of Social Work*, 4: 7–23.

Rubin, D. (2007) The design versus the analysis of observational studies for causal effects: parallels with the design of randomized trials, *Statistics in Medicine*, 26: 20–36.

Scott, D. (2002) Adding meaning to measurement: the value of qualitative methods in practice research, *British Journal of Social Work*, 32(7): 923–30.

Schon, D. (1983) *The Reflective Practitioner*. New York: Basic Books.

Schweinhart, L., Barnes, H. and Weikart, D. (1993) *Significant Benefits: The High/Scope Perry Preschool Study Through Age 27*. Ypsilanti: The High/Scope Press.

Shaw, I. (2000) Book review, *Health and Social Care in the Community*, 8(4): 285–86.

Shaw, I. (2003) Qualitative research and outcomes in health, social work and education, *Qualitative Research*, 3: 57–77.

Shaw, I. (2007) Is social work research distinctive?, *Social Work Education*, 26(7): 659–69.

Shaw, I. (2008) Merely experts? Reflections on the history of social work, science and research, *Research, Policy and Planning*, 26(1): 57–65.

Shaw, I. and Norton, M. (2007) *Kinds and Quality of Social Work Research*. London: SCIE.

Shaw, I. and Norton, M. (2008) Kinds and quality of social work research, *British Journal of Social Work*, 38(5): 953–70.

Sheldon, B. (1978) Theory and practice in social work, *British Journal of Social Work*, 8: 1–22.

Sheldon, B. (1983) The use of single case experimental designs in the evaluation of social work, *British Journal of Social Work*, 13: 477–500.

Sheldon, B. (1984) Evaluation with one eye closed: the empiricist agenda in social work research – a reply to Peter Raynor, *British Journal of Social Work*, 14: 635–7.

Sheldon, B. (1986) Social work effectiveness experiments: review and implications, *British Journal of Social Work*, 16(2): 223–42.

Sheldon, B. and MacDonald, G. (1992) Implications for practice of recent social work effectiveness research, *Practice*, 6(3): 211–18.

Sheppard, M. (1995) Social work, social science and practice wisdom, *British Journal of Social Work*, 25: 265–93.

Sheppard, M. (1998) Practice validity, reflexivity and knowledge for social work, *British Journal of Social Work*, 28: 763–81.

Shepard, M. and Pence, E. (1999) *Coordinating Community Responses to Domestic Violence*. Thousand Oaks, CA: Sage.

Sibbald, B. and Roland, M. (1998) Understanding controlled trials: why are randomised controlled trials important?, *British Medical Journal*, 316: 201.

Sinclair, R. and Bullock, R. (2002) *Learning from Past Experience: A Review of Serious Case Reviews*. London: The Stationery Office.

Skehill, C. (2000) Notes on the history of social work: an examination of the transition from philanthropy to professional social work in Ireland, *Research in Social Work Practice*, 10(6): 688–704.

Skehill, C. (2003) Social work in the Republic of Ireland: a history of the present, *Journal of Social Work*, 3(2): 141–59.

Smale, G., Tuson, G. and Statham, D. (2000) *Social Work and Social Problems*. Basingstoke: Palgrave Macmillan.

Smith, J. and Deemer, D. (2000) The problem of criteria in the age of relativism, in N. Denzin and Y. Lincoln (eds) *Handbook of Qualitative Research*. Thousand Oaks, CA: Sage.

Smith, R. (1987) The practice of diversion, *Youth and Policy*, 19: 10–14.

Smith, R. (2003) Claimants, applicants, customers or supplicants?, in T. Buck and R. Smith (eds) *Poor Relief or Poor Deal?* Aldershot: Ashgate.

Smith, R. (2004) A matter of trust, *Qualitative Social Work*, 3(3): 335–46.

Smith, R. (2005) *Values and Practice in Children's Services*. Basingstoke: Palgrave.

Smith, R. (2007) *Youth Justice: Ideas, Policy Practice*. Cullompton: Willan.

Smith, R. (2008) *Social Work and Power*. Basingstoke: Palgrave.

Smith, R. and Anderson, L. (2008) Interprofessional learning: aspiration or achievement?, *Social Work Education*, 27(7): 759–76.

Smith, R., Monaghan, M. and Broad, B. (2002) Involving young people as co-researchers: some methodological issues, *Qualitative Social Work*, 1(2): 191–207.

Soydan, H. (2008) Applying randomized controlled trials and systematic reviews in social work research, *Research on Social Work Practice*, 18: 311–18.

Stanley, N., Manthorpe, J. and White, M. (2007) Depression in the profession: social workers' experiences and perceptions, *British Journal of Social Work*, 37(2): 281–98.

Strang, H., Sherman, L., Angel, C., Woods, D., Bennett, S., Newbury-Birch, D. and Inkpen, N. (2006) Victim evaluations of face-to-face restorative justice conferences: a quasi-experimental analysis, *Journal of Social Issues*, 62(2): 281–306.

Strauss, A. and Corbin, J. (1990) *Basics of Qualitative Research: Grounded Theory Procedures and Techniques*. London: Sage.

Sulman, J. and Dumont, S. (2006) Health inequalities and social development in Africa: the Iolonioro local development initiative, *ESRC Research Seminar: Social Work and Health Inequalities Research*, available at: http://www2.warwick.ac.uk/fac/cross_fac/healthatwarwick/research/devgroups/socialwork/swhin/esrc_seminar_series/seminar_2/sulmanpaper.pdf.

Swigonski, M. (1993) Feminist standpoint theory and the questions of social work research, *Affilia*, 8(2): 171–83.

Swigonski, M. (1994) The logic of feminist standpoint theory for social work research, *Social Work*, 39(4): 387–93.

Taylor, B. (2006) Factorial surveys: using vignettes to study professional judgement, *British Journal of Social Work*, 36(7): 1187–207.

Taylor, C. and White, S. (2000) *Practising Reflexivity in Health and Welfare*. Buckingham: Open University Press.

Taylor, J., Williams, V., Johnson, R., Hiscutt, I. and Brennan, M. (2007) *We Are Not Stupid*. London: Shaping Our Lives.

Tedlock, B. (2000) Ethnography and ethnographic representation, in N. Denzin and Y. Lincoln (eds) *Handbook of Qualitative Research*. Thousand Oaks, CA: Sage.

Tew, J. (2008) Researching in partnership, *Qualitative Social Work*, 7(3): 271–87.

Thomas, A. (2008) Focus groups in qualitative research: culturally sensitive methodology for the Arabian Gulf?, *International Journal of Research & Method in Education*, 31(1): 77–88.

Todhunter, C. (2001) Undertaking action research: negotiating the road ahead, *Social Research Update*, 34. Guildford: University of Surrey.

Toroyan, T., Roberts, I., Oakley, A., Laing, G., Mugford, M. and Frost, C. (2003) Effectiveness of out-of-home day care for disadvantaged families: randomised controlled trial, *British Medical Journal*, 327: 906.

Trevillion, S. (2008) Research, theory and practice: eternal triangle or uneasy bedfellows?, *Social Work Education*, 27(4): 440–50.

Trinder, L. (1996) Social work research: the state of the art (or science), *Child and Family Social Work*, 1(4): 233–42.

Turner, M. and Beresford, P. (2005) *User Controlled Research: Its Meanings and Potential*. London: Shaping Our Lives.

Unrau, Y. (2006) Research on placement moves: seeking the perspective of foster children, *Children and Youth Services Review*, 29: 122–37.

Webb, S. (2001) Some considerations on the validity of evidence-based practice in social work, *British Journal of Social Work*, 31(1): 57–80.

Webber, M. and Huxley, P. (2004) Social exclusion and risk of emergency compulsory admission: a case-control study, *Social Psychiatry and Psychiatric Epidemiology*, 9(12): 1000–09.

Weber, M. (1957) *The Theory of Social and Economic Organisation*. Chicago, IL: Free Press.

Weber, M. (1978) *Economy and Society*. Berkeley, CA: University of California Press.

Weeks, L., Shane, C., MacDonald, F., Hart, C. and Smith, R. (2006) Learning from the experts: people with learning difficulties training and learning from each other, *British Journal of Learning Disabilities*, 34: 49–55.

Weinbach, R. and Grinnell, R. (2007) *Statistics for Social Workers*. Boston, MA: Allyn & Bacon.

Whyte, G. (1991) Decision failures: why they occur and how to prevent them, *Academy of Management Review*, 5(3): 23–31.

Williams, J., Jackson, S., Maddocks, A., Cheung, W-Y., Love, A. and Hutchings, H. (2001) Case-control study of the health of those looked after by local authorities, *Archives of Disease in Childhood*, 85: 280–5.

Willmott, H. (2008) *Qualitative Document Analysis*. Available at: http://dialspace.dial.pipex.com/town/close/hr22/Principles%20of%20Qualitative%20Research/Qualitative%20Document%20Analysis.ppt.

Wilson, K., Ruch, G., Lymbery, M. and Cooper, A. (2008) *Social Work*. Harlow: Pearson Longman.

Youth Justice Board (2008) *About the YJB: Prevention Cohort Study*. Available at: http://www.yjb.gov.uk/en-gb/yjb/Whatwedo/Research/PreventionCohortStudy.htm.

INDEX